D0937048

AFRICAN POWDER KEG

RONALD MATTHEWS

African
Powder Keg

Revolt and Dissent in Six Emergent Nations

THE BODLEY HEAD
LONDON

© Ronald Matthews 1966
Printed and bound in Great Britain for
The Bodley Head Ltd
10 Earlham Street, London, WC2
by C. Tinling & Co. Ltd, Prescot
Set in Monotype Baskerville
First published 1966

Contents

1. Stating the Problem, 7
2. Algeria, 22
3. Ghana, 58
4. The Congo (Brazzaville), 88
5. Gabon, 115
6. Dahomey, 134
7. Malawi, 161
8. Conclusions, 190
9. The Latin American Parallel, 216

Algiers
Tunis
Oran
Tunisia
Ifni
Morocco
Algeria
Libya
U.A.R.
(Egypt)
Sp. Sahara
Mauritania
Mali
Niger
Chad
The
Sudan
Fr. Somaliland
Senegal
Upper Volta
Fed. Rep. of
Niger
Ethiopia
Gambia
Guinea
Ghana
Togo
Dahomey
Central African
Republic
Somali Rep.
Portuguese Guinea
Sierra
Leone
Liberia
Ivory
Coast
Accra
Cotonou
Porto Novo
Fed. Rep. of
Cameroon
Fernando Po
Rio Muni
Libreville
Gabon
Congo
Congo
Uganda
Kenya
Equator
Rwanda
Burundi
Pointe Noire
Cabinda
Brazzaville
United Rep. of
Tanzania
Zanzibar
Angola
Zambia
Malawi
Zomba
Mozambique
Rhodesia
South-
West
Africa
Bechuanald
Prot.
Swaziland
South Africa
Basutoland
Malagasy Rep.

N

AFRICA

miles

0   500   1000

Stating the Problem

THE LIFE OF an African head of state or premier could not be called a particularly secure existence as 1965 passed on its way. The three years that had just gone by had seen a series of *coups d'état* or plots or political murders directed against the local régimes reported from more than twenty African states, or well over half the independent countries of the continent. The August 1963 Congo (Brazzaville) rising led to the overthrow of President Fulbert Youlou, and the October 1963 Dahomey demonstrations to the eviction from the Presidency of Mr Hubert Maga. In the December 1962 plot in Tunisia, President Bourguiba owed his life, if the official version is correct, to a certain amount of luck, President Nyerere disappeared from circulation for twenty-four hours during the January 1964 mutiny in Tanganyika, while the August 1962 plot in Ghana involved an attempt on the life of President Nkrumah, a new bid to assassinate whom was reported in 1964. Nor was there any sign of a halt in the succession of incidents: it was rare for a quarter to pass without a new one hitting the headlines of the world press. The close of 1964 saw the public execution in the Republic of Niger of four members of the banned Sawaba opposition party, which had launched an insurrection. The opening of 1965 witnessed the assassination of the Premier of Burundi, whose predecessor in office was promptly arrested on suspicion of complicity, and an Algiers court's sentencing of Ait Ahmed, one of the nine 'historic leaders' who had launched the seven-year war of liberation against the French, for mounting a rebellion against his former companion in captivity, President Ben Bella; in June, Ben Bella himself was overthrown by a military *coup*, while, in August, President Nasser announced the discovery in Egypt of a large-scale plot against his régime. The regular succession of acts of violence calls to mind the observation credited to the then Brazilian Emperor when he visited the Philadelphia exposition in 1876: 'Many Latin

American countries,' Dom Pedro II is said to have remarked, 'have more revolutions per minute than the machines you are showing me here.'

Some of the challenges the African Governments faced had genuine popular backing behind them. The trade unions turned out in the streets of Brazzaville against President Fulbert Youlou; Ait Ahmed's rebellion enjoyed very wide support in his native ethnic enclave of Kabylie, and not a little sympathy outside it from elements opposed to the Ben Bella régime's out-and-out Socialist policy. Others appear to have been rather the work of cabals, whose underground operations had no parading crowds to lend them strength. It was probably natural that the sentencing to death or prison of the men who were convicted of plotting against President Bourguiba of Tunisia should have evoked no protests; with two exceptions, the prisoners were all small men with no sort of hearing in the countryside. But there was just as little effervescence when the discovery of two successive plots against President Houphouet-Boigny, of the Ivory Coast, led to the arrest of no less than nine cabinet ministers.

Whether the threat he might have to face tomorrow originated with a mass movement or with the machinations of conspirators, the danger to an African head of state was just as great. And the position of the leaders of French-speaking sub-Saharan Africa was made no easier, as 1964 went out, by the decision of the Government in Paris to reduce the number of its troops stationed there by more than three-quarters, from 27,800 to 6,600. The redeployment of the French forces and the disappearance or the slashing of their expenditure on the spot would deal a serious blow to the local budgets which might well, as a recent experience showed, have political repercussions in countries which were most of them so poor; even more important was the fact that the locally-raised forces in all the new republics were small, and were not always dependable. The President of Togo had lost his life in January 1963 in a mutiny by his army which had political overtones; the President of Gabon had been deposed by a military *putsch* in February 1964 and had only recovered his office thirty-six hours later, when sufficient French troops had been flown in to restore him. The unreliability of their own soldiers was regarded by the Governments of at least two French-speaking African states, those of the Ivory Coast and of the Congo (Brazzaville), as a sufficient hazard to warrant the raising of 'people's militias' to ensure order in their place, while across the continent, in English-speaking Malawi, Premier Banda was declaring that the only people in whom he felt real confidence were the 5,000 armed women of the force he had christened his 'Amazon Army'.

Africa is, of course, a continent of very considerable natural resources. With an area representing twenty-two per cent. of the land-surface of the globe at their disposal, Africa's 261 million inhabitants formed in 1961 a mere eight per cent. of the world's total population. Pressure of the birth-rate on food and other supplies is therefore far less than it is in Europe or Asia, though national income per head is still extremely low. What is more, there seems no reason at all why this poverty should continue indefinitely. Africa has got twenty-eight per cent. of the world's potential reserves of hydro-electric power. Its petrol- and gas-production is rising. Its deposits of fissile materials are more than ample. A high proportion of these riches is still unexploited or under-exploited, but that position is swiftly changing. And it might not unreasonably be suggested that the political instability from which the continent has been suffering since its new states acceded to independence is due to the fact that a fair proportion of them were in the economic stage, on the border of penury and solvency, which historical experience has shown to be the most propitious to the outbreak of revolutions: it is not the starvelings who rise from their slumbers; it is the prisoners of want who have already perceived that the doors of their prison are opening before them. This interpretation of events is belied by the fact that the African states which have been the scenes of *coups* and conspiracies in the past three years have by no means been confined to those which are beginning to envisage economic independence as a possibility. Some of the victims were indeed, according to the 1961 figures of the International Development Association, approaching the national income per head which experts regard as marking the verge of unassisted 'take-off': such were Gabon, with $200 per head per year; Ghana, with $199; and the Ivory Coast, with $184. Far more of them, however, were still plunged in the kind of poverty whose meaning is barely intelligible to Western minds: these ranged down from Cameroon, with its $86 per head annual income, through Togo, with its $70, and Tanganyika, with its $59, to the Congo (Brazzaville), Chad and Dahomey, all with no more than $40.

Whether they were still on the verge of starvation or on the eve of easier times, however, all these countries had certain things in common. One was conspicuous waste on the part of the authorities. Up and down the continent, the visitor could see costly presidential palaces, sometimes more than one to a president, and ceremonial guards stifling in gold-braided uniforms. He could watch the cabinet ministers of states that cannot afford enough tractors riding about their business – or pleasure – in Mercedes cars which had been bought at fantastic prices to run over roads that would be regarded in the West as cart-tracks. He might find himself invited to parties marking the annual celebration of independence day, where hundreds of guests would eat dishes and sip drinks worthy of the Ritz, and imported from abroad at Ritz prices, within half a mile or less of shanty-towns whose inhabitants had barely enough food to keep life going. In the Balkanized Africa of the 1960s, he would observe that the ex-French group of states could boast of fifteen Governments, more than 150 ministers, several hundreds of members of ministerial secretariats and far more deputies for a set of territories whose total population was considerably less than that of the former colonial power and their wealth infinitely smaller. Gabon, for instance, with its half-million population, has 47 deputies, or one for just over 10,000 inhabitants, and their pay per head is higher than that of British M.P.s. And though an African deputy works, if that is the proper word, for maybe three months out of the twelve, he will be paid as if he toiled continuously from 1 January to 31 December, and there are not a few African countries where six months of his hardly exhausting labour, which is supplemented by advantages in kind, bring him in as much as the ordinary peasant can hope to earn in thirty years. All the same, there is no record of an insurrectionary movement in an African state having been unleashed by the inauguration of a new presidential palace, or of underfed crowds breaking into a lavish official reception and satisfying their hunger from the plates on the over-garnished tables, or of angry demonstrators invading a parliament building while its deputies did happen to be sitting and calling on them to account for the vast – by local standards – salaries they drew for the job of regularly saying Yes to Government measures.

Possibly this may be ascribed in part to the fact that those of the population who could read would never find in the well-disciplined local press any reference to, let alone criticism of, this scandal of conspicuous waste, or to the chronic overspending on unexceptionable objects which is just as constant a feature of existence in African lands. The traveller through the continent would meet African officials who were not only drawing the same scales of pay as their English or French predecessors, but the identical generous overseas allowances, while their juniors would be subsisting on the old native scales and often enough resorting to corruption to eke things out. He might encounter the same privileged functionaries flying first class to Europe on business, a luxury which the British Government does not concede even to its ambassadors. He would find countries which need more than anything else to expand education building schools in brick and concrete when they could construct four or five times as many for the same outlay if they contented themselves with dried mud or the local wood as materials. He would find that funds advanced from Europe for the elimination of the ever-spreading shanty-towns were being used to run up blocks of flats whose rents far exceeded anything that the slum-dwellers could afford to pay, and that much more was being spent in this and other ways on the urban population, a minority in every African state, than on the vast majority of people who lived in the countryside. His travels would show him that the tiniest territories wanted to have not only their own consumer industries, but their heavy industries too, with the three largest countries of the Maghreb, their combined population totalling less than 25,000,000, each solemnly setting up its own steelworks. But for all this investment in the future, he would learn, if he kept his ears open in the right places, that the high-ups did not seem to possess unlimited faith in that future's stability: he would be told of presidents, and some ministers too, building up substantial savings in Swiss banks, while their wives bought themselves villas on the shores of the Lake of Geneva.

The waste and the overspending were the work of a new privileged class, which up and down Africa was taking the place of the vanished or vanishing European administrators and professional men. It was a privileged class that seemed to feel far less conscience about its duties than its predecessors. Doctors are sorely needed in the *bled* and the bush, but a high proportion of Africans who have pursued their medical studies in Europe will return home – if they do – feeling that the capital is the only place suitable for the exercise of the qualifications that their country has paid for them to acquire. The members of this African élite feel themselves obliged to extend their patronage over their families and friends: in sub-Saharan Africa, the staff of a minister's secretariat will tend to be drawn from their boss's tribe. They tend to feel contempt for manual work, and even in the stifling height of summer heat, they wear the jacket and tie which underlines their superiority to the ordinary man. What is more, far too many of them are corrupt, and while the sanction of possible bankruptcy can be trusted to keep this plague down to a reasonable minimum in capitalist countries, it is not present in the Socialist economies to which many of the African countries purport to be aspiring. Bribery is so ever-present that there is even a stock phrase, 'the corruption index', for what it will cost a foreign businessman to see a minister. Education is a crying necessity in all the underdeveloped countries if they are ever to lift themselves up out of their underdevelopment. But in most of the new African states, that education does not even pretend to be geared to the agriculture which is the livelihood of three-quarters and more of their inhabitants. If children, as they do in many places, walk miles to school every morning and afternoon, it is because their parents are aware that schooling is the only way for them to accede to the ranks of the officialdom that forms the bulk of the privileged class. But the coming into existence of this new upper crust has not so far evoked any particularly dangerous reactions. True, it needs very little provocation to draw from peasants up and down the continent the disillusioned comment: 'Independence wasn't meant for us; the only people who've got anything out of it have been those townees.' That is no more than resignation, though, and resignation is at the opposite pole from revolt. The only concrete expression that this disillusionment has so far found has been widespread peasant tax strikes in some African countries.

There is, however at least one other common element to be found in almost all the newly-independent African states and, in fact if not in form, in one whose independence is more than a century old: the single-party system. Just how the single party's political monopoly had been established made no difference at all to its authority. That monopoly might be a *de facto* one, or it might be written into the constitution, as is happening in more and more African states. This last development is a paradoxical one, since most of the constitutions, imitating their European models, specifically guarantee the rights to freedom of expression, of the press and of meeting which can hardly exist under a one-party régime. Whatever its formal status, the party, under its single leader – for few people believed that other people's arguments in its theoretically supreme central committee or political bureau had any chance of being listened to unless they won the support of that predominant figure – was in fact the sole repository of real power. The decisions taken by that central committee were far more important than the empty debates in the parliament whose members almost certainly owed their positions to party nomination.

As often as not, this primacy of party institutions was given open recognition. Nkrumah stated in 1959 that since Ghana's ruling Convention People's Party made the Government and not the Government the C.P.P., members of the C.P.P. Central Committee would in future take precedence over non-Central Committee Ministers at all public functions. In Mali the next year, President Modibo Keita described the Administration as being the emanation of the Government party. Under the constitution plebiscited by the Algerian electorate in the autumn of 1963, Algeria's single party, the F.L.N., selected the candidate for the presidency of the Republic and all the candidates for the National Assembly, and also laid down the national policy and supervised the activities of the state, the Assembly and the Government.

It will be suggested in this book that most if not all the plots and *coups* which have been reported from African countries over the past three years have been due in great measure to the existence of this single party or to an attempt to set it up. The one incident which might be put forward as an outstanding exception to this rule – the arrest in July 1963 of almost all the leaders of Morocco's left-wing opposition party for an alleged plot against the monarchical régime – would appear on examination to be no exception at all. Few impartial observers on the spot believed that there had been any such machination by the National Union of Popular Forces as the authorities asserted, though almost all the prisoners were tortured in an attempt to get them to confess to conspiring. The party meeting into which the Casablanca police burst had in fact been called to declare a boycott of the impending local council elections on the grounds of what was represented as gross official interference with the freedom of the electoral campaign. And though the Moroccan constitution of December 1962 specifically forbade the establishment of a single-party system, it can plausibly be argued that the Government's restrictions on electoral liberties, followed by its round-up of the National Union of Popular Forces leadership, amounted to an attempt to procure *de facto* one-party status for the so-called 'King's Party', then officially if somewhat oddly named the Front for the Defence of Constitutional Institutions.

Defenders of the single party will maintain that its existence provides no ground at all for conspiratorial activities. Would-be conspirators would achieve far more by joining its ranks, they say, for there is complete freedom of speech in meetings of party members till policy on a given issue has been decided by the party as a whole. Those of us who lived in Stalin's Russia and heard the same sort of assertion made there will be a little chary about accepting it. What is more, there are facts about some at least of the plots which cast further doubt on this plea. A number of the conspiracies reported led to the arrest and sentencing of distinguished figures who, if speech within the single party had been really free, would have found it far easier to have made their views heard than would any ordinary party member, and who might therefore have been expected to use their rights to put their case across: no one but a fool plots when he can persuade. The nine cabinet ministers arrested over the two 1963 Ivory Coast plots did not stand alone. The Ghana plot of August 1962 was followed by the arrest not only of two ministers, but of the executive secretary of the single party. The trial that followed the alleged Senegal plot of December 1962 saw the then Prime Minister and four of his cabinet colleagues in the dock. The February 1963 Liberian plot was followed by the arrest of the Army's commander-in-chief and the dismissal of the Secretary for Defence; in Mali, two Malian former members of the French Cabinet were arrested and sentenced after July 1962 riots, and died in 1964 under, to say the least of it, somewhat disturbing circumstances. In Burundi the assassination of the Prime Minister in January 1965 was followed by the arrest not only of his predecessor in the premiership, but of the Minister of Communications, the General Secretary of the local trade unions and the Director of Information. All this rather suggests that the underlying motive that inspired many of the plotters was that they were unable in fact to obtain a hearing within the single party for their grievances against the administration and saw in subversion and violence the only way out.

The author was in 1964 granted permission to attend sample cell meetings of the Tunisian single party, which is now known as the Socialist Destour and which was at the time preparing for its first congress for five years; he was allowed freely to select his cells. The proceedings at the two cells he picked, one in a small country town, in which there were few young people and no women, and the other in the capital, where there were quite a number of women and a fair proportion of youngsters, may perhaps shed a little light on the inside working of the single-party system. First, the chair at both meetings was taken by a representative of the party organization in Tunis, though the officials and other members of the cell committee were seated at the committee table. Second, the participants had no hesitation at all in bringing up local grievances even when, by Western standards, their complaints might have been judged out of order. Third, there appeared to be a quite normal rotation among office-holders. The fourth thing that struck a Western observer was that, though the next party congress was imminent and quite important decisions would almost certainly be taken at it, there was no attempt at all to put forward resolutions to be discussed on the congress floor. An official from the party's central headquarters explained that in principle the newly-elected committee of each cell, which picked the cell's delegates to the congress, would instruct them on the points to raise in the light of the grievances raised at the cell meeting; and he added that the average Tunisian party member had probably too little experience of political affairs to engage in the complicated task of framing resolutions.

Nevertheless it was still a little surprising to an outsider that neither cell meeting indulged in any sort of general political discussion, or adopted or gave its backing to the least motion to be put before the approaching congress, which it was already known would be far from a run-of-the-mill gathering. It was the first congress to meet since the 1962 plot against President Bourguiba's life, and it would be called on to ratify, as in fact it did, the consequential decisions taken in 1963 by a National Council – a small-scale delegate conference – and which were aimed to increase democracy in the ranks of the party and to link it up more closely with the machinery of government. The congress was also certain to consider Mr Bourguiba's suggestion to the 1963 National Council that, in order to improve the quality of the party's work and the intellectual level of those who chose the congress delegates, membership should be divided into two classes, ordinary members and active members. The President had proposed that the latter should be chosen annually from among ordinary members who had proved their competence, and that there should be guarantees against any favouritism in their selection. Neither the National Council's decisions nor the President's proposals were even mentioned in the speeches from the floor at either cell meeting, though they must have been present to every intelligent party member's mind.

It was a little difficult for a Westerner to understand this omission in a party which claimed to practise internal democracy. In England, it would be inconceivable, if issues so vital were coming up before the next Labour Party Congress, that they would not be hammered out beforehand in the humblest party branch meeting. It will be said that Tunisia, unlike England, has no political tradition; but that would not be quite true. The Socialist Destour Party is by far the senior of all the single parties in Africa: it had fifteen years of vigorous activity behind it when Nkrumah founded the Convention

People's Party in 1949. In 1964, it was considerably older than was the Labour Party when Ramsay Macdonald was invited to form the second Labour Government at the close of the 'twenties. During its three decades of existence, it had known twenty-one years of open or clandestine political agitation, punctuated by spells of resistance work, and nine years of political power. Yet the proceedings at the Tunisian cell meetings unmistakably suggested that important policy decisions within the party did not come up from the rank and file and were not even submitted for its approval; they were imposed from above.

If such a line was followed in the Socialist Destour, which was, with Sekou Touré's Guinean Democratic Party, streets ahead of the other African single parties in its organization and in its members' understanding of the implications of their membership, imposition of policy by the leadership was virtually certain in other countries, where party ideology barely existed and where the apparatus of the party counted for nothing at all by comparison with the man who led it. Moreover, while sparse membership naturally makes a party an obedient instrument in the hands of its boss, indiscriminately large membership can have just the same effect. Thoughtful Ghanaians can be heard to maintain that just because the Convention People's Party has roped citizens into its ranks by hundreds of thousands, it means far less than its sister parties in Guinea and Tunisia. It would therefore be less accurate to describe Ghana as a single-party country than as a country dominated by a single man. Some students of the African scene have divided Africa's political organizations into two classes, which they have christened 'mass parties' and 'élite parties', the former having an internal set-up not unlike that of Western parties and going out for members, and the latter being more in the nature of cliques following in the wake of a leader who is often enough the African who took over from the former colonial authorities at the moment when they finally withdrew. What has just been said about Ghana suggests that there may not be as much difference as all that between the internal working of the two kinds of organization.

This book will start off by telling the story of plots or *coups d'état* which have been reported from a sample half-dozen

African countries during the three years ending with the middle of 1964. It will then try to see what lessons are to be learned from the facts recorded, and will present views, largely African views, on the arguments for and against the single-party system. It will also give consideration to what appears, on the surface of it at any rate, to be a parallel in another part of the world to the sequence of events reported from Africa and will inquire whether common causes were at work.

It will be worth while to conclude this introductory chapter with a brief sketch of the atmosphere in an African single-party country as it would appear to a casual visitor who kept his eyes and his ears open. It is unlikely that the visitor would have cause to realize he had arrived in such a country when he went through the customs and passport formalities at the airport. He almost certainly would when he opened his morning newspapers the following day. First of all there would be little if any difference between the assessment of news values in the various dailies – if there was more than one – the sort of difference one observes between conservative and liberal, or popular and serious newspapers' judgements of the value of a story in Great Britain and the United States. Secondly, though news from the outside world would be printed, it would quite likely fall into second place unless it concerned events of indisputable importance, such as the re-election of President Johnson or the deposition of Mr Khrushchev: the most prominent positions on the front page would in a high proportion of single-party countries go to the activities of the head of State, or of the party he directed, unless they have been enjoying an unusually idle day. Finally, if the visitor had access to any outside source of information, such as B.B.C. news bulletins or responsible foreign newspapers, he might easily discover that information which most editors would have considered interesting to local readers had in fact been held out for reasons which it would sometimes need a little background to identify. Thus, for example, it was natural that the well-controlled Algiers press should have published only the shortest and most misleading accounts of the press conference of July 1963 in which Ait Ahmed announced that he was launching a new party in opposition to the Ben Bella Government. It was a little surprising at first sight that the Tunisian papers should have printed nothing at all about it, though Algeria is Tunisia's neighbour and a Tunisian news agency correspondent was at the conference, taking copious notes of Ait Ahmed's statements. Everything became clear when it was realized that Tunisia was strenuously seeking to improve her relations with Algeria, which had been seriously compromised earlier in the year when President Bourguiba had accused Mr Ben Bella of harbouring some of the plotters who had sought his life, and that the Tunisian authorities probably thought that this reconciliation would be helped if their press did not carry the story of the new opposition leader's onslaught on the F.L.N. chief. It should be added that unless the visitor to a single-party country has access to a radio set, he may not be able to check on the local news-censorship. A fair proportion of the single-party states stop the sale of papers coming in from abroad if they contain any information or opinions which are displeasing to the local régime. Nor will they confine their attentions to sensational sheets, which will hardly find it worth while referring to political events in African countries unless they can blow up an eddy of local discontent into the beginning of a plot. In French-speaking states, no paper has suffered more from such hold-ups than that most responsible of all organs, the Paris *Monde*.

The only other obvious sign that would indicate to the visitor the kind of country to which he had come would be the omnipresent portraits of the local leader. Naturally they would be up and framed in Government offices and those of enterprises dependent on the Government, but the odds are that this would be far from the end of the display. There are capitals in which not a single café or restaurant or hotel is without the precious picture, where it will be looking out at the passer-by from shop-fronts and office-fronts right down the streets, sometimes more than one from a single window, and where party agents will distribute new copies or a fresh photograph when the time comes round. Other signs of the single-party atmosphere take a little more discovering. If the visitor meets any local acquaintances he may have in a café, he may be a little surprised by the guarded nature of their conversation, which will tend to collapse into evasions or commonplaces if any at all important matter of local politics is raised. He will get no answer on the spot if he inquires the reason for this discretion, though he may be told in the street later that there are certain subjects it is wiser not to talk about in public. Only if he gets on intimate terms with his local friends will he learn the real reason for their reticence: that plain-clothes police are sure to be present in such places as the better-frequented cafés – the author has met them in the press gallery of at least one parliament – and that they have been known to pick up for interrogation people whom they have overheard talking indiscreetly. Unless he has a particular interest in political or social affairs, the stranger in a single-party country may need some time before he becomes aware that everything in it is under party control, from women's organizations to federations of students, from employers' associations to trade unions, and that the trade unions are likely to be firmly slapped down if they indulge in what most people would regard as the normal syndical activity of pressing for wage increases when the cost of living rises. He would need to be well in with an informed foreign resident to learn of the political arrests that are a regular feature of life in at least some single-party states, arrests whose victims, by no means all of whom have been indiscreet enough to talk in public places, are rarely if ever brought up for open trial.

It is true that such opposition to the single-party régimes as exists, in clandestinity or in exile, is not always endowed with the tactical sense it needs if it is to overthrow the tyranny against which it is protesting. An African acquaintance, a man of outstanding intelligence who has been too level-headed ever to identify himself as a critic of his country's internal set-up, was all the same discreetly approached to help with the organization of its underground opposition. His first suggestion was that the party concerned should modify its title by incorporating into it the word 'Liberal'. In this way it might hope to obtain support from the Liberal International. The opposition leader who had made the approach said No at once. A change in the party's appellation, he said, would be unfair to those of its members who had suffered or were still suffering imprisonment for their loyalty to it under its old name. His solicitude for the feelings of his movement's martyrs can be respected, but his political judgement seems open to question.

It is also true, however, that the single-party régimes cannot count with any sort of certainty on the loyalty even of those who are spending their whole time putting out frenzied propaganda for the party and its objectives. There is good reason to assert that most of the journalists who in such countries as Ghana and Guinea daily write reams of this sort of nonsense are fully aware of the vacuity of the material they are turning out. An acquaintance* asked a journalist in one such African single-party country, an intelligent man and a very good writer, why he continued scribbling the absurdities he was obliged to produce for the local official paper. The answer he gave was a roundabout one, but it boiled down to this: The writer was aware that he was probably at the moment the only worth-while journalist in his country. He knew that, with his talents, it would not be too difficult for him to fix himself up with some sort of job abroad. But that simple and apparently satisfying way out of a situation in which he was forced to devote his gifts to propagating what he knew were falsehoods would hardly, as he saw it, be fair to his own countrymen. It would mean that if his country ever were to find freedom, there would be nobody on the spot to run its liberated press as it should run, which he could quite certainly do. The argument is not without its validity, and it can only be hoped that the writer does not have to wait as long to express himself freely as did Ilya Ehrenburg in Russia.

* Here, and elsewhere throughout this book, the author has felt himself unable to reveal his personal sources of information, since such disclosures might have involved those sources in grave trouble with their authorities at home.

2

Algeria

AT HALF PAST two on the morning of 19 June 1965, three senior officers of the Algerian armed forces burst into the bedroom of President Ben Bella in the unpretentious flat he occupied in a block just opposite the Algiers Presidential palace. They paid no attention to the President's protests. 'Get dressed quickly, and no nonsense,' they told him. 'We arrest you in the name of the Revolutionary Council.'

No one knew on that morning of 19 June just who composed the Algerian Revolutionary Council, or how it had come into existence. It wasn't till more than a fortnight later, on the third anniversary of Algeria's independence, that its 26-man membership was officially revealed, not till a week later again that the names of the Government it had installed in power were published. It was common knowledge from the start, of course, that the head of the Council was Colonel Houari Boumedienne, first Deputy Premier, Minister of Defence, and second only to Ben Bella in the hierarchy of power; Boumedienne who, with his austere appearance and faintly Chinese looks had been as much as anyone else responsible for Ben Bella's accession to power just under three years before, at the cost of a near civil war that had cost the newly independent Algeria hundreds of dead.

Why had Boumedienne ousted from office the man he had done everything he could to instal there in the summer of 1962? It can safely be asserted that there was a great deal in common between the motives that had inspired him to the two antithetical actions. In 1962, he had put his forces in the field to back Ben Bella as the national leader against Benyussef Ben Khedda, then Premier of the Algerian Provisional Government, because the latter had just dismissed him and his two fellow-officers from their positions as chief and deputy chiefs of staff of the Army of National Liberation. In 1965, with the same two officers among those behind him, he staged a faultlessly organized military *coup* to overthrow Ben Bella because he believed that the President was going to go even further than he had so far done in the period since independence to eliminate the Algerian army from political life, and that once again he himself was in danger of being a victim. One of those who gave Boumedienne the strongest support was the young ex-army officer who had become Foreign Minister and who was certain to lose his post; another was an older ex-officer who had been forced out of the Ministry of the Interior the previous year. The Revolutionary Council might produce every sort of subsequent justification for its *coup*, but those on the spot regarded the most important element in it as being that of a personal settling of accounts.

Moreover the men involved in the coup knew they must act quickly if they were to act with the least hope of success. Within a matter of days, the Afro-Asian summit conference, 'the second Bandoeng,' was due to meet in Algiers: the streets of the city were filled with posters individually welcoming each of the fifty-odd participating nations. Any moment might see the signature with France of agreements on the working of Algeria's petrol deposits and on French economic aid to Algeria, which would be followed by an official visit to Paris by the President. The two events would add enormously to Ben Bella's prestige. If Boumedienne and his fellows let themselves be evicted from office, what hope had they of staging a come-back against a man who had taken the chair at a gathering whose participants ranged from Nasser to Nkrumah, from Soekarno to Chou En-lai, and who had been received in Paris by General de Gaulle?

It could be and indeed was argued that the *coup* was in some sense a response to a wave of popular discontent. The proclam-ation broadcast by the Revolutionary Council within a few hours of its taking power described Ben Bella as a 'diabolical dictator', and declared that the revolutionaries had 'acted in response to the people's anguished appeal' and aimed to fulfil the Algerians' most cherished hope, that of recovering their stolen freedom. It is true that the first three years of Algeria's independence had not been particularly happy ones. Opening with weeks of civil strife, they had been punctuated by two armed insurrections, one of them headed by a former prison companion of Ben Bella's, the other by a colonel who had a brilliant wartime record as a commander of the Army of National Liberation inside Algeria. Correspondents who had succeeded in getting between the Government lines and the rebels during the second heard the local population saying: 'If we'd known things were going to end up like this, we'd never have fought the French.' The authorities had met with next to no success in tackling the mass unemployment which was one of the main problems facing the country. Production on the workers-managed nationalized farms, which were one of the Ben Bella régime's proudest achievements, had fallen both in quantity and in quality, and agricultural exports still represented fifty per cent. of Algeria's sales abroad. Official inefficiency was growing, a serious matter in a State where more and more activities were coming under Government control; corruption was on the increase too. Arrests on political grounds, which had begun in 1963, had been steadily increasing.

The fact remained, however, that in the period immediately before the coup, Ben Bella had shown at least some signs of recovering a popularity he had seemed at one moment to be losing. He had reached an agreement with a one-time group of rebels, he had freed a number of prominent political prisoners, he had publicly appealed for national reconciliation. If the Revolutionary Council had been acting in response to a surge of public indignation against the President, one would have expected Algerians to have come out on the streets to hail the army that had liberated them. Nothing of the sort happened. The only popular reaction for the twenty-four hours that followed the *coup* was complete inertia. Then, up and down the country processions, small in Algiers – where they were said to have enjoyed Communist backing – bigger in the provinces, began to thread their way through the streets. The slogans they shouted were not what the Revolutionary Council may have hoped; they were 'Up Ben Bella!' 'Boumedienne murderer!' The tanks that had been discreetly withdrawn from the streets reappeared. Troops opened fire in Bone and Oran, Souk Ahras and Tebessa, among other places, and the dead ran into around 100; there is evidence that in Algiers individual soldiers were killed by civilians, while in Tlemcen, where the military were overwhelmed by the crowds, they took off their steel helmets, held up their hands and shouted:

'Hit us if you like, but we're with you.' Less than a week later, the demonstrations had ceased. That was not unnatural in a country which seven years of merciless war had disinclined for any sort of civil strife. But on the anniversary of Algeria's independence, which occurred on 5 July, the new authorities did not dare to permit the kind of march-past which had been a regular affair in the past, for fear of pro-Ben Bella incidents, and though in previous years Algerian flags had been hung out on almost every balcony, there were precious few flags to be seen in 1965. Weeks and weeks after the coup, one could hear Algiers housewives saying of their new head of State: 'He doesn't bear looking at on the T.V.' Which, indeed, he gave them precious little opportunity of doing, for when he broadcast, it was invariably from a manuscript; he held this below the level of the table at which he was sitting and it was only at the rarest intervals that he looked up and enabled viewers to have a look at his eyes.

Algeria, with its long Mediterranean coastline, is four and a half times the size of France, though more than three-quarters of this area is occupied by the Saharan territories. In the past, its chief resource has been agriculture, whose products include a large quantity of excellent wine. Its soil is, however, insufficient, wind and water erosion have been carrying away the equivalent of 100,000 acres into the sea every year, and re-afforestation is a crying need. Algeria has also considerable mineral resources. She is already getting ample revenue from the petrol and natural gas in her Saharan territories, while she can also boast of iron ore deposits estimated at hundreds of millions of tons near Tindouf, on the Moroccan frontier, zinc, antimony, mercury and manganese and high quality phosphates.

In historical times, the first known people of Algeria were the Berbers, a white race believed to be akin to the nations of southern Europe: Berbers, with a small admixture of Arab and Negro blood, still form the vast majority of the country's inhabitants, though the only place where their language continues to be spoken today is the mountain area of Kabylie. Algeria became a part and a very prosperous part of the Roman Empire a century before Christ: when Christianity came, one of its greatest theologians, St Augustine, was an Algerian

Berber. The seventh century brought the Arab conquest and, after a number of intermediate phases, Algeria came in the sixteenth century under the rule of a succession of Deys who were theoretically subject to the Sultan of Turkey. The Deys were the elected representatives of the country's ruling castes of corsairs and Turkish troops, and by the eighteenth century, Algeria was treating on an equal footing with the great Powers of Europe.

Then, in 1830, French troops landed on the Algerian coast. Ostensibly their expedition was no more than a punitive one, a retort for a three-year-old insult to France by the Dey. In fact, once Algiers had been occupied and the Dey had surrendered, King Louis Philippe and his advisers thought they would profit from the collapse of the local régime by taking its place. Over the decades that followed, therefore, French troops progressively conquered the whole of the country and expropriated its Moslem inhabitants' lands. It was not till 1871 that the final rebellion against the occupants was put down.

By that time, Algeria had been given the status of three departments, or counties, of France, and European immigrants were pouring in; as early as 1848 it was estimated that one-third of the cultivable lands of the country were in European hands. The settlers very soon acquired a strongly defensive common mentality: among other things, they bitterly attacked the Government's spending of money on the education of Moslems. It wasn't till after the first world war, for which Algerian Moslems were mobilized as conscripts, that the first Algerian nationalist movement was founded, by Messali Hadj, the son of a shoemaker, who had emigrated to France and married a French Communist there. Messali was doomed to spend a good deal of his life in prison, but members of one of the organizations formed by him were eventually responsible for launching the war in Algeria in 1954.

The second Algerian nationalist leader to raise his voice was a chemist named Ferhat Abbas, who in his 1942 *Manifesto of the Algerian People* claimed absolute equality for all the inhabitants of the country, and a few months latter added a demand that at the end of the war an Algerian State should be set up, whose Constitution should be drafted by a Constituent Assembly. Naturally his demands were turned down: the

French community in Algeria, who by now numbered around a million, saw themselves as a perpetually dominant minority and were convinced that the natives preferred it that way. General de Gaulle, however, in 1944 issued an ordinance which provided that all Moslems over twenty-one should have the right to vote for the French Chamber, though they would vote on separate lists from the French citizens, and for different candidates. The French National Assembly in 1947 enacted a new Algerian Constitution which had its liberal elements. There might thus have seemed a reasonable hope of Algeria evolving peacefully towards some form of autonomy.

Two facts, among a number of others, were to stand in the way of such an evolution. The first was an incident in north-eastern Algeria in 1945 which sparked off the massacre by Moslems of more than a hundred French civilians and thus provoked weeks-long reprisals by French troops in which not fewer than 15,000 Moslems were killed. That provoked feelings of bitterness among Algerians which it was very hard to forget. The second fact was that in all the elections which took place in Algeria after 1947, to the Algerian Assembly set up under the new Constitution, to the French National Assembly and to the local councils, the French authorities quite shamelessly faked the results where Moslem candidates were concerned. It was thus that in March 1954, nine young Algerians established the Revolutionary Council for Unity and Action which set about organizing the armed insurrection that was designed to conquer for their fellow-countrymen the freedoms they could not win by constitutional means, the insurrection that broke on the world in November 1954. Rather less than two years later, a conference of revolutionary leaders inside Algeria laid down a general platform of action for the rebels. In October of 1956, a conference in Tunis of Algerian, Moroccan and Tunisian leaders that might have paved the way to peace was frustrated when the French army forced down at Algiers the plane carrying the four Algerian delegates to the meeting and made them prisoners: the then French Premier, the Socialist Guy Mollet, had not the courage to repudiate the action which had been taken behind his back. A little more than eighteen months after that, an insurrection in Algiers by Europeans who feared that the Paris Government was going

27

to settle with the Algerian rebels led to the accession to power of General de Gaulle. And after a series, first of peace feelers and then of initially unsuccessful peace talks between the new French Government and the rebels, the two sides signed in the French watering place of Evian a series of documents which brought the war to an end.

Few people would have imagined, on the March day of 1962 that witnessed the signature of the Evian agreements, that another five months would see Algeria a prey to something very near civil war. A civil war, what is more, not between Algerians and Europeans but between conflicting leaders of the Federation of National Liberation, or F.L.N., the name by which the Algerian rebel movement had been known. Yet almost as soon as the agreements were reached a succession of events occurred which pointed plainly to divergencies of view within the F.L.N. leadership, and between some at least of these leaders and the commanders of the Army of National Liberation, or A.L.N., whose strongest and best-armed units were stationed outside Algerian soil, near the frontiers with Algeria of Tunisia and Morocco. It was stated and never denied that Ben Bella and his nationalist companions of captivity in the French chateau of Aunoy, all of them members of the Provisional Government in exile, had been kept fully informed of the progress of the Evian discussions and had approved their outcome. Yet when the five men were released, they did not fly direct to Tunis, the headquarters of the Provisional Government, as might have been expected. They went to Rabat, where Premier Ben Khedda and his other fellow-Ministers had to fly to greet them, and it was more than three weeks before Ben Bella finally landed up in Tunisia. Then it was not till over a month after his liberation that Ben Bella paid his first genuine tribute to the Evian agreements, when he described them to the official Algerian news agency as 'positive for the Algerian people': earlier he had talked of the agreements' 'positive and negative aspects'. Again it needed little discernment to see the strong sympathy that existed between Ben Bella and the officers and men of the A.L.N. on Moroccan and Tunisian territory: on his trip to Morocco, Ben Bella and his prison companions were invited up to visit the A.L.N. camp at Oujda, an invitation which was not extended to Ben Khedda and the rest of the Algerian Cabinet. And forty-eight hours after Mohammed Yazid, the Algerian Information Minister, had denied the existence of any differences between Ben Bella and the rest of the Provisional Government, an incident occurred which strongly suggested that there were considerable differences, in the field of propaganda at any rate, between the Provisional Government and the A.L.N. general staff: the A.L.N. issued direct to the press a communiqué on alleged violations by the French of the Evian cease-fire agreement which went far beyond a similar statement put out earlier by the official Algerian news agency.

No one who visited the A.L.N. headquarters at Ghardimaou could fail to be impressed by the revolutionary atmosphere which pervaded it, an atmosphere which seemed far more Left-wing than the sentiments expressed by the Ministers of the Algerian Provisional Government back in Tunis. 'Independence is a stage: Revolution is our end' read the most prominent notice on the Political Commissary's notice-board. The Algerian revolt did indeed *start* with the aim of independence, a young officer explained. But the people had seen what had happened in other newly-independent countries: in Tunisia and Morocco, poverty still continued side by side with privilege, and the A.L.N. was determined that shouldn't happen at home. 'We'll never be Communists,' another voice claimed – but a picture of Fidel Castro was one of the only two portrait photographs on the walls. And a political officer explained the army's activities by observing: 'There's a saying: The A.L.N. lives in the people like a fish in water' – which happened to be a saying, about the Chinese Communist army, by Mao Tse-tung.

The clash between Premier Ben Khedda and the majority of his Ministers on one hand and Ben Bella and the A.L.N. high command on the other did not, however, find public expression till the meeting in Tripoli in June of the National Council of the Algerian Revolution, or 'nationalist parliament', as it had been known up to then: the meeting was held in Tripoli because the Libyan authorities make no bones about stopping journalists from entering their country. There were two main items on the National Council's agenda. The first was the approval of a social and political programme for independent Algeria, which had been worked out by specialized commissions and was to be the platform of the F.L.N. candidates at the Constituent Assembly elections due to be held at the end of July, and this was adopted unanimously. The second item, which led to the trouble, was the transformation of the F.L.N. from a Resistance organization into a political party.

It led to trouble because Ben Bella proposed that the F.L.N. party should be run by a seven-man political bureau on which he and his friends would have enjoyed absolute predominance: neither Ben Khedda nor any of his supporters were on the list of members suggested. The composition of the political bureau was of extreme importance, since it was to have the choosing of the F.L.N. candidates at the Constituent Assembly elections. And the proposal confirmed the suspicions of one of Ben Bella's former prison companions, Mohammed Boudiaf, a deputy Premier of the Provisional Government, that Ben Bella was out for absolute power, suspicions which were almost certainly shared by other Provisional Government ministers. Soundings at the National Council are said to have shown that Ben Bella's proposal would have obtained a majority of votes, though not the two-thirds majority necessary for its adoption: among those who supported it were the three members of the A.L.N. general staff, Colonel Boumedienne, who denounced the Evian agreements and as good as accused the Provisional Government of having betrayed the nationalist cause, and Majors Slimane and Mendjeli. In fact, no vote was ever taken, since Ben Khedda, after having been covered with abuse by Ben Bella, walked out of the meeting with the ministers who supported him and returned to Tunis.

There is little doubt that Ben Khedda was in the line of F.L.N. tradition when he opposed the Ben Bella proposal. An F.L.N. congress held inside Algeria in secret two years after the war started had decided on the principle of collegial leadership within the organization. Two excellent reasons could be urged for this: firstly, no F.L.N. leader then possessed the overwhelming popularity with which Bourguiba had returned to Tunisia and secondly Messali Hadj, founder of the first Algerian nationalist movement, had made himself intolerable to his followers in his later days by his authoritarian behaviour as single party boss. If there had been any uncertainty whether Ben Bella's proposed political bureau would in fact have meant collegial leadership or one-man rule, it was speedily dissipated after the man who was to become Algeria's first President returned to his country.

What was it that divided Ben Bella and Ben Khedda? It may be suggested that their contrasting backgrounds had something to do with it. Ben Bella's education had stopped early: on the days, before his arrest, when he was looking young, he suggested nothing more than an upper form schoolboy with a gift for games, and indeed he used to play excellent football. He served in the French army during the war and was awarded the *medaille militaire*, which an N.C.O. can only win if he displays conspicuous courage. In 1949, he had already joined the Algerian nationalist movement and organized an attack on the Oran general post office with the aim of getting money for the cause: the *coup* was successful, but Ben Bella was captured and sentenced to life imprisonment, which he failed to serve only because he escaped from jail in 1952 and made his way to Cairo. Ben Khedda, a chemist by profession, is an intellectual with a deceptively mild appearance. Ben Bella had been one of the nine 'historic leaders' who might be called the founding fathers of the Algerian revolution, but through no fault of his own he had spent all of the wartime years outside Algeria. Ben Khedda, on the other hand, had been in the thick of events there. He played a prominent part in organizing the 1956 F.L.N. congress, which defined the objectives of the movement and established the National Council of the Algerian Revolution, and he helped to direct the 1956–57 battle of Algiers, the months-long campaign of bombings that stopped only when General Massu and his parachutists were drafted into the city. With that background, he could obviously count on the support of the political leaders who, like himself, had been active inside Algeria during the war.

Their contrasting backgrounds were, however, no more than a minor element in the conflict between the head of the Algerian Provisional Government and the man who was to replace him. The key to the conflict was that for something like a year there had been serious differences of opinion between the Provisional Government and the commanders of the A.L.N. in Tunisia and Morocco, which its 25,000 men, with their modern armament, made a force far more formidable than any inside Algeria. The army commanders did not approve the way the peace negotiations were going. Before Ben Bella and his fellow-prisoners had been liberated from the chateau of Aunoy, they had contacted him there and agreed with him that as soon as he was set free, he should take their part inside the Provisional Government. He had in fact done his best to reconcile the two sides, and it was not till more than a year later that he came out with a violent and public attack on the Provisional Government as a whole during its stay in Tunisia. 'The Provisional Government,' he then said, 'filled whole cemeteries with the best of Algeria's cadres because they disagreed with it.'

June was almost out, however, before the general public had its first inkling of the crisis that had riven the Algerian nationalist leadership in Tripoli. For some time past, the A.L.N. radio station at Ghardimaou had been making violent attacks on the Provisional Government: in the second half of June, it stepped these up, after the truce agreement which the Provisional Executive in Algeria had reached with the French terrorist Secret Army Organization, with the approval of the Provisional Government in Tunis. In the last week in June, a conference of the military and political leaders of three of the *wilayas*, or provinces, into which the F.L.N. had divided Algeria, plus representatives of the F.L.N. federations in France and Tunisia, met and passed a resolution repudiating the authority of the A.L.N. general staff. That was just what Ben Khedda wanted. The following day, the Algerian Provisional Government voted for disciplinary action against Colonel Boumedienne and his two assistants. Mohammed Khider, another prison companion of Ben Bella's, not only opposed the proposal, on the grounds that the Provisional Government had failed to get a vote of confidence from the 'nationalist parliament' in June, but resigned and left the country, and two days later Ben Bella too slipped out of Tunisia, to Tripoli. Nothing appeared in the press about the breach between the two sides, but it was open.

And late on the evening of 30 June, the Algerian Provisional

Government issued an order of the day to the A.L.N. which at last revealed the fact. The order stated that Colonel Boumedienne, Major Slimane and Major Mendjeli had been dismissed and deprived of their rank. It accused them of 'criminal activity,' intended to undermine the Provisional Government's authority and to establish a dictatorship, and it ordered the A.L.N. to obey only the Provisional Government, or officers loyal to it. The A.L.N. general staff replied with a statement declaring the Provisional Government's order to be null and void and instructing the troops to obey its commands only. It was under these hardly propitious circumstances that Premier Ben Khedda and his Government flew into Algiers on 3 July.

The Provisional Government Premier had, indeed, made two last moves to save his position, one conciliatory and the other tough. At the mass meeting held in Tunis on the evening of 2 July to bid farewell to the Algerians, there was an unexpected member of the audience: Wing Commander Ali Sabri, Vice-President of the United Arab Republic, who had flown in from Cairo a bare hour before with a mission from President Nasser to reconcile the two sides. Just before midnight, Wing Commander Sabri and Belkacem Krim, one of the Deputy Premiers in the Algerian Provisional Government, flew into Libya with Ben Khedda's approval to try and persuade Ben Bella to return to Tunis and fly back to Algiers with his colleagues: they failed. Ben Khedda was no more successful with his tough move. Shortly after he had dismissed the A.L.N. commanders, he asked the French to order their troops in Algeria to prevent Colonel Boumedienne's forces from crossing the frontiers from Tunisia and Morocco. Paris said no; it wasn't intervening in Algerian internal affairs any more.

So on the morning of 3 July, men of the A.L.N. in Morocco crossed the frontier and paraded in Oran, where crowds cheered the name of Ben Bella. On 4 July, the A.L.N. forces in Tunisia crossed the border too. What is more, immediately after his dismissal, Colonel Boumedienne had made a secret trip to southern Algeria. He had contacted Colonel Chaabani, head of the Saharan *wilaya*, one of the most famous commanders of the nationalist forces inside Algeria, and persuaded him to disregard the Provisional Government's orders. The nationalist forces in the Aurès mountains, to the north, lost little time in following Chaabani's example. Their commander, Colonel Tahar Sbiri – who three years later was to participate in Ben Bella's arrest – publicly stated that he and his men considered Ben Khedda to be 'the head of the counter-revolutionaries' and regarded Ben Bella as their real chief. The Provisional Government Ministers were cheered to the echo by enormous crowds when they drove into Algiers from the airport on 3 July. But Ben Khedda knew only too well that they were in for trouble.

Just what could he count for in the way of support? Not even all the troops inside Algeria, for Boumedienne had won over some of their commanders and the forces in others had been immobilized by the entry of the A.L.N. from outside. Probably the only men on whom he could really rely were those of the Kabylie *wilaya* – the Kabyles, who speak the language current in Algeria before the Arab conquest, form quite a sizeable linguistic if not ethnical minority – the Constantine *wilaya* and the Algiers *wilaya*. Yet for all that, the situation had its hopeful elements: for one thing, whatever the commanders might think, there was considerable ill-feeling between the forces inside Algeria and those who had come in from outside. The forces from outside looked down on the *wilaya* fighters, who hadn't had their doctrinal training. The forces inside resented the fact that, as they saw it, the troops outside had never helped them in their tough struggle in the *djebels*. 'When the French were hunting us down,' they said, 'Boumedienne kept for his men the arms that were meant for us. It didn't worry him if *we* were wiped out: all he wanted was to pave the way for his seizure of power with his well-armed troops and their tanks and artillery.' Finally, the troops inside Algeria had fought for independence and agrarian reform: those outside had been indoctrinated to regard the aim of their struggle as an out-and-out Socialist revolution.

So Ben Khedda made a last attempt to reach a settlement with his opponents. Early in July, two of his Ministers flew to Rabat, where Ben Bella had now arrived, and had two days' discussions with him and Khider, who might be said to have become his *eminence grise*. Ben Bella made two demands: cancellation of the dismissal of the A.L.N. commanders and an immediate reconvening of the 'nationalist parliament' that

34

had never finished its business in Tripoli. Ben Khedda's Ministers had other proposals to make: for one thing, they didn't feel that the men who had met in Tripoli still fully represented the country. It was eventually agreed that the necessary decisions should be left to a meeting of the heads of all the Algerian *wilayas* which was convened in the town of Orleansville. Meantime Ben Bella and his swelling train of supporters – one somewhat unexpected figure who joined these was the hardly revolutionary first Premier of the Provisional Government in exile, Ferhat Abbas – drove into Algeria and set up their headquarters in the north-western hillside town of Tlemcen, in the area where Ben Bella had been born.

The *wilaya* leaders' meeting came to nothing: the representatives of the *wilayas* supporting Ben Bella walked out. The same evening, Ben Bella did his best to trump the Algiers Provisional Government's claims to be the only constitutional authority. His Information Officer read to the press a proclamation which declared null and void all the decisions taken by the Government in the past month, declared the sole legitimate executive of the F.L.N. to be the seven-man committee proposed by Ben Bella in Tripoli, and called on Ben Khedda and his supporters to accept the position. On both sides of Algeria A.L.N. troops supporting Ben Bella were probing or advancing; in Algiers, there was every sign that the Provisional Government was breaking up. But Ben Bella seemed in no hurry to move into the capital: he merely shifted his headquarters to the great West Algerian port of Oran. And talks between the two sides started up again, with Khider the Ambassador-at-large on the Ben Bella side.

On 1 August, agreement was reached. Attempts by the Ben Khedda side to get one of the still titular Premier's supporters on the political bureau failed, but Mohammed Boudiaf, who was just as suspicious of Ben Bella's ambitions, consented to occupy the place on it which he had previously declined. Elections to a Constituent Assembly, it was agreed, should take place before the end of the month. Finally, the National Council of the Algerian Revolution, as representative of the F.L.N., was to meet a week after the polls 'to examine the question of the political bureau'. Ben Bella flew into Algiers, was received with wild enthusiasm and drove straight to the seat of the Provisional Government, where he publicly shook hands with Ben Khedda. The Provisional Government announced that its powers would in future be exercised through the political bureau, and it was stated that nominations for the elections would close on 18 August. When the single list of candidates was in fact submitted on that date, it might have been thought that all the trouble was over.

It wasn't. When Ben Bella came into Algiers, he had announced that normal life was going to resume: a civil administration would be installed and the *wilayas* would disappear. That might appear perfect good sense. But it sounded as a death-knell in the ears of the commanders of the two *wilayas*, the Algiers area and Kabylie, who had retained a measure of independence of Ben Bella and his military backers. They knew perfectly well that the reconversion of the *wilayas*, necessary though it might be in the end, would at the moment spell the final triumph of the armies from beyond the frontiers over the internal *maquis* who had borne the real burden of the struggle for freedom. They therefore agreed between themselves that they would accept no demobilization and no reconversion till Algeria had solid and legally established institutions. A few days later, the dispute came out into the open. The Algiers *wilaya* organized a public meeting the keynote of whose speeches was: 'Bar the way to personal power!' The political bureau called a gathering of their own, at which demonstrators arrived bearing banners with such inscriptions as 'The A.L.N. back to barracks!' During the night, troops of the *wilaya* occupied the Algiers radio station, while its officers prevented the newspapers reporting the political bureau demonstration. Finally the political bureau came out with a communiqué denouncing the *wilaya*'s attempt to assert its authority in Algiers by force of arms, stating that it was no longer in a position to exercise its powers and consequently postponing the elections till conditions of real peace existed.

That put the fat in the fire; but the struggle between the two sides that followed remained for a few days a war of press conferences, with each side accusing the other of lack of respect for democracy, and the Algiers *wilaya* taxing the political bureau with wanting to get a prefabricated parliament at all costs. On 29 August, however, heavy and continuous rifle and machine-gun fire broke out in the heart of Algiers: on one side was a battalion of troops loyal to the political bureau who had been brought into the capital at the beginning of the month and gone under cover in the Casbah, the old Moslem city, and on the other the men of the Algiers *wilaya*. The *wilaya* authorities immediately declared a curfew, the first to be imposed since independence. The following day the political bureau ordered the troops loyal to it to move into Algiers. A column would advance on the capital from the west and a column, headed by Colonel Chaabani, from the south: the troops in the Constantine area, to the east, refused to take part in the operation and 'fire on their brothers'.

The political bureau's reaction was predictable. What wasn't predictable was the reaction of the Algiers population to the proclamation of the curfew. They flatly refused to observe it. An hour after curfew time, a stream of demonstrators, a high proportion of them women, paraded through the streets shouting rhythmically: 'Seven years, that's enough!' – they had a right to expect an end of violence after having endured seven years of it. No attempt was made to stop them; indeed, troops and police along the route they took ostentatiously removed the magazines from their tommy-guns. It wasn't the last demonstration of its kind, either; what is more, the trade unions in Algiers decided to call a general strike if civil war should in fact break out.

Behind the trade unions' threat and the night march through the streets lay a general resentment that Algeria's independence should have appeared to turn sour the moment it had been achieved: the rejection of violence may be compared to the general attitude of the population when Ben Bella was deposed. Only very simple-minded Algerians can have expected the establishment of a new heaven and a new earth to follow immediately on the hoisting of the green, white and red colours over the public buildings of Algiers. What they felt they did have a right to expect was that their leaders should at once set about tackling the enormous material problems facing Algeria, particularly since these leaders – their agreement at Tripoli on a development programme for their country bore witness to this – appeared to be divided far less by political than by personal issues. And a whole series of very big problems was facing the Algeria of summer 1962. One of these was unemployment, which had risen to 2,000,000: the country's economy had been running down for a year and more. Another was that the unemployed weren't getting their unemployment pay, any more than old age pensioners were drawing their pensions or employed parents their family allowances: most of the social insurance offices concerned, together with their records, had been bombed out by the French terrorist Secret Army Organization weeks before independence. A third problem was that, under Secret Army Organization pressure, no direct taxes had been collected since early in the year, and no income tax returns had so far been sent in. And that did not take into account the decline in foreign trade, the paralysis of many administrative offices by the mass departure 'on leave' of their French officials, nor the continued kidnapping of Europeans by heaven knew who, not to speak of the necessity to start ahead right away with the F.L.N.'s agreed programme of nationalizations and social reforms.

The advance on Algiers had, however, been ordered, and it went on. To start with, at any rate, it was bloodless: Colonel Chaabani's troops entered the town of Boghari, some 120 miles south of Algiers, in company with the Algiers area *wilaya* forces who had been supposed to bar the way to them, surrounded by a crowd of civilians rejoicing that there had not been a clash. That didn't last long, however. Heavy fighting developed both south and west of the capital, and it continued for several days after Ben Bella suddenly appeared in Algiers and announced to a crowd in the square outside the former French Government General buildings that the crisis in Algeria's political leadership was over once for all, and that the political bureau was returning to Algiers for good. He had in fact reached a ceasefire agreement with the two opposition *wilayas*, but he had to fly to the front himself by helicopter to see it was observed. The agreement allowed the fixing of a new and final date for the Constituent Assembly elections. The date set was 30 September, and when the list of candidates was made public, it proved to be considerably different from the list which the political bureau – after consultation with all the *wilayas* – had submitted just under a month before. The first list would have yielded an Assembly including most of the tendencies in the Algerian nationalist movement. Almost all the critics of Ben Bella had been eliminated in the new list; indeed, one in four of the candidates put forward in August had been replaced by new names.

All the same, speech was still free in the Algeria of September 1962. In the most frequented bar in Algiers, an Algerian businessman could be heard observing that he didn't think Algeria was sufficiently well off in competent politicians to afford to eliminate from its first parliament, and so from its first Cabinet, such figures as Ben Khedda, and the two members of the Provisional Executive – who had been doing the practical work of governing Algeria since Evian – who had been dropped with him. In the Algerian trade union headquarters, a labour leader said that if the new Government didn't satisfy the workers' legitimate demands, the unions might come out against it, and might even form a Labour Party, on the lines of that in Great Britain. Ben Bella had already made plain his intention that the F.L.N. should be the only party in Algeria, but not everyone had yet taken the position for granted.

Speech was equally unfettered when the Constituent Assembly opened at the end of September, despite the fact that the single list of candidates who automatically became deputies had been hand-picked by the political bureau with a view to eliminating the maximum number of critics. Far from behaving as a rubber stamp body, the Assembly repeatedly came out in opposition to the political bureau line. Thirty-six deputies abstained from voting when Ferhat Abbas stood for the Speakership: more abstained, or even voted against, when Ben Bella stood for the Premiership the next day. Thirty-six-years-old Ait Ahmed, the Benjamin of the now defunct Provisional Government – he had resigned all his official positions back in the summer on the grounds that the Algerian people were sick of their leaders' post-independence disputes and wanted to see a completely new team in power – hadn't the least hesitation in holding a press conference in one of the two biggest Algiers hotels. Ait Ahmed denied that he was going to take the lead in a regular opposition to the Government, but said that he would be holding regular press conferences in the future – which would hardly have been necessary if he intended always to take the Government line – and added that if minority opinions weren't given their say in the Assembly, there would be a danger of Algeria's turning into a police State.

But though 1 November saw the celebrations of the eighth anniversary of the launching of the Algerian revolt go off with great enthusiasm, there was an increasing number of small signs that the police State might indeed be on the way. That the new Algeria would be a single-party State, Ben Bella had made clear once more in a press conference he gave at the close of the festivities. He and his collaborators, he said, were agreed that the multi-party system was not valid for Algeria: their idea of democracy was that the ordinary man would be free to speak his mind within the single national party and shouldn't be stifled by party officialdom. The Communist party, he implied, would have to go, and indeed it was banned shortly afterwards, though its daily paper, *Alger Républicain*, by far the liveliest in Algiers, was permitted to survive.

One sign of the evolution towards a police State was the coming into existence of an underground opposition movement, the Revolutionary Socialist Party, which it was later learned had been organized by Mohammed Boudiaf. Its activities appeared to be confined to the distribution of cyclostyled leaflets critical of the Government, but its existence would hardly have been necessary if speech within the F.L.N. had really been free, and such underground parties are found only in police States. But it was in the field of trade union activities that the trend towards an authoritarian régime was most clearly seen. In September, a trade union spokesman came out openly against the system prevalent in most newly-liberated African countries, under which the unions are under the control of the single Government party. At the end of October, the trade unions' organ was confiscated for twenty-four hours after it had appeared with an article complaining of attempts by F.L.N. representatives to interfere with union activities. In December, the same weekly printed an editorial in which it bitterly denounced the 'scissionist work' within the unions of certain elements of the F.L.N. and complained of the avalanche of 'prefabricated resolutions' that had recently been appearing in the official F.L.N. daily, purporting to come from branches which had never previously signified their existence to union headquarters, and denouncing the alleged lack of representativity of the unions' provisional secretariat. It should have been easy to guess from that what would happen when the unions' first congress met in Algiers in mid-January 1963. There was a violent debate between delegates who wanted the unions to be completely free and those, who appeared to be in a majority, who believed that they should be subject to the F.L.N. Tempers were hardly improved by a leaflet distributed by the pro-autonomy delegates, who accused the F.L.N. of a plot to sabotage the congress by swamping the hall with people who had no right to be there, and keeping genuine delegates out, an accusation which received additional support when, shortly before the first afternoon session began, 600 unemployed mobilized by the F.L.N. streamed into the hall. Naturally the final resolutions were not in favour of autonomy, and a secretariat which could be counted on to follow the F.L.N. lead was elected. Though at the unions' next congress, two years later, even that docile leadership was replaced.

Mid-March of 1963 saw the French exploding an atom bomb in the Algerian Sahara: at the end of the month, Ben Bella announced that the big French landed properties in Algeria were to be taken over and run by workers' management committees. It was a popular method of retaliation, but firstly there was reason to believe that it had been taken in response to pressure from below, from militant members of the trade union movement, and secondly, the original proposals for workers' management had been drafted by Ait Ahmed, who was soon to come out as an opposition leader.

There were increasing grounds for opposition to the new régime by any Algerian who had an independent mind: more and more facts suggested that Ben Bella was using the heroic stature to which the A.L.N. had built him up for its own purposes to achieve something very like personal power. In April Khider resigned, under pressure from the Premier, from the general secretaryship of the F.L.N. political bureau, which promptly voted Ben Bella into his place. Three obvious comments on the move come to the mind. Firstly, Khider had played a key part in the leadership crisis of the preceding summer in helping the A.L.N. instal Ben Bella in power – and no aspiring dictator likes to be under a debt of gratitude. Secondly, on two of the issues suggested as grounds for differ-

41

ences between the two men, Ben Bella was within a matter of months to adopt the views that Khider held. Thirdly, now that he was general secretary of the Government party's political bureau as well as head of the Government, Ben Bella had attained a position of concentrated power as strong as Nkrumah's was in Ghana or as Stalin's had been in the Soviet Union.

Up to now there had been few if any political arrests since Algeria became independent. June 1963 saw the first of these. Mohammed Boudiaf, leader of the underground Socialist Revolutionary party, was picked up in the street by plain clothes police and, after some days of detention, deported with three of his party companions, first to the edge of the Algerian Sahara, and then deep into the Sahara itself, where the temperatures at midsummer are stifling. None of the four had been subjected to any form of trial. They had not even been told why they had been arrested, and when their repeated letters to the authorities failed to elicit any explanation, they started a hunger-strike which they kept up for more than a month; this alone was responsible for their transfer to the north, where they were taken to hospital and then confined under more humane conditions. Questioned by Ait Ahmed in the Assembly, Ben Bella said he had incontrovertible proof that the four men had been involved in a plot against the régime; later he told the congress of Algerian students that they were being treated like kings. When they were finally released in November – after Boudiaf had refused to agree to his expatriation to Switzerland – they had still not been given the slightest intimation of the reasons for their five months-long imprisonment.

Boudiaf's opposition party had been an under-cover one. Less than three weeks after his arrest, Ait Ahmed – who described it as the act of 'a blind and obstinate tyrant' – announced in a press conference his decision to take the lead in what he called an open opposition to the Ben Bella régime. Ait Ahmed met the press in his home town of Michelet, 3,000 feet up in the Kabylie mountains; he hadn't given the conference in Algiers, he explained, because fellow-members of the F.L.N. had warned him that he was in danger, not just of being arrested, but of being liquidated if he stayed on there.

Ait Ahmed attacked the Ben Bella Government on a number of different grounds. Firstly, he said, the Premier was out for power, and power for life, at all costs. Secondly, he had made a horrible mess of the country's financial, economic and social affairs: one pointer to this was the persistence of mass unemployment. Finally, freedom of speech had ceased to exist. Even deputies in the Assembly, Ait Ahmed said, were afraid to speak their minds: that seemed a slight exaggeration, though fewer of them were coming out against the Government line than had done so nine months before.

It was when he talked of the organization of his opposition movement – later christened the Socialist Forces Front – that Ait Ahmed was least convincing. He spoke of holding local and regional party meetings which would pave the way to a Government of National Union, and of boycotting the elections to the next Assembly then due – though they were postponed by a year – in September. But it seemed wildly improbable that the Ben Bella Government would tolerate the holding of meetings designed to promote its downfall, or allow any publicity to be given to Ait Ahmed's indictment of the authorities; indeed, the next day's Algiers papers printed only four paragraphs of his two hours long series of statements and completely omitted his key declaration that he was going to lead an open opposition. It looked therefore as if Ait Ahmed would be compelled to carry out his propaganda work underground and would sooner or later be forced into the use of violence. And that is in fact what happened less than three months later.

The next prominent leader to come out against Ben Bella was Ferhat Abbas, veteran Algerian nationalist leader, the first Premier of the Algerian Provisional Government in exile and, since the autumn of 1962, Speaker of the Constituent Assembly. It had always been a little difficult to understand why such an essentially moderate political figure – in France, Abbas would have been a member of the Radical-Socialist party – should have come out against Ben Khedda and in favour of Ben Bella in the summer of 1962, except for interested reasons: one possibility is that he had hoped to act as an adviser to the politically inexperienced Ben Bella and to exercise a moderating influence on the Government party's revolutionary policy. By the summer of 1963, Abbas was undeceived. In two successive speeches in his constituency, he said firstly that Algeria's Socialist revolution was going a little too fast, and secondly that he would retire from public life if the authorities didn't give the Algerian people freedom of speech and of the vote. It wasn't till the middle of August that he carried out his threat. That was a fortnight after 4,000 local leaders of the F.L.N. from all over Algeria had met in the biggest Algiers cinema and discussed and unanimously approved the draft Constitution for Algeria prepared by the political bureau. The draft provided for a President of the Republic who would at the same time be Premier and who could obtain from the National Assembly delegated powers for legislation, who would in fact be the uncontested chief of the country. It also contained a section defining the position of the F.L.N. as Algeria's single party and laid down that it would select the candidate for the Presidency of the Republic and all the candidates for the Assembly, define the main lines of national policy and not only inspire but supervise the activities of the Government. The curious may ask why the cinema meeting should have been necessary, when Algeria already had a Constituent Assembly, whose main task was supposed to be the voting of the Constitution. The obvious aim was to bulldoze the Assembly deputies, who were present at the cinema meeting and who had occasionally shown a slight if decreasing independence, into voting the F.L.N. draft, though there were two others before them, including one by Abbas himself.

Explaining his resignation from the Speakership in a letter to the deputies, Abbas declared that the submission of the draft Constitution to the party leadership before it had been submitted to the Assembly itself was a breach of the law. He added that the system under which parliamentary candidates, who automatically became deputies, were chosen by the party would turn them into 'robots, opportunists and courtiers'. 'We aren't yet a police State,' he said, 'but if we don't look out we soon shall be.' A couple of days later, the political bureau of the F.L.N. expelled Abbas from the party.

Naturally the Assembly voted the Constitution, after a

44

five-day debate at the end of the month, but it didn't go through unanimously: 139 deputies voted for the document, eight abstained and twenty-three had the courage to vote against. Most of the thirty speakers who might have been expected to be critical supported the draft on the grounds that 'it was in line with the present political evolution of the world'. There were the bold, however. One of them came out strongly against the personality cult and in favour of collegial leadership: to place all executive power in the hands of a single man was a grave mistake, he said. Another speaker declared that he was all in favour of a strong executive under certain circumstances and would willingly vote it special powers if this appeared necessary. What he did oppose was a draft which definitively conferred fantastically wide powers on the President. Finally, the Abbé Bérenguer, who had acted as an F.L.N. spokesman in South America during the war, said that history was full of revolutions that started with freedom and ended in slavery.

The results of the Constitutional referendum were equally predictable. Officials gave the number of registered electors as 6,314,451 of whom 5,122,854 were stated to have voted, 5,016,692 in favour of the Constitution: there appeared some reason to believe that the figures had been faked and that the total of abstentions had been considerably higher than represented. Shortly afterwards, leaders of the F.L.N. from all over Algeria, meeting in the same Algiers cinema, unanimously adopted Ben Bella as sole candidate for the Presidency of the Republic. The candidate seized the occasion to say that he had always been against the personality cult. 'If there's any people in the world that'll never stomach a dictatorship, it's the Algerian people,' he said.

Ait Ahmed wasn't going to stomach it, anyway. Speaking to a crowd of 4,000 in the Kabylie town of Tizi Ouzou on the last Sunday in September, he came as near as his habitual ambiguity would permit him to launching a revolt against the Government. He didn't call on the people to take to arms. What he did say was that he wanted to see the establishment of a provisional Directory composed of the five ex-prisoners among the top leaders of the Algerian nationalist movement – Khider, who had been forced out of the general secretaryship of the F.L.N., Boudiaf, who was at the moment under detention, Bitet, who had just resigned from the Government, himself and Ben Bella. And it was pretty obvious that negotiations would never induce Algeria's first President to agree to the replacement of himself and his assistants by such a team: only force could work the trick.

It was obvious too that there was force behind Ait Ahmed and his Socialist Forces Front. Alongside him on the platform, besides two Assembly deputies, was Colonel Mohand Ou el Hadj, commanding the troops in the Kabylie area, whose men mounted guard over the meeting and the roads around. Talking to journalists later, Ait Ahmed said there was no question of his movement being a Kabylie secessionist one. It wasn't an area that was revolting; what was happening was that a section of the Algerian people was resuming the revolutionary movement that had been smashed by the crisis of 1962. He added that though he regarded the Ben Bella Government as illegal, there was no question of his setting up a new administration in the areas which had come over to him. Referring a week or so later to the mission of mediation between himself and the Government which certain Kabylie deputies had undertaken, Ait Ahmed said there was no question of talking things over within the party, because the party was no more than an instrument of the régime. 'We refuse to talk in the party,' he added, 'because the party is one of the things we want to discuss.'

Ben Bella's first reaction to Ait Ahmed's revolt was to minimize it: twenty-four hours later, in a radio and T.V. speech, he used what was becoming a favourite gambit of his and denounced it as a plot with international ramifications. Finally he told a 60,000 crowd in Algiers that the last French-owned farmlands in the country, two and a quarter million acres of them, were being nationalized. The measure, which was executed with considerable brutality, would have been carried out sooner or later anyway, but it had been speeded up in response to Ait Ahmed's allegation that the revolution was being braked down. Ten days after Ait Ahmed had made his Tizi Ouzou speech, Government troops blocked all the roads leading into Kabylie; then they occupied his home town of Michelet, and he and Mohand Ou el Hadj took to the mountain crests from which the latter had defied the French during the war. In any case, the revolt soon faded out of the public mind, for in the meantime the Algerian-Moroccan frontier clash had broken out.

The frontier clash was a bit of luck for Ben Bella, for it ended by splitting Ait Ahmed and his military supporters. Ait Ahmed did indeed issue a leaflet calling on the Government to withdraw its forces from Kabylie so that his supporters could go to the front, though he also put forward a number of political demands, including the formation of a Government of National Union and the liberation of Boudiaf and his fellow-prisoners – who were in fact released in November. Mohand Ou el Hadj and other Kabyle officers didn't confine themselves to talk. They went to the front themselves, and six months later, after the first F.L.N. party congress, Mohand Ou el Hadj vainly appealed to Ait Ahmed to call off his revolt and to join in with the régime in building Socialism. There was, however, what appeared to be one positive reaction to the Socialist Forces Front revolt. Though Ait Ahmed had called for a more revolutionary policy, a high proportion of the people who supported or sympathized with him did so because they wanted less Socialism, not more – tradesmen who feared nationalization, small craftsmen, anyone who possessed the least bit of capital. Well, at the turn of the year, Economics Minister Boumaza told the Assembly that though in the long run the private sector of the economy was bound to disappear, Algeria was willing to give guarantees for private property for a certain period of time. People began to talk of an Algerian N.E.P. – and then the trouble at Oran blew up.

It all started in a very small way, with a protest by street vegetable sellers whom a new by-law had forbidden to hawk their wares on certain streets where traffic was particularly heavy. The vegetable sellers were joined by unemployed working on a local relief work project, who had come to an end of their current fortnight-a-month's employment and who wanted payment of their 'wages', and the two groups went to the town hall with their grievances.

The next day, the complaints developed into what looked very like a demonstration by the opposition to the Government. The demonstrators, who were by no means confined to the two sets of men with precise grievances, marched on the prefecture shouting slogans hostile to Ben Bella, the local prefect and Socialism, and there were cries of 'Long live Abbas! Long live Khider!' – known opponents of the Ben Bella régime, who had resigned or been forced to resign from their official positions on account of their differences with it. Bands of youths armed with sticks joined the procession, obliged tradesmen along the route to the prefecture to shut up their shops, stopped trolleybuses and broke a few windows, and then French flags are said to have appeared. Two thousand people got to the prefecture: then the town hall was invaded, and certain offices in it were sacked. For the greater part of a day, the demonstrators had the town to themselves, and not a single party leader, trade union official or representative of the administration so much as showed his nose.

The demonstration came as something of a shock to the authorities. There had, indeed, been clashes between unemployed and troops in other places more than once in the previous twelve months, though not all of these had been reported in the press. But Oran was not particularly hard hit by unemployment: Constantine was far worse off. Nor had Oran, the capital of the area where Ben Bella was born, ever been regarded up to then as an opposition centre. It looked as if the fortuitous events that had precipitated the demonstration had allowed it to crystallize a feeling that was likely enough widespread in the country: the resentment of the poor and the workless at the fact that during its eighteen months in power, the F.L.N. appeared to have become the party of a new privileged caste, smartly clad and driving in bright new cars – and asking the ordinary man to make sacrifices for the triumph of Socialism.

The Government was quick to hit back. Three hundred people were arrested in Oran and a special tribunal was set up to try them: the latter measure conformed with a Cabinet decision reached just after the demonstration to establish at the seat of each appeal court a 'revolutionary criminal court' which would deal with 'crimes susceptible of impeding the normal working of institutions or involving an unusual disturbance of public order'. Ben Bella described the Oran events in a speech as the result of a conspiracy in which foreign Powers

48

had been involved. 'I warn you,' he told his hearers, 'there is going to be shooting. The man who has killed is going to be killed himself.' And he had a dig at Ferhat Abbas – whom Algiers radio had already linked with the disturbances – without actually naming him.

None of the main opposition leaders turned up at the F.L.N. Congress which started in Algiers on 16 April 1964, though participation was open to any former member of the Provisional Government in exile or to any former *wilaya* commander. Perhaps the reason was that the critics simply had not got a common alternative programme to offer: their hostility to the régime was based almost entirely on their unwillingness to accept a Ben Bella dictatorship. The congress discussions, which took place behind closed doors, do not seem to have been vastly exciting. The opposition leaders would likely enough have agreed to the definition of the F.L.N.'s aims given in the programme that was voted. This laid down that the task of the F.L.N. was to establish a Socialist State on a basis of 'scientific Socialism', though during a necessary transitional period, banks would not be nationalized, neither would small farms, while mixed economy companies would be encouraged. The system of workers' management, the basis of Algerian Socialism, must be extended to every sector of the economy, it was stated. The passages in the programme to which opposition spokesmen would undoubtedly have objected were those which concerned the party. The F.L.N., it was laid down, must directly supervise the activities of the 'national organizations' – of labour, of tradesmen and industrialists, of women and of youth; the trade unions must abandon wage and other claims in favour of 'positive participation in economic life'. Finally, while there must be free speech within the F.L.N. there must be no toleration for 'exploiting class arguments'. Anyone who is familiar with the periphrases in which Communism sometimes likes to characterize its aims could guess what that meant: the party was being turned into a totalitarian party and Algeria into a totalitarian State. Incidentally, on the last day but one of the congress – which unanimously elected Ben Bella general secretary of the F.L.N. – the sole remaining independent daily in Algiers came under the control of the party. It wasn't a right-wing organ. It was the fellow-travelling *Alger Républicain* – but its correspondence columns had in the past printed detailed criticisms of the actions of the authorities as they concerned the ordinary citizen such as appeared in no other daily in the country. There was just one sign at the congress that Ben Bella still found it advisable to conciliate potential sources of scission within the party. The eighty-man central committee of the F.L.N. which the congressists elected included such hardly orthodox figures as Mohand Ou el Hadj, who six months before had been in open revolt, and Colonel Chaabani, whose possible defection had been a matter of gossip; what is more, the two officers were both elected to the inner political bureau.

Meantime, with the Moroccan frontier crisis over, the Socialist Forces Front announced in a communiqué at the end of February that it was resuming its struggle against Ben Bella's 'dictatorial régime'. A fortnight later it reported clashes between its commandos and the authorities, and the kidnapping of some local F.L.N. leaders, one of whom had been tried and executed; later a sub-prefect was kidnapped and killed. The killings went on. At the end of May an officer of the A.L.N. – now known as the National Popular Army, or A.N.P. – was shot down in the streets of Ait Ahmed's home town of Michelet, where the local F.L.N. organization had ceased to exist and nobody was willing to take the risk of reforming it. June saw a Socialist Forces Front car wounding two police guards when it shot up the People's Palace in Algiers, the former residence of the French Governors-General, where the Algerian Government had given its official receptions since independence and which was just opposite the block of flats where Ben Bella lived. There might indeed be no question of Ait Ahmed and his followers staging a march on Algiers. But Ben Bella could hardly tolerate indefinitely the existence of an insurgent centre in the mountains well under a hundred miles from the capital, particularly when what appeared to be reliable sources spoke of 'pocket *maquis*' of the discontented springing up at points all over the country, including even the area immediately round Algiers. So as summer came in, Kabylie was put under the same sort of military occupation it had known under the French, and lorries and jeeps full of A.N.P. soldiers were to be seen patrolling its roads everywhere.

They did their work. Once June was out, little more was heard of the Socialist Forces Front. But Ait Ahmed's movement wasn't the only danger the régime had to cope with. On the last day of June, Khider, who two years before had played a leading part in promoting Ben Bella's accession to power, told a Paris press conference that he had now completely broken with the régime in Algiers and was henceforth devoting himself to the fight for Algeria's freedom. The Algerian Government, he said, was leading the country to disaster in every field, as the result of the increasing trend towards absolute and personal power: the country was now living under a police régime in which freedom of expression had ceased to exist. Khider said his statement was a personal one, though he added that he had made contact with, among other people, Ferhat Abbas, Boudiaf and Ait Ahmed.

On the same day, Colonel Chaabani, who two years before had done almost as much as any military man to make Ben Bella's definitive entry into Algiers possible, had taken to the *maquis* in southern Algeria. Chaabani, who was an out-and-out fighter, had been one of the most conservative among the Algerian nationalists: he was a devout Moslem, with not very much time for democracy or Socialism. The indications were, however, that personal grievances rather than political principles had been responsible for his revolt. He had known that the Government had been planning to cut up the military area for which he had been responsible and to relieve him of its command, and he was generally believed to have joined the new F.L.N. political bureau a month before in the hope that he would be able to block the move. He wasn't successful, and though the Government tried to sweeten the pill by appointing him to the army general staff, he didn't apparently regard that as adequate compensation for the loss of something he had come to regard as a personal domain.

The second anniversary of Algeria's independence did not, thus, go off as gaily as it might have done. Ben Bella made a fighting speech, in which he said that his enemies had the support of the French petrol kings, and that he had 'written proof' that Ait Ahmed was being backed by Europeans. The

F.L.N. central committee requested the President immediately to assume the personal powers he had a constitutional right to exercise in case of 'imminent danger to the nation'. Finally it was announced that Ferhat Abbas, the last man who would ever have embarked on extra-legal action against a régime of which he notoriously disapproved, had been put under house arrest in his Algiers villa. The police had detained him as he was about to board a plane: the authorities apparently feared that he was going to join the other opposition leaders who were meeting abroad.

The detention of Ferhat Abbas didn't stand alone. Bitat, who had been a Deputy Premier less than a year before, was put under house arrest also. The same thing happened to Amar Bentoumi, who had been Minister of Justice till the summer of 1963, and his brother, who was one of the deputies for Algiers. Mohammed Khobsi, former Minister of Trade, was soon to disappear into captivity, as was Abderrahman Farès, head of the Provisional Executive that had administered Algeria in the months following the Evian agreements, while it wasn't long before Abbas was removed from his comfortable Algiers villa and disappeared into detention, it was presumed, in the Sahara. And it wasn't on the shoulders only of the big names that the hands of the police fell. A visitor who returned to Algeria after a few months absence was often shocked to learn the number of his acquaintances who had 'disappeared' in the interval, and when he inquired – not from official sources, which remained mute – why they should have been picked up, he was told that they were probably overheard criticizing the régime. Plainly the Government was getting tough.

August 1964 came in with the announcement that practical steps were being taken to organize the 'people's militia' whose establishment had been decided in June by the F.L.N. central committee. Its commander was to be appointed, naturally, by the party general secretary, Ben Bella. Ben Bella had also just taken over another job, which would normally have been the responsibility of the Minister of the Interior: the appointment of prefects. The President's aim, it was suggested, was to prepare the way for the postponed elections, now due in September. The Minister of the Interior, an army man, didn't like this trespassing on his prerogatives; he resigned, and less than a year later he was one of the group of officers who evicted Ben Bella from power.

Colonel Chaabani's revolt proved to be a short-lived one. He was captured less than a fortnight after he had launched it and executed almost exactly two months later. One could see the death sentence coming in advance. For some days before the colonel came up for trial the newspapers, now all safely under the Government wing, had been demanding the liquidation of the traitor, just as they would have done in the Russia of Stalin's days. Just about the same time they were publishing the single list of candidates proposed to the public for election to the new National Assembly. Not a single non-conformist could be identified among the lot of them. There was obviously no danger of Algeria's second parliament indulging itself in real debates or criticisms of the Government. The electorate seemed to realize how little the polls meant. At the first plebiscite and at the first elections in 1962, long queues of men and women had lined up in front of the polling stations before they even opened. This time the voters arrived in driblets, all through the day, except in the places where the police roused them at dawn to vote. The official figures of the results, always subject to suspicion in a single-party country, represented eighty-five per cent of the registered electors as having voted. Abstentions were undoubtedly far higher in Kabylie and other opposition centres. Less than a month later, half-way through October 1964, it was announced that Ait Ahmed had been arrested in Kabylie – 'denounced by the population', Algiers officials said, an assertion which seemed faintly unlikely. The arrest was a triumph for Ben Bella, but it changed the facts little. The Socialist Forces Front had for months past ceased to exist as an opposition. Nevertheless, as soon as the arrest was known, telegrams of congratulation flowed into the F.L.N. political bureau, just as they would have done in the Soviet Union – or in any other African single-party country. In a single-party State, it is always as well to be on record as having come out behind the authorities at such a moment.

The following March, Ait Ahmed was condemned to death after a four-day secret trial by the Algiers revolutionary criminal court. He was convicted of having plotted insurrection; his defence was that the flouting of the constitution justified his action. A number of foreign lawyers, French, Moroccans and Senegalese, had volunteered to participate in his defence. They all walked out of the court in protest against what they described as the irregularities of the procedure. Two days later, the death sentence on Ait Ahmed was commuted on the occasion of the feast which has been described as 'the Moslem Christmas', the Aid el-Kebir.

It would have been hard for Ben Bella not to have commuted the death sentence on a man who had been, with him, one of the nine 'historic leaders' who had launched the Algerian revolt. He made a further advance towards liberalism as summer came in. At the start of June it was announced that Ferhat Abbas, Amar Bentoumi, Abderrahman Farès and a number of other prominent political prisoners had been liberated. Ben Bella stated that he had reached a peace agreement with the surviving leaders of the Socialist Forces Front in Kabylie. Finally, appealing for national reconciliation, he used a phrase that led many people to believe that, three months after the death sentence had been passed on him, Ait Ahmed was to be freed. It was in the wake of these liberal gestures that Ben Bella was ousted from power by the army in June 1965. Ousted by an army under the headship of a man whom he had described in private conversation no more than eighteen months before as 'a staunch ally and a real friend'.

The liberal gestures may in fact have been the last straw for the army. Ben Bella had over the previous months been taking more and more power into his own hands. He had taken over not only the Ministry of the Interior but the Ministries of Information and of Finance: these departments were being run, none too efficiently, by permanent officials, and there was said to be outrageous over-spending in all of them. The army had won less than no popularity by its virtual occupation of Kabylie, on Ben Bella's orders. It now seemed more than possible that at any moment the President might appear on the television screen side by side with Ait Ahmed, announce their reconciliation and represent himself as the champion of national unity and the army – which had done no more than execute his instructions – as its enemy. Was such a piece of wild injustice to be tolerated? What is more, though the Government had been extremely incompetent – the workers-managed co-operative farms which it had set up had paid their members no dividends after their first, in January 1964 – the army was generally agreed to be the most efficient institution in Algeria. It even had its model chicken farms, which supplied its men with excellent poultry at low costs.

All the same, the man whom the army removed from power was a man whom they had done more than anyone else to build up into a national figure. Those who were closest personally to the deposed President suggested two reasons why he had been led to arrogate more and more power to himself. One was of a general nature: it was no more than Acton's dictum 'All power corrupts; absolute power corrupts absolutely' – in other words Ben Bella's experience of almost uncontrolled authority had led him more and more to resent any curbs on it. Another was more individual: in his early period in office, the President had met with disappointment after disappointment from Algerians whom he had trusted with high office, and who had turned out to be drinkers and womanizers, and for that reason he had felt that it was in the national interest that he should personally take over more and more of the running of the country. In any case, he had completely changed in his manner over the three years since he had assumed the Premiership. An adviser who saw him frequently testified that he had been able to discuss everything with Ben Bella at first; later on, when he had raised such topics as the arrest of Ferhat Abbas, which he condemned, the President had headed him off by asking: 'But what do you want for yourself?'

What is more, when Ben Bella had one by one evicted from office all the people who had helped to install him in power, he had made one grave mistake. He had seriously over-estimated his own popularity. He had more than once told responsible interlocutors: 'Nobody in this country dares touch me. If they did, the people would turn out on the streets at once.' Well, apart from a short-lived series of generally minor demonstrations, the people simply didn't.

His successors met with one immediate failure. The Afro-

Asian summit conference which had been due to meet in Algiers in a matter of days was almost immediately postponed to the, in English eyes, hardly propitious new date of 5 November, the date on which Guy Fawkes had been discovered in 1605 in a cellar under the British Houses of Parliament preparing to blow them and the King up. Even that did not work. At the last moment a meeting in Algiers of the foreign ministers of a number of the states invited decided that the summit should be postponed *sine die*. And this though, from the summer on, Algerian Ministers who had, according to their own accounts, quite enough to do clearing up the internal mess that confronted them, had been sent flying all over the globe to make certain that all the participants invited would in fact turn up. The new Premier, Colonel Boumedienne, had over the past three years been trying to associate within Algeria's post-independence army officers and men of two groups who back in 1962 had been bitterly opposed: the forces who had spent all the war fighting inside Algeria and those who had passed most of that period on its frontiers. Both sides were given representation in the Revolutionary Council. Few competent observers, however, felt any sort of certainty that Ben Bella's successors in office would be able to exercise their powers to any better effect than he had done. Some maintained that speech was freer under the new Government, which did indeed liberate a large additional number of political prisoners; others that another type of people were speaking freely. What is certain is that within a couple of days after the *coup*, the members of the National Assembly, all elected as strict Ben Bellists, had voted a resolution cravenly supporting the new régime, which they would hardly have done unless they had been subject to pressure or feared it. While three months later, political arrests, reportedly followed by torture, were starting up all over again, and the Algerian students' organization and the trade unions were reported to be both at odds with Ben Bella's successors in power.

Those who heard Colonel Boumedienne read a statement to the press when the new executive secretariat of the F.L.N. was installed at the end of July noted three things about it. Firstly, the colonel made one completely untrue statement about the reasons for the revolution: that the F.L.N. in

Algeria had been in magnificent shape at the moment of liberation, and that then Ben Bella had taken the party over for his own profit and spoiled it – in fact the party, as it existed at the moment of liberation, had been smashed by the civil war which Boumedienne had done everything to promote. Secondly, the new Premier said that the Algerian trade unions had got to eliminate what he called the 'workerist' spirit, that is, not to put forward claims on behalf of their members. Finally, speaking of the National Union of Algerian Women, the colonel said that in organizing the women of Algeria, 'it must safeguard our moral principles by avoiding any kind of mimicry or exhibitionism' which sounded very like telling the women of Algeria to stay at home. All of which hardly seemed to indicate a particularly honest or liberal outlook by the new Government of unhappy Algeria.

3

Ghana

THE STORY OF the accession to independence of Ghana, formerly the British colony of the Gold Coast, has a personal angle to which there is probably only one parallel among the other countries of Africa. The figure who was brought in from England to help promote its liberation movement ended by imposing himself as a leader and within a matter of years had branded his former employers as traitors. Soon after its foundation in August 1947, the United Gold Coast Convention, the first serious nationalist body in the country, invited a youngish man over from London to undertake the work of organization for it. He was thirty-eight-years-old Kwame Nkrumah, B.A. and Bachelor of Theology at one American university, and M.Sc. at another, and on his arrival he assumed the general secretaryship of the movement. Less than two years later, he had broken away and formed his own party, which commanded a far wider following. In 1951, he was released from his second term in prison for political offences to head the first Gold Coast Government under a new Constitution, by 1957 he had won his country independence, and by the summer of 1960 he was President of what had now become the Republic of Ghana and general secretary of the movement he had founded, the Convention People's Party. His official title today is Osagyefo Dr Kwame Nkrumah, the President, and Osagyefo means 'he who never fails'. Dr Danquah, the principal founder of the United Gold Coast Convention, which originally invited Nkrumah over to Ghana, died in jail as a political prisoner at the beginning of 1965.

The beginning of 1965 also saw a Ghana court sentencing five men to death under circumstances which would have been regarded as unusual, to say the least of it, in any other country. The five men included a former Ghana Information Minister, a former Ghana Foreign Minister, and the former executive secretary of the Convention People's Party. The unusual aspect of the case was that the two ex-ministers and the former party official had all been tried previously by a special division of the Ghana High Court on the identical charges of conspiracy to commit treason, and had been acquitted in December 1963. Nkrumah had immediately dismissed the Chief Justice, who had presided over the trial – the Constitution in fact gave him the right to revoke the appointment of a Judge as Chief Justice – a fortnight later the National Assembly voted an Act empowering the President to quash any decisions of the special court, and on Christmas day, an odd day to choose, he declared the judgement null and void.

In a New Year's Eve broadcast a week later, Nkrumah explained his action in terms that even a Soviet statesman would have hesitated to employ. 'In the performance of their duties,' he said, 'judges of the Supreme Court and the High Court are not interfered with by the Chief Executive. But under our Constitution, the office of Chief Justice is not solely judicial. It is also quasi-political. It involves active co-operation and understanding with the President in securing justice, law and order, peace and stability.

'A treason trial by its very nature is political, and can lead to unrest, disturbances and even violence. For this reason our Government was bound to be interested in the treason trial. The failure of the Chief Justice to take the President into his confidence in regard to the judgement of the Special Court showed a serious disregard for the office of the President. His failure also to recognize the effect that the judgement, whatever it was, would have on the peace, stability and order throughout the country for which the Government would be responsible is a clear indication of his lack of political responsibility.

'The judges of the High Court, by their failure to take me into their confidence, meant to create discontent and terror throughout the country. The country cannot tolerate a dishonest and corrupt judiciary. There is a possibility of a retrial of the persons involved in this particular case.'

Those who followed the first trial of the five men said that it became increasingly doubtful as it went on whether the two ministers and the party executive secretary had had anything to do with the assassination attempt against Nkrumah which was the basis of the charges. The jury at the second trial had plainly learned the lesson of Nkrumah's New Year's Eve broadcast just over a year before. They retired for fifty minutes only before they came back with an unanimous verdict that all five were guilty.

The Republic of Ghana, with a 330-mile-long coastline on the Gulf of Guinea and an average depth inland of 440 miles, has an area of 91,000-odd square miles and a population of around seven million. Parts of the Gold Coast, as it was called earlier, have been known to the West for upwards of 500 years, its chief attractions to European traders lying in the slave trade and in gold. Till the development of modern sanitary knowledge, its warm, damp climate favoured the spread of malaria and of tropical diseases, and it was long known as 'the White Man's grave'.

Like most other African countries south of the Sahara, Ghana is divided into a number of ethnic groups, five in all, while as many main languages are spoken, not to mention dialects. The chief regional dividing lines, as in other countries on the west coast of Africa, are roughly parallel to the coastline. In the coastal area, with its relatively long contact with Europe, a literate middle class with a European education sprang up earlier than it did to the north. The rich central area formerly came under the Ashanti Confederation, a military theocracy which at one time dominated most of the Gold Coast. The Northern Region contained more widely diverse tribal and linguistic groups. The northerners feared the southerners, for they had been the chief victims of the slave trade, which had almost wiped out their tribal organization, while the southerners despised the backward northerners. Any nationalist leader with the least discernment must thus have realized that, once independence had been won, it would require a great deal of tact and conciliation to weld the country into a unitary state. One of the principal charges against Nkrumah is that he set about achieving Ghanaian unity not so much by tact and conciliation as by force.

Four or five European nations were at one time or another interested in commerce with the Gold Coast, and set up trading posts there. The castle of Christiansborg, for example, which dominates the sea in the outskirts of Accra, and is now one of Nkrumah's official residences, was built by the Swedes and the

Danes. Gradually, however, Britain drew into the lead over her rivals. The coastal area became a British protectorate before the middle of the nineteenth century, and it was turned into a crown colony in 1874. That brought Britain into conflict with the Ashantis, whose ruler, the Asantahene, was captured and deported to the Seychelles at the end of the nineteenth century, though his subjects succeeded in hiding away from the invaders the symbol of his sovereignty, the famous Golden Stool. Both in the coastal and the Ashanti areas, the stool, like the throne in Europe, was regarded as the symbol of chiefly authority, and the formal accession to power of a chief was known as his 'enstooling'. In January 1902, Ashanti was annexed and a British protectorate was established over the Northern Region, while in 1915 a central administration for the Gold Coast as a whole was set up, and Ashanti and the Northern Region became provinces of the colony. Finally, after the First World War, part of the former German colony of Togoland next door was mandated to Britain by the League of Nations; in a plebiscite in 1956, its inhabitants voted themselves into the Gold Coast.

Ghana is not a poor country, though it shares the weakness of other African states in depending too much on a single crop. In Ghana it is cocoa, of which the country is the largest single producer in the world. But Ghana has other resources too, palm oil and copra, ground-nuts and rubber, while it possesses large deposits of minerals. Ghana is the second largest producer of gold in Africa, and it also exports diamonds, manganese and bauxite; its bauxite reserves are said to amount to more than 200 million tons.

It was not until after the Second World War that the independence movement started, but the Gold Coast, as it then was, had shown signs of vigorous political life long before that. The educated classes had shown considerable opposition to the 1925 Constitution, which for the first time gave the country a certain right to elected representation. It is true that of the fourteen unofficial members of the twenty-nine-man legislative council only nine were Africans, but it was not so much this that the critics resented. They complained that among the nine Africans the chiefs in the countryside had twice as many representatives as the municipalities, for they feared that the former would be tools in the hands of the British governor and that thus any distant hope of national independence which existed would be compromised for ever.

The Gold Coast made a big contribution to the Second World War. Out of its then 4,000,000 population it gave no less than 65,000 men to the various services and subscribed generously to War Loan and the Spitfire Fund. It was therefore not unnatural that it should receive a political reward when peace returned. This came with the 1946 constitution, which gave elected Africans a clear majority on the legislative council and provided for a legislative union of the Gold Coast and Ashanti. The inauguration of the new constitution was hailed as a triumph, but less than two years later there were serious disturbances in many parts of the country.

It was because they were already dissatisfied with the constitution even in 1947 that a group of upper-middle-class citizens that summer set up the United Gold Coast Convention. Dr Danquah, one of its founders, had in the inter-war years established the Gold Coast Youth Conference, which was designed to awaken young people to the needs of their country. The U.G.C.C. leaders complained that the thinking African was seriously disappointed that his representatives on the new legislative council could criticize Government policy but could do nothing to frame or indeed to change it. Events had already shown, they went on, that it had been a grave mistake to concede to the Africans a majority on the council without giving this body some measure at least of responsibility. For the people at large had substantial grievances against the Government; in particular, they resented its apparent impotence to bring down the high prices and curb the profiteering which had resulted from the war and post-war shortages. The nationalism of the U.G.C.C., however, was of a very conservative type by comparison with that of the parallel movement which already existed in Tunisia, and with those which were soon to take root in Morocco and Algeria. The U.G.C.C. leaders constantly insisted that their aim was the earliest possible self-government for the chiefs and the people, but they stressed just as strongly that this was to be achieved by legal and constitutional means only. A turning-point in the history of the U.G.C.C., and of the country as a whole, came in

December 1947 when Francis Nwia Kofie Kwame Nkrumah – to give the present President his full name – became the party's general secretary.

Who was Kwame Nkrumah? His father was a goldsmith, and he was born in 1909 in a village in the extreme south-east of the Gold Coast, was baptized a Roman Catholic, became a pupil-teacher at the age of seventeen, after eight years in elementary school, entered and graduated from a teachers' training college, and between 1930 and 1936 held a succession of teaching posts, ending up on the staff of a seminary. He had already conceived the idea of going to America to complete his studies, and with the help of relatives was able in the autumn of 1936 to cross the Atlantic and enrol as a student at the eighty-year-old Lincoln University, the first institution in the United States to give higher education to Negroes.

The little money with which young Nkrumah had arrived was soon gone, and, though he was awarded a scholarship, he was forced to earn extra money writing essays for fellow-students and kept himself in the long vacation by working as a steward on ocean liners. In 1939 he took his B.A. in economics and sociology, and that autumn became an assistant lecturer in philosophy at Lincoln; he was simultaneously reading theology at his own university, where he became a Bachelor of Theology in 1942, and philosophy and education at the University of Pennsylvania, fifty miles away, from which he got a M.Sc. degree in 1943. He then started reading for a doctorate of philosophy, and by 1945 had completed the course and passed the preliminary examinations; all that remained for him to do was to write the necessary thesis. In fact, an attack of pneumonia brought on by overwork – he had been working from midnight to eight a.m. in a shipyard to help pay his expenses – prevented him from ever completing this, and the doctorate he holds is an honorary one, which Lincoln University conferred on him in 1951, when he was already the leading political figure back at home.

In the U.S., Nkrumah had also embarked on political activities, and in these three of the themes on which he insisted when he took over power had already emerged: zeal for African unification, a devotion to Left-Wing Socialism and a demand for personal allegiance. He founded and became first president of the African Students' Association of America and Canada, whose organ, *The African Interpreter*, endeavoured to revive a spirit of nationalism and to promote a movement towards African unity. In addition, he tried to acquaint himself with as many political organizations as possible, ranging from the Democrats and Republicans to the Communists and Trotskyites. His reading of Marxist literature had already convinced him that Marxism offered the best solution of the problem of imperialism. The object of his various political contacts was not, however, a philosophical but a strictly practical one. 'My aim,' he explains in his *Autobiography*, 'was to learn the technique of organization. I knew that when I eventually returned to the Gold Coast I should be faced with this problem. I knew that, whatever the programme for the solution of the colonial question might be, success would depend on the organization adopted.'

In May 1945, Nkrumah left for London. His idea was to read Law and complete his doctoral thesis, but in fact he soon found himself caught up in political activities. He became vice-president of the African Students' Union and soon started helping to organize the Fifth Pan-African Congress, which was held in Manchester in October 1945. The congress, in large part owing to Nkrumah's preparatory work, was very different from the four which had preceded it. The previous congresses, Nkrumah says, had been promoted and supported mainly by middle-class intellectuals and bourgeois Negro reformists. The Fifth Congress was attended by trade unionists and farmers, representatives of co-operatives and students, and it rejected both capitalist and reformist solutions to the African colonial problem and unanimously adopted a doctrine of African Socialism based on the tactics of 'positive action' without violence. Nkrumah was appointed secretary of the Working Committee set up after the congress to help give effect to the programme it had adopted, and of the West African secretariat established at the suggestion of such figures as Kojo Botsio, then a Gold Coast resident in England, who a few years later was to become a minister of Nkrumah's – and was to be purged in 1961.

Possibly one of the most interesting of the other bodies which Nkrumah organized or worked for during his London period was a students' group known as The Circle and described as 'the Revolutionary vanguard of the struggle for West African unity and independence'. The first of the seven rules to which a member pledged himself was: 'I will irrevocably obey and act upon the orders of the Grand Council of The Circle' – Nkrumah was the chairman. The seventh read: 'I accept the leadership of Kwame Nkrumah.'

One day Nkrumah received a letter from the Gold Coast from Ako Adjei, a former fellow-student in America who was later to become another of his ministers and to be condemned to death in 1965. Adjei asked Nkrumah whether he would return home and take on the job of general secretary of the United Gold Coast Convention. He explained that the big problem of the U.G.C.C. was how to establish contact between a leadership composed of the intelligentsia and the people at large, and he said that, knowing of Nkrumah's activities in America and England, he had recommended him to the executive for the general secretary's post.

Nkrumah took his time. He made inquiries about the U.G.C.C. and found that it was backed almost entirely by 'reactionaries, middle-class lawyers and merchants', with whom it would be impossible for a man with his own revolutionary background and ideas to work. Dr Danquah, one of the chief founders of the movement, insisted, however, and after a number of consultations Nkrumah finally agreed to go out. Probably the chief reason was that, in his own words, it looked like 'the dawn of action at the end of a long and intensive training'. He was equally clear about his attitude towards the differences that seemed more than likely to arise between him and the conservatively-minded heads of the organization that was going to employ him. 'I was very sure of the policy I was going to pursue,' he says, 'and fully prepared to come to loggerheads with the executive of the U.G.C.C. if I found that they were pursuing a reactionary course.' Dr Danquah and his associates could not know it, but they had bitten off more than they could chew.

Nkrumah arrived back home at a very interesting moment. There was general discontent over the scarcity of imported goods and their extremely high prices. Swollen shoot disease was wreaking havoc among the cocoa plantations and, with cocoa prices high, the generally illiterate farmers were unwilling to destroy their diseased trees as a Government order required. As soon as he arrived, therefore, Nkrumah started a tour of the country urging the necessity for self-government. At the end of February 1948, matters came to a head. A shop-boycott movement launched by an Accra sub-chief had indeed induced the local tradesman to promise to cut their profit margins by from fifty to seventy-five per cent for a trial period of three months. The man in the street, however, interpreted this undertaking as a pledge to reduce *prices* by this proportion; when he found that they had dropped only by one-sixth, he was in an ugly mood. To add to the trouble, on 28 February discontented ex-servicemen had organized a demonstration in Accra, and police opened fire on them. Tempers went by the board at once. There was an orgy of shop-looting in Accra and other towns, which led to damage to property estimated at £2,000,000, while 29 people were killed and 237 injured. The U.G.C.C. had in fact had nothing to do with the shop-boycott campaign, but it was so synchronized with the new general secretary's assumption of his post that it was natural for the authorities to conclude that he was the instigator. The Government therefore promptly arrested and deported to remote areas in the north six of the chief U.G.C.C. leaders, including Nkrumah and Danquah, who were soon popularly hailed as 'the Big Six'.

Since the cause of the riots fairly obviously lay some way below the surface, a commission was immediately sent out from England to investigate. It was the Watson Commission, and its members reported, among other things, that the 1946 Constitution had been outmoded at birth, for it had been drafted in the light of pre-war conditions; they suggested the establishment of an enlarged legislature and of an executive council with a majority of African ministers which would be responsible to it. The Gold Coast Government decided not to implement these recommendations until they had been considered by a representative African body. The committee entrusted with the job submitted in 1949 a report very much on the lines of the Watson Commission's recommendations, and the Government promptly adopted its main proposals, which covered Ashanti and the Northern Region too. Moderate opinion welcomed the decision. Nkrumah declared that 'Ghana must have freedom, and freedom now'. It should be added that the only member of the Big Six who had not been called to serve on the African committee was Nkrumah.

His colleagues and employers of the U.G.C.C. are most unlikely to have regretted this omission, for over the months they and he had steadily been moving apart. It is true that during his first six months as general secretary he had increased the number of U.G.C.C. branches in the country from a theoretical thirteen to an actual five hundred. It is true that he was tireless in his travelling and extraordinarily successful as a public speaker. But the U.G.C.C. executive had come to realize that the man they had hired to work for them was not going to be content merely to accept orders from above. During the couple of days that Nkrumah and the other members of the Big Six were in prison together after their arrest following the February 1948 riots they made plain – according to Nkrumah – their feeling that it was his fault that they had been detained. Things became no easier when the six were released on the arrival of the Watson Commission. Nkrumah started to organize youth groups to act as a vanguard for the U.G.C.C. and to attract younger people into it, and the groups were later federated by the Committee of Youth Organization, or C.Y.O. He soon acquired the impression, however, that his employers resented the existence of the C.Y.O. 'because it was composed of the less privileged, or radical, section of the people, and went completely against their more conservative outlook'. Another of his initiatives which they disliked was his establishment of the Ghana National College at Cape Coast, to take in secondary-school boys who had gone on strike against the arrest of the Big Six and been expelled in consequence. In July 1948 Nkrumah was hauled up before his U.G.C.C. bosses on a series of charges. A proposal that he should resign his post and be provided with a passage to London was turned down because some members of the executive believed that he had a strong personal following, and that his removal might result in the complete breakdown of the U.G.C.C. Finally they hit on the curious compromise of relieving him of the post of general secretary and appointing him treasurer instead. The day their decision came into effect saw the appearance of the first number of the daily paper Nkrumah had decided to found as an organ of the movement, despite the executive's objections. It was the *Accra Evening News*, its editor was Komla Gbedemah, and the fighting motto it carried on its front page was: 'We prefer self-government with danger to servitude in tranquillity.'

Nkrumah had very likely hoped that the infiltration into the U.G.C.C. of the supporters he was vigorously recruiting would permit him to recover his position as general secretary. He was mistaken. When the party conference met at Easter 1949, it refused to reinstate him. So on 12 July 1949 Nkrumah announced to a huge public meeting in Accra his foundation of a new organization, the Convention People's Party. The first of the six objectives which the new body set itself was 'to fight relentlessly by all constitutional means for the achievement of full self-government *now* for the chiefs and people of the Gold Coast'.

This objective plainly put the C.P.P. into direct conflict with the proposals of the latest inquiry committee as adopted by the British authorities; these have been described as offering the Gold Coast merely self-government – with luck – before long. In mid-December 1949, Nkrumah warned the Governor that unless the British were prepared to grant the Gold Coast immediate Dominion status within the Commonwealth, the C.P.P. would embark on a campaign of strikes, boycotts and non-co-operation based on the principle of absolute non-violence. The campaign was launched in January 1950, violence naturally occurred, most of the C.P.P. leaders were arrested and Nkrumah was sentenced to three periods of twelve months' imprisonment, to run consecutively.

The C.P.P. naturally did not approve the new Constitution, but with great good sense it stated its willingness to take part in the first elections for the Assembly set up under it, which were fixed for February 1951. With Nkrumah still a prisoner – though he managed to smuggle out to his followers advice and even an election manifesto scribbled on sheets of toilet paper, and to have himself entered as a candidate – Gbedemah set about organizing to win the C.P.P. an incontestable victory. Party propaganda was certainly not lacking in imagination. A 'prison graduate's cap' was awarded to released political prisoners. There was a party flag, green, white and red, a party salute, and a party cry of 'Freedom!'. The propaganda vans that drove about were painted in the party colours, party colour cloths, handbags and belts were put on sale, and framed photographs of Nkrumah were sold everywhere. The results were a triumph for the C.P.P. It won thirty-four out of the thirty-eight seats filled by direct election and contested on a party basis. Nkrumah was elected for the Accra Central constituency by the largest individual poll till then recorded in Gold Coast history, 22,780 votes out of a possible 23,122. The day after the figures were announced, the C.P.P. executive successfully approached the Governor for Nkrumah's release, and less than twenty-four hours later the Governor was asking him to form a Government. Nkrumah was given the title of Leader of Government business, but just over a year later his style was changed to that of Prime Minister.

The Nkrumah Government went ahead with a moderate development policy which aimed, among other things, at providing a basic six-year primary-school course for every child in the country, and in April 1954 a new constitution came into force which marked another step towards full self-government. The constitution set up an all-African Cabinet, which was to be responsible for everything but external affairs and defence, and a legislative assembly of 104 members, all to be chosen by direct election. Just before the first polls under the new arrangement, there was a development which should have been a warning to Nkrumah, though he did not appear to have taken any heed of it: a new party was formed. It was the Northern People's Party, a frankly regional organization, and behind its formation lay the northern population's traditional fear of the southerners and their distrust of what they described as the dictatorial tendencies of the C.P.P. It had given itself little enough time to campaign, but for all that it won twelve of the seventeen seats in the Northern Region. Naturally the C.P.P. easily got the overall majority it had expected, 71 out of the 104 seats in the House. When it came to the total votes cast, however, the number falling to the C.P.P. was 391,817 and the other parties' share was no fewer than 314,903, which could hardly be represented as a walk-over.

Barely three months after the elections, there was a new

warning for Nkrumah. A second opposition party, the National Liberation Movement, was formed, this time in Ashanti. There had been a historical antagonism between the inhabitants of Ashanti and the coast, but the particular Ashanti grievance which brought exasperation with the C.P.P. to a head was the Government's tabling in the Assembly of a bill which sought to fix the maximum price of a sixty-pound load of cocoa at seventy-two shillings for four years, though the world price was climbing steeply. There were excellent arguments for the measure. In the first place, the additional revenue obtained through it would provide indispensable capital for the development of the country as a whole. Further it could be regarded as a sensible attempt to check inflation, as world prices of cocoa climbed to the equivalent of £12 10s a load. The Ashanti farmers, who owned some of the richest cocoa lands in the country, could hardly be expected to see things that way. They felt it was monstrous to fix the price of cocoa at a price exactly the same as that of the previous season on so swiftly rising a market; they also thought that a much larger share of the additional revenue obtained should go to them. What is more, it was asking for trouble for the Government to take its action almost immediately after elections in which everyone's hopes had been raised.

Very soon the N.L.M. was demanding a federal form of government which would give a measure of autonomy to the country's four regions; it also pressed for a two-house legislature whose upper house, in which the chiefs would be represented, would be able to check what was represented as 'the creeping dictatorship' of the South. The N.L.M. won some measure of support in the Northern Region and Togoland, where the same fear of the South was felt. Then in October 1954, the Asantahene, the traditional ruler of Ashanti – the kingdom there, abolished at the end of the nineteenth century, had been restored in 1935 – signed a petition to Queen Elizabeth with fifty of the chiefs on his council asking for the appointment of a commission of inquiry into federal government for the Gold Coast. Meantime an epidemic of violence between supporters of the N.L.M. and of the C.P.P. had broken out in and around the Ashanti capital of Kumasi.

Mere common sense should have impelled Nkrumah to

70

enter into contact at once with the new opposition. In fact, it was not till December that he broadcast an invitation to the N.L.M. leaders to confer with the Government on regional devolution. By that time he was too late: they refused. A select committee of National Assembly deputies was then appointed to consider the situation; deputies of the only opposition party as yet represented in the House, the N.P.P., declined to sit on it on the grounds that there would be a certain C.P.P. majority against them. The Government next invited a British constitutional expert out to give his advice. The N.L.M. leaders would not appear before him on the plea that a measure concerning local administration just put through by the Government clearly showed that Nkrumah's offer to consider their case could not be taken seriously. When the visiting British expert reported – he found, not unreasonably, that federation would be far too costly for a country with a bare five million inhabitants – the N.L.M. turned down the invitation to attend an inter-party conference called to consider his recommendations; one of their chief reasons was that the Government had also invited to the meeting 'bodies which had been created by the party in power' in order that they might be sure of majority support.

This negative N.L.M. attitude may be deplored, but extraordinary bitterness had by this time developed between the two sides. The C.P.P. *Evening News* printed a report of what it described as a secret meeting held under the chairmanship of the Asantahene at which the N.L.M. had decided to eliminate Nkrumah. The N.L.M. now had its own daily, the *Liberator*, and this published a reply to 'these homeless tramps and jackals' that 'the Ashantis are thinking of better things and have no time to attempt the life of a damned Colonial Prime Minister'. The N.L.M. was also developing a whole series of parallel organizations, patterned on those of the C.P.P. It had an Ashanti Farmers' Union, a pro-N.L.M. section of the local youth body, a women's section and its own tough private police, while there were also a party flag, party songs, slogans and propaganda vans, and a party salute.

Nkrumah could not, however, wait indefinitely for the freedom he had promised his people. In April 1956 he published his Constitutional proposals for the independence of the

Gold Coast under the name of Ghana. Ghana was the appellation of an African empire which is represented as having dominated a wide area of the western Sudan in the dark ages, and whose tribes are stated to have been the ancestors of some of the Gold Coast population. The opposition were quick to hit back. They welcomed independence, but they insisted that before it was granted there should be satisfactory guarantees against the domination of Ashanti and the Northern Region by southern politicians. The British Government therefore decided that independence would be granted only when the people of the Gold Coast had enjoyed an opportunity of expressing their views in a general election on the proposed new Constitution.

The elections were fixed for July 1956, and Dr K. A. Busia, a scholar of chiefly family who had taken over the leadership of the N.L.M., made an excellent case for his party on the eve of the polls. In the light of after events, some of his statements seem to have a prophetic quality. Dr Busia said that the N.L.M. had been formed in order to promote a federal form of government for the Gold Coast, to safeguard the country against dictatorship and provide constitutional checks on the centralization of power. The N.L.M. wanted independence, he declared, but it wanted that independence as 'a happy unity of equals': it did not want a small clique to dominate the country. Within less than a year, Busia's suspicions were to receive support from Nkrumah's own pen. In the preface to his *Autobiography*, published in London in March 1957, Nkrumah speaks of the need for a Socialist society in a newly-independent underdeveloped country and goes on: 'But even a system based on social justice and a democratic constitution may need backing up, during the period following independence, by emergency measures of a totalitarian kind. Without discipline, true freedom cannot survive.'

Busia also attacked corruption in the C.P.P., and here too he had a case. A commission of inquiry appointed late in 1953 to investigate allegations that public funds were being misused did indeed find that this sort of conduct was not general. But it also reported that J. A. Braimah, then Minister of Communications and Works, had accepted £2,000 in notes from a contractor who had been awarded the job of building a training college. Braimah was later convicted of corrupt conduct but acquitted on appeal. About two years later, another commission was set up to go into similar charges against the monopoly Cocoa Purchasing Company which was, among other things, the Cocoa Marketing Board's agent for issuing loans to farmers. This second commission found that the Cocoa Purchasing Company was controlled by the C.P.P. and had been used for winning adherents to the party by granting loans largely to political sympathizers. It also reported that most of the irregularities it had investigated would have been prevented if the Government had taken a firm stand to check conduct of this type back in 1953. Moreover, anyone who had any information was well aware of the big houses which Ministers had built themselves in Accra and for which they drew rent allowances, and the luxurious way of living of many party leaders, while there were whispers that, far from Braimah's conduct having been an exception, it was essential for anyone who wanted to get a Government contract to slip the appropriate sum to the minister concerned or to his secretary.

All the same, the election results were a far bigger success for the C.P.P. than might have been expected. It secured all forty-four seats in the Gold Coast, eight out of twenty-one in Ashanti, eight out of thirteen in the formerly mandated Togoland which had just plebiscited its way into integration, and eleven out of twenty-six in the Northern Region. Of the opposition parties, the Northern People's Party led with fifteen seats and the National Liberation Movement followed with twelve. There is a case for believing that the N.L.M. might have scored a bigger success had its leaders made sure of their Ashanti base before they tried, as they did, to penetrate the South as well. Not a few southerners were led to regard the N.L.M. as the spearhead of a new Ashanti invasion of their part of the country. Faced with the election figures, however, the British Government, which had wanted to see a 'reasonable majority' of the electorate agreeing on the proposed Constitution before it set a date for Ghana's independence, had no choice. In September it announced that it intended that independence should come about on 6 March 1957.

That did not end the trouble. The opposition had wanted to

see independent Ghana defended from the possible dictatorship of a single-chamber parliament (which in fact followed) by such means as a second chamber for chiefs, increased powers for the four regional assemblies which were to be set up, guarantees of an independent judiciary and genuine safeguards against any unduly easy amendment of the Constitution. The document tabled by Nkrumah granted none of these demands, and after the Assembly had voted for it by the predictable majority the N.L.M. and the N.P.P. sent a joint resolution to London threatening to secede from the new state. The position looked really serious, and then in January 1957 the Colonial Secretary, Lennox-Boyd, visited the country and appeared to have succeeded in reconciling the two sides. His chief argument was that, despite their differences, they both wanted the same thing, independence for Ghana, and in fine, high-sounding phrases he expressed his confidence that, given goodwill and trust, their contrasting political threads could be 'closely and lastingly woven together into a rich and colourful pattern of independent nationhood'. In the compromise that resulted from his mission, the C.P.P. made the most concessions. The final draft of the Constitution maintained the unitary state, but it gave additional powers to the four regions and, far more important, did its best to protect Ghana's charter of independent nationhood by making amendments to certain basic clauses of it dependent not only on a two-thirds vote of the National Assembly, of which the C.P.P. were assured in advance, but on the agreement of two-thirds of the regional assemblies, of which they had no assurance at all. So finally the opposition leaders agreed to take part in the independence ceremonies of March 1957.

Any illusions they may have harboured about the permanent security of public liberties were soon to be dispelled. Evidence dating back more than a year before independence made it plain that even within the party ranks the voicing of dissentient views had ceased to be possible. In January 1956, the C.P.P. Accra regional executive had submitted to Nkrumah a memorandum on the grievances of the Ga-speaking community in the capital. The memorandum made four points. First, it was difficult and improper to criticize the party in public. Second, members were given no opportunity of criticizing

74

the party internally. Third, any attempts to offer suggestions or make criticisms about the party were accepted by those in office as implying disloyalty. Finally, the party authorities had never been known to invite criticism from below; on the contrary, communications between the ordinary members and the party bosses were limited to instructions periodically issued to the former from the latter concerning organizational work. With freedom of speech so restricted within the party, it could hardly be expected to survive very long outside.

What pressing danger inspired this throttling of liberty, which was soon to become evident to the world as a whole? There was no danger that could be seen. Through Lennox-Boyd's mediation, Nkrumah had reached an agreement with the two opposition movements, and their leaders had every interest in the world in observing it. All that was needed to satisfy the complaints of the Gas in the party was a little plain common sense. One plausible explanation of the escalation of tyranny that followed may be very briefly expressed: just as absolute power corrupts absolutely, so does the vision of absolute power which had pretty plainly been in Nkrumah's mind even before he returned to his homeland. To have stood by the terms he had offered the opposition would have implied a certain curb on his liberty of action, and he did not want to accept it. To have given satisfaction to Ga and other critics within the party would have meant the same thing, and there was no reason why a budding dictator should show any more regard for his supporters than for his opponents.

So the Ga movement gathered strength and stimulated un-rest among other discontented groups, and after Krobo Edusei became Minister of the Interior in the summer of 1957 a whole series of repressive measures was taken. In the first place, to increase the power of the C.P.P. in the provinces, Regional Commissioners were appointed there – and those nominated were not expert administrators but party bosses. Further, in order to deprive the opposition of the basis of their support up-country, an act was passed in December 1957 which forbade the existence of all parties organized on a regional, tribal or religious basis – and both the N.P.P. and the N.L.M., despite the efforts of the latter to extend its activities outside Ashanti, were in fact regional parties.

Finally, measures were taken to centralize the authority of the Government, though the principal among these would never have had the disastrous effects on public liberties that in fact followed from it had it not been for the opposition's complete lack of tactical sense. In April 1958, there appeared the report of the commission which had been entrusted with making recommendations about the establishment and authority of the elected regional assemblies which were to replace the interim bodies set up in 1957. It will be remembered that the agreement of two-thirds of these assemblies was required for the amendment of certain basic clauses of the Ghana Constitution. When the Government severely restricted the range of powers which the commission had recommended these assemblies should have, the opposition boycotted the October 1958 elections to them. Anyone with the least political insight could have predicted the result. The C.P.P. gained control of all four assemblies, which then approved a Bill removing the restrictions on constitutional changes, the Bill went through the National Assembly with the necessary two-thirds majority, and in 1959 a Constitutional amendment abolished the regional assemblies and vested unrestricted powers in a simple majority of the Assembly.

That was not all, however. A whole series of measures was adopted which permitted the taking of action against individual members of the opposition. The most important of these was the Preventive Detention Act of July 1958. Under this act, it became possible to detain a person for five years, without any right of appeal to the courts, for 'conduct prejudicial to the defence and security of the State and to its foreign relations'. Supporting the measure, Nkrumah said that the Government was determined to preserve both justice and freedom. But, he went on, twice within the year preceding the tabling of the bill, opponents of the Government had been acquitted by the courts on political charges on technical legal grounds; this setting at large of dangerous characters simply could not be allowed to go on. In November 1958, the Government started to use the Act, and detained thirty-eight members of the opposition. They were alleged to have plotted to kill Nkrumah, though no attempt was ever made to prove the charges. After this, Nkrumah began to use the Act on a widening scale and on even slighter evidence, first against the opposition, and then against a succession of C.P.P. leaders.

By 1960, the opposition members in the National Assembly had fallen, through arrests, departures abroad and opportunistic crossings over to the Government side, to half their original thirty-two. When, however, the Government in 1960 put forward a new, presidential Constitution, and Nkrumah was nominated the C.P.P. candidate for the presidency under it, his critics decided to hit back. The N.P.P. and the N.L.M., who had three years before joined forces under the banner of the United Party, not only called on the electorate to reject the Constitution but also nominated Dr Danquah as rival candidate for the presidency – Danquah who thirteen years before had invited Nkrumah out to the Gold Coast. Danquah did not have an easy campaign. He was denied permission to reply over the radio to Nkrumah's recommendation of the draft Constitution. Local chiefs and district commissioners refused his propaganda van entry into a number of areas. For all that, he had a considerable potential backing. Part of this backing was ethnical, and included the Gas of Accra, whose discontent at the lack of free speech had become apparent four years before. Another part of Dr Danquah's support came from discontented trade unionists, in revolt against the 1958 Industrial Relations Act, which made it necessary for workers to obtain the authorization of the Ministry of Labour before they went on strike. And the first results to come in, those from Accra, stongly suggested that Nkrumah was not going to have a walk-over. Only forty-five per cent. of the registered electorate voted, and among those who did vote, 16,804 pronounced for Nkrumah and 9,305 for Danquah. The figures of the Yes and No votes in the constitutional referendum were almost the same. Abstentions had therefore been extremely high and the opposition vote surprisingly large. Yet the Coast had always been the great C.P.P. stronghold. There was an obvious danger that the results from the other three regions might amount to an open defeat for the Government party.

Voting figures which came in from there in the next two days strongly suggested that the authorities had realized the peril and had taken every possible precaution to avert it. The percentage of registered electors going to the polls rocketed up in some constituencies to eighty and occasionally ninety per cent., and the proportion of those who picked Danquah dropped away to nothing, even in areas where he had every reason to expect overwhelming support. Thus, in one rural Ashanti constituency where the opposition candidate had in 1956 got 8,334 votes against the C.P.P.'s 1,390 in a seventy per cent. poll, the presidential election results represented the poll as having been ninety per cent. and Nkrumah as having obtained 22,676 votes against Danquah's 137 – a little difficult to credit. When the final figures came in, they purported to show that 88·5 per cent. of the voters had pronounced for the new Constitution and 89·1 per cent. for Nkrumah as president.

The next year, however, was to see the Nkrumah régime confronting a labour challenge far more serious than the political one. This second challenge was the more surprising because since the start of the 'fifties Nkrumah's agent John Tettegah had progressively taken over the Ghana trade unions as an appendage of the C.P.P. By 1958, the key posts in most of the twenty-four federations affiliated to the Ghana T.U.C. were held by C.P.P. men, which was one reason why there was no openly unfavourable reaction to the Industrial Relations Act of that year. It was not only the trade unions who were being called to heel either: the National Ghana Farmers Council and the National Co-operative Council were also brought under the C.P.P. sway.

The origins of the 1961 labour trouble lay in a dangerous economic crisis. Primary and secondary education had been free since the previous year, and with the additional costs of an enormously expanded civil service and the pay and expenses of ministers, deputies and advisers, budgetary expenditure for 1961–62 was eighteen per cent. and more up on the preceding year. The Government therefore announced a series of drastic austerity measures. Taxes on a wide variety of articles, from beer and tobacco to tea and textiles, were increased by from fifty to a hundred per cent., and new customs duties were imposed, while in addition a forced loan was introduced under which a percentage of workers' pay was to be deducted at source and invested in Government securities. The austerity measures, which the Assembly naturally voted without the least demur, were bound to lead to an all-round increase in prices, but ten days after they were announced the Government issued a statement that all wages were to be frozen till further notice. What is more, though there was known to be smouldering opposition to the austerity plan among ordinary workers, the C.P.P. made not the least attempt to launch a propaganda campaign to put it across.

The trade union leaders might know which side their bread was buttered, but the ordinary workers were not going to stand for being treated in this way. Three days after the date when the first austerity measures were due to enter into force, the dockers at Takoradi and Sekondi came out on strike, and the two great ports were paralysed. Up country, at the Ashanti capital of Kumasi, the railwaymen came out too. The movement spread rapidly, and before long there was not a train running in the country. In many places, co-operative workers joined the strike, there was trouble in the mines, and acts of terrorism occurred up and down the country.

The Government hit back at once. Police and tanks were sent to Kumasi and strong forces took over a good part of the two ports. An emergency decree made striking the equivalent of sabotage, which was punishable by a long prison sentence. Nkrumah was out of the country, but the Minister for Presidential Affairs, speaking in his name, warned all employees of the Government and of nationalized enterprises that unless they returned to work at once they would be dismissed. Appeals and threats alike had little effect. Hundreds of strikers were arrested; the rest went on. Tettegah, speaking as general secretary of the T.U.C., used the radio daily to denounce the 'counter-revolutionaries' and 'imperialists' who were responsible for the trouble, meaning the ordinary members of his own organization. His fine phrases went unheard. In the end, it was hunger only that forced the men back to work. The Government waited for a couple of months for feelings to die down, and then had a number of strikers tried and sentenced for high treason. Finally, a White Book published at the end of the year did its best to show that the strike was part of a great foreign-financed conspiracy against the Ghana régime, which included a plot to kill Nkrumah, to hand back nationalized properties to their former owners and to reinstall a British Governor in Accra.

Part of the reason for the 1961 crisis was that though the C.P.P. now boasted no less than two million titular members, it was becoming less and less effective as a popular force. True, the party was omnipresent: there was hardly a pie into which it did not stick its finger. True, its monetary resources seemed to be unlimited. True, its leaders enjoyed outstanding prerogatives: since 1959, members of the party Central Committee had taken precedence over non-Central Committee ministers at public functions. All the same, the C.P.P., which had never succeeded in recruiting more than a handful of the country's intellectual élite, was progressively losing its character as a commoners' party. In April 1961, Nkrumah had said in a broadcast that C.P.P. members must not use their party membership for personal gain. But the limits he sought to impose on them were an indication of how far the party, in its upper ranks, had become a group of the privileged. For a ruling from the President's office laid down that no single party member should own more than two houses of a combined value of £20,000, or more than two motor-cars.

And just after the strike movement petered out, the party was purged of a number of its leading figures on the grounds that they had exceeded these limits. In a public speech, Nkrumah accused six of his ministers of abusing their positions to amass private fortunes and called on them to resign. Among those the President hit out at were two figures who were regarded as ranking immediately after himself in the C.P.P. hierarchy: Gbedemah, who had been a brilliant party organizer, and Botsio, who had known him in his London days. A third target was Krobo Edusei, the Minister of the Interior.

Gbedemah protested his innocence in the National Assembly. He was speaking in a debate on a bill to establish a Special Criminal Division of the Ghana High Court, which would deal with political offenders and from whose judgements there would be no appeal. The measure was described by the Government spokesman as containing 'the seed of the true welfare of the people of Ghana'. Gbedemah, who had served as a Minister continuously since the first cabinet Nkrumah formed, was too well in the know to be taken in by that sort of catch-phrase. It was supposedly to safeguard the hard-won freedom of the people of Ghana that the Preventive Detention Act had been passed back in 1958, he said, yet, as he spoke, how many people were not languishing in prison under its provisions? 'If we are to learn from that experience,' Gbedemah declared, 'when the present bill goes on the statute book, the last flickering flame of freedom in our country will be forever extinguished. We may any of us be pulled out of bed at a moment's notice to face a firing squad after a summary trial and conviction.' Gbedemah did not wait to see the official reaction to his outburst. He left the country as soon as he had finished speaking, before any attempt could be made to curb his freedom. Not everyone was as lucky. Danquah was only one of a number of opposition figures arrested for their alleged participation in the plot that was stated to have lain behind the September 1961 strikes.

Almost all the early leaders of the C.P.P. had now been evicted from office and, since it was plainly hopeless to attempt to oppose the Government by constitutional means, terrorism started up. The beginning of August 1962 saw an attempt on Nkrumah's life at Kulungugu, as he was motoring back from the Togo frontier. At the start of September, there was a bomb outrage outside his chief official residence, Flagstaff House. Five days later the National Assembly voted a law imposing the death penalty on anyone caught carrying a firearm or explosives without a licence; a week later again troops and tanks took part in a methodical comb-out of the capital for terrorists, while a dusk-to-dawn curfew was declared and motor traffic in town was forbidden. There was burning and looting, and foreign correspondents who reported what had happened were expelled. All the same, no trace was found of the terrorists, who began to change their tactics: instead of continuing their attempts on the President's life, they started a campaign of haphazard bomb explosions up and down Accra in order to create an atmosphere of general panic, while subversive inscriptions and subversive leaflets began to appear. The next bomb attack against Nkrumah himself did not occur till the beginning of 1963, and it was not the last such incident. The terrorists did, indeed, completely fail in their probable objectives of killing the President and driving the C.P.P. from power. But the succession of acts of violence, most of which cost a number of innocent lives, and the brutal repression, that was the only official reply to them, had opened a progressively wider breach between the Government and the ordinary citizen. It had done less than nothing to promote unity within the C.P.P. and it had led an increasing number of Ghanaians to flee their country. By the beginning of 1963, there were thousands of these voluntary exiles in the neighbouring Republic of Togo, which had been officially accused of complicity in one of the plots against the régime, thousands more in the Ivory Coast, and colonies of expatriates in other West African countries and in London.

Shortly after the Kulungugu attempt on Nkrumah, three more leading figures in the régime were arrested and accused of complicity in the crime. They were Information Minister Tawia Adamafio, C.P.P. Executive Secretary Hugh Horatio Coffie-Crabbe and Foreign Minister Ako Adjei, who had been a fellow-student of Nkrumah's in America and who had invited him back to Ghana fifteen years before. The three men were not allowed to consult legal advisers before their trial was under way; when that stage had been reached, no lawyer would accept a brief from them on the grounds that proceedings were too far advanced. All the same, the affair saw the temporary eclipse of the extreme anti-Western element in the party, with which the three arrested men were associated. It is true that the party press continued its violent verbal attacks on neo-colonialism, but practical steps were taken to attract foreign investments. Thus, a measure introduced in April 1963 gave foreign firms which set up in Ghana guarantees against expropriation, the right to repatriate their profits and a number of tax allowances. Internally, there was some evidence of greater freedom of debate in the National Assembly. There seemed reason to hope that the Government had embarked on a political and economic course which would bring greater freedom and the stability which normally accompanies this, and which the foreign capitalists to whom Ghana was bound to look for aid would therefore regard as encouraging.

Only too soon these hopes were to be disappointed. On 9 December, the Special Court which had been trying the C.P.P. Executive Secretary and the two ministers acquitted all three. Nkrumah responded by dismissing the Chief Justice and annulling the verdict, but that was not the only repressive measure taken. The maximum period of preventive detention was increased from five to twenty years, and it was laid down that henceforth any Ghanaian who wanted to leave the country would have to obtain a special authorization before he did so. What is more, Nkrumah announced in a New Year's Eve broadcast that the Government had decided, 'in the interests of the people', to take advantage of the situation created by the treason trial acquittals to make certain amendments to the Constitution. One of these amendments empowered the President at his discretion to remove any judge of the High Court or the Supreme Court; hitherto he had been able only to revoke the appointment of a judge as Chief Justice. The second amendment provided that 'in conformity with the interests, welfare and aspirations of the people, and in order to develop the organization, initiative and political activity of the people, there shall be one national party in Ghana, which shall be the vanguard of our people in the struggle to build a Socialist society . . . the Convention People's Party'.

The authorities took every possible precaution to ensure that the referendum should yield the result expected of it by the largest at all credible majority. Every voter's ballot paper was marked with the same serial number as appeared in the registration book opposite his name and address: it would thus be the simplest thing in the world to discover who had voted No and who had abstained. That was not all. In a number of polling booths, party officials either sealed or removed the No box. Newspaper men who had made a tour of the polling stations found that in some at least of them, the number of citizens who had voted, as shown in the registration books submitted for their inspection at the close of the poll, was half or less than half the official figures later announced by the authorities. These figures purported to show that, taking the country as a whole, 92·8 per cent. of the registered electors had voted, which was just credible, and that 2,773,920 of the voters had pronounced in favour of the constitutional amendments and 2,452 against, which nobody could be expected to swallow. All the same, in February 1964, Ghana became a Convention People's Party Republic, in which the party flag, overprinted with a black star, became the national flag. As for the tiny minority group in the National Assembly, and the opposition United Party outside it, they had been finished with once and for all. When the country's first parliamentary elections since independence took place in June 1965, all the 198 candidates nominated by the party's central committee were declared to have been returned unopposed.

Party propaganda has done its best to instil into the people of Ghana something very like a worship of Nkrumah. Naturally his head appears on stamps and on coins, and a statue of him stands outside the parliament house, with his hand uplifted in the C.P.P.'s 'freedom salute'. Young Pioneers, the youth branch of the party, lead schoolchildren in starting their school day with an expression of faith in him. The chorus leader intones 'Nkrumah does no wrong' and the children's response varies from 'Nkrumah is our Messiah' to 'Nkrumah never dies.' The President has a whole range of titles: The Indomitable, The Infallible, The Man of his Word, The Man of Action and The Pacifier. What is more, an attempt has been made to inculcate the belief that Nkrumah has transferred part of the breath of his life to his son, Gorkeh Gamal Kwame, who was six years old in 1965; the transfer is said to be proved by the fact that since it, the President's face has lost part of its expression.

For all that, as 1965 came in, Nkrumah was an isolated man. He was isolated in his own country. He appeared to be secluding himself in Christiansborg Castle, well guarded by soldiers – the police who had formerly looked after him had been disarmed after the attempt on his life by one of them outside Flagstaff House in January 1964. He was progressively becoming isolated in Africa. Almost as soon as Ghana had achieved independence – the only sub-Saharan states then enjoying that status were Ethiopia, Liberia and the Union of South Africa – Accra had become the capital of Pan-Africanism, for Nkrumah had been the principal originator of the idea of the United States of Africa. With the end of the colonial régime in more than thirty other African lands, Ghana lost its privileged position, but that was not all. The first Pan-African summit meeting, held in Addis Ababa in May 1963, flatly rejected Nkrumah's idea of a Pan-African parliament and government.

And in 1965, the Ghanaian authorities were forced to make the most humiliating concessions to avoid a mass boycott by other African states of the latest African Unity Organization summit conference, which was held in Accra in October. Ghana's neighbours had accused it not merely of harbouring political refugees from their territories, but of training them in subversive activities: an attempt early in 1965 on the life of the Niger President, Diori Hamani, was only one of a number of crimes said to have been inspired by Accra. In order to persuade the doubtful Powers and their friends to come to Accra in September, the Ghanaians had to agree not only to expel from their territory all such people as they might regard as undesirable, but to allow the General Secretary of the African Unity Organization to verify that the appropriate measures had in fact been taken. Even so, no more than nineteen African heads of state or premiers turned up, while most of the French-speaking sub-Saharan states were not represented at all, and Nkrumah's proposal for an all-African executive council, was turned down.

It would be absurd to pretend that the Nkrumah Government's record has been a purely negative one. In its first years, at any rate, it could boast of considerable achievements. In 1957, non-Ghanaian high officials in the central administration, the judiciary and the police formed seventy-five per cent. of the total. By 1963, the figure was down to less than one per cent., and the civil service is generally acknowledged to be extremely efficient. The number of children in school had enormously increased, though possibly the educational standards had fallen off a little, and the number of hospital beds had been doubled. Industrial production regularly increased up to 1962, and a start had been made with processing local raw materials on the spot, and with diversifying production.

All the same, what the exiled opposition described as reckless overspending was progressively undermining Ghana's credit abroad. Her foreign currency reserves were down to less than a fifth of what they had been on independence; her external debt had risen to nearly £200 million. And she showed no sign of tightening her national belt, where Government expenditure was concerned, anyway. The year 1964 saw this country of a bare seven million inhabitants committed to opening its sixty-first overseas mission, in North Korea, of all countries. The 1965 Budget showed a deficit of £66 million. Some of Nkrumah's economic development plans appeared to level-headed observers to be the wildest fantasy, as when he talked of making Ghana independent not only in consumer goods, but in the manufacture of machines for making consumer goods. Repression was still going on: one of the latest signs of it was the establishment of a Government committee to ensure the removal from bookshops and the libraries of schools, colleges and universities of 'all publications which do not reflect the ideology of the party, or which are hostile to its ideals'. Nkrumah did not appear to trust even his ministers: when he went to London in June 1965 for the Commonwealth Prime Ministers' Conference, the whole of his Cabinet were penned up for three weeks in the Kwame Nkrumah Ideological Institute at Winneba in order, or so it was stated, 'to examine themselves, to consolidate their knowledge of Nkrumaism and to study the history and the meaning of African Socialism'.

And of course scandals involving corruption were still continuing. One of the latest, which was revealed by the report of a commission of inquiry in October 1964, concerned irregularities in the granting of import licences. The Finance Minister, who had at the operative time been responsible for trade also, resigned, while a number of senior civil servants were dismissed. In May 1965, two Ghanaian industrialists and a member of parliament were sentenced to terms of more than twenty years' imprisonment each for an import fraud which was said to have netted £1,000,000 for the three of them. There are Ghanaians who think that the real reason why the C.P.P. lost its hold over the masses in the late 1950s was this notorious canker of corruption within it. It had by that time come to be regarded as an old boy stronghold, and his failure to establish a corruption-proof party, a plain man's party, might well be regarded, they argue, as Nkrumah's biggest failure.

In 1965, therefore, Ghanaians were talking against their Government, though they were not doing so in public, and the press was as docile as ever. Discontent was not confined to the towns, where prices were rising because of shortages and the increase in the amount of money in circulation. The farmers were complaining too. Cocoa planters were reported at the turn of 1964 and 1965 to have agreed to a four-shillings-per-load levy on their cocoa. They had done nothing of the sort: the levy had simply been imposed on them by the official farmers' organization. Nationalization was not being a conspicuous success: only four of the long list of State enterprises appeared to be paying their way.

What of the future? The Army had up to 1965, with one exception, remained neutral in the dispute between the President and the opposition; so had the civil service. There thus seemed very little danger of the President's being overturned by such a *coup d'état* as had cost the life of Sylvanus Olympio, the Head of State of the neighbouring Republic of Togo, though Nkrumah was apparently growing nervous about this: in August 1965 he took over direct command of the defence forces, following reports that two generals had been talking against him. The real threat appeared to be that pressure from elements within the C.P.P. which could eventually develop into an opposition movement might compel Nkrumah to pay a lot more attention to public opinion in his administration of the country – and that would go clean contrary to the whole of his behaviour in the past. This peril was a real one, too, for as 1965 opened, more and more people were joining the C.P.P. in order to subvert it from within.

More and more Ghanaians too were abandoning their country, even men in secure and senior positions. At the turn of 1964 and 1965, the Deputy Editor of the official *Evening News* was sent over to East Germany on a news assignment. It would be difficult to imagine a non-Governmental job more desirable than his. All the same, the official daily's Deputy Editor got permission to call in at London on the way to see a brother – and as soon as he arrived he declared very firmly that he was not going back to Ghana.

4

The Congo (Brazzaville)

ON THE AFTERNOON of 15 August 1963, the President of the Republic of the Congo (Brazzaville), Abbé Fulbert Youlou, resigned his position after three days of increasingly violent demonstrations against him. The demonstrations had been launched by local trade unionists, the strongest single element among whom was represented by the Christian trade unions. The Congo people in general and labour in particular had a whole series of grievances against the forty-six-year-old Abbé, who had been responsible for his country's affairs, first as Head of the Government and then as Head of State, for almost six years. The administration was notoriously corrupt, and the President drank, and womanized and robbed the Treasury with as much enthusiasm and as little discretion as any of his subordinates. It had done nothing at all to promote the coherent development of what is one of the poorest countries in Central Africa, and urban unemployment was a grave and chronic problem. Following the discovery, or more probably the invention, of a Communist plot by the President's somewhat curious French advisers in 1960, a series of repressive measures had been enacted which permitted the gagging of the press and the internment of people regarded as dangerous to public security. But the main cause of the trouble that started on 13 August was twofold. The Abbé had announced his intention of setting up a single party in the Congo and had called a round-table conference to discuss the matter. There were plausible arguments for his plan, since the basis of the existing Congo parties was less ideological than ethnical, and as late as 1959 99 people had been killed and 177 seriously injured in the course of four days of inter-tribal rioting in Brazzaville. There appeared to be much less justification for the Abbé's second step. On 6 August, he had issued a decree under which, till the single party was in fact established, a ban was imposed on all public meetings which 'might have a political character or be contrary to the principle of national indivisibility'. The trade unions regarded this decree as a violation of the fundamental rights recognized by the United Nations Charter, and on 7 August they decided to call a general strike in protest against it six days later.

In January 1964, the Pan-African Union of Christian Workers held a congress in Brazzaville, and speakers hailed the city as 'the capital of the first revolution in which free trade unionism – that is, trade unionism not run by the Government – had played a decisive part'. The delegates had congratulated themselves a little too soon. The following July, the men who had overturned President Youlou because of his attempt to set up a single party and stifle free speech put a bill through the National Assembly which accorded permanent single-party status to the political organization – the National Revolutionary Movement, or M.N.R. – which they had founded, and which had won, if that is the correct word, all the seats at the parliamentary elections called after the Abbé's deposition. The next month the M.N.R. central committee called for the press, invited them to work in with the régime and immediately showed the extent of its distrust of them by telling them that a censorship was being set up. Finally, on 5 November, the Congo President and Prime Minister, the diplomatic corps and delegates of countries ranging from Ghana to the Soviet Union and from Algeria to Communist China were present at the constitutive congress of the single trade union movement which the régime had decided to set up, despite the refusal to co-operate of the Christian trade unions which had played the leading role in the revolution which had overturned Fulbert Youlou. Speeches delivered at the congress left little doubt about the character which that régime had by now assumed. A spokesman for the M.N.R. Youth Movement hailed what he called 'our brothers in the struggle in the Soviet Union and China' and demanded that those who tried to obstruct the road to 'scientific Socialism' should be brought before a 'people's court'. The first general secretary of the new trade union body denounced apolitical unionism and called on the Government to take action against counter-revolution in all its forms. The end of the congress, he went on, should mean the end of the Christian trade unions, and he concluded: 'We don't want to hear any more of wage-claim trade unionism. We

89

want to train the workers in the practical methods of applying scientific Socialism.' Just over a fortnight later, the national president of the Christian trade unions, Fulgence Biyaoula, was arrested in a car driven by a Roman Catholic priest and there is reliable evidence that he was subjected to torture by electricity before he disappeared into jail.

One of the most outspoken critics of the Youlou administration had been not a politician but a Congolese priest, the Rev. Louis Badila, editor of the Catholic weekly *La Semaine Africaine*. The weekly was not a political organ, but it did comment on current events and came down heavily on those threats to public and private liberties which a Christian who understands the implications of his religion is bound to resist. It had in consequence at least once been confiscated by the Youlou Government because of the frankness of its observations.

Father Badila did not change his objective attitude in the least after President Youlou's successors had been installed in power. By August 1964, indeed, he was appearing in court on charges of libelling the new President, Alphonse Massemba-Débat, in a political article, though he was discharged. On 8 November the *Semaine Africaine* published an open letter by its editor to the President which constituted an extremely serious attack. Father Badila said that the people of Brazzaville had marched unarmed on Youlou's palace in protest against an abuse of personal power that was turning into a dictatorship. Today these people felt they had been betrayed. Their aim had been national unity, but unity combined with diversity, and fifteen months later those who had appropriated the revolution were trying to reduce everything to uniformity, parties and trade unions, non-political movements and even teaching. And the writer declared that those in power were throwing people into prison arbitrarily, and torturing them arbitrarily, while they had aroused general discontent by their endless delay in bringing political prisoners to trial. Nevertheless, it was not an unfriendly letter. It ended: 'The Congo isn't lost, Mr President. . . . But help us to get it out of this crisis.'

Just a fortnight later, Father Badila recounted to the readers of the *Semaine Africaine* a little story that showed, in down-to-earth terms, the meaning to the ordinary citizen of the repressive activities taken by the administration which he had denounced in his letter to the President. His article dealt with a visit he had paid to a village outside Brazzaville, where an old couple had told him, after many precautions, that 'they' had come and picked up a neighbour. 'We daren't talk too loud about it,' the husband said, 'for you never know. "They" might come and pick us up too. I've known men of our age threatened with denunciation by children, simply because they wanted to know why a man round the corner was arrested without trial or sentence. . . . Yes,' the old man continued after an interval, 'our children are threatening to jug us.'

One of Father Badila's comments on his experience was an extremely pertinent question. Had Africans, he asked, got rid of white colonialism only in order to replace it by black colonialism? The article was, however, the last he was to write. A day or two after it appeared, he was himself picked up, tortured and flung into jail, and under his successor in the editorial chair the *Semaine Africaine* gave the authorities no further trouble.

The Republic of the Congo (Brazzaville) covers an area of just under 128,000 square miles; it lies on the west bank of the river Congo and has a short coastline on the Atlantic. Its population, twenty per cent. of it urban, is rather over 800,000, the biggest towns being the capital, Brazzaville, with more than 100,000 inhabitants, and Pointe Noire, the commercial capital, with around 60,000. Despite its fine modern buildings, Brazzaville has been described as 'a great window opening on nothing', for it has no sort of supporting hinterland. The country's resources are, indeed, extremely limited, the principal among them being wood from its great tracts of tropical forest, sugar-cane and cabbage palms, though traces of petroleum and diamonds have also been found, and it lives to a considerable extent on its transit trade. For all that, the Congo has at its disposal more than 1,100 miles of metalled roads, 800 miles of navigation on the Congo, 300 miles of railway, the only railway in French Equatorial Africa, to which it once belonged, and by far the biggest port in the area. The fact that it enjoys these facilities is to a great extent due to the contributions in money and manpower made by the neighbouring states of the former

French Empire, which were largely dependent on the use of its transport.

Like most other countries in sub-Saharan Africa, the Congo has a population which is divided into a number of ethnic groups. About one-third of the inhabitants of the Republic live in small villages scattered through the northern forest, and for the most part these belong to the M'Bochi tribal group. Another but smaller division of the population consists of the Vili tribes, who inhabit the area round Pointe Noire, on the Atlantic. The third and most important population group is that of the Bakongo, who straddle the Congo river, and whose most important branch in the Congo (Brazzaville) is that of the Lari. The Bakongo have been described as to a considerable extent responsible for such progress as the country had made in the past, for they are one of the most evolved and enterprising peoples in Central Africa and have shown a capacity for adapting themselves to a Western-type economy without losing their own traditions or social structure.

The first colonists in the area were the Portuguese, who at one time set up there an Empire of Saõ Salvador, whose emperors were local chiefs converted to Catholicism. Naturally a big slave-trade developed later. It was not until the end of the nineteenth century, however, that the first attempt to colonize the country seriously began. Behind it was the French explorer, Savorgnan de Brazza, who, after a number of expeditions, in 1880 signed on behalf of France a treaty of friendship with the Makoko, or King, of the Bateké under which the latter accepted French protection. A French law voted two years later founded the colony of the French Congo, of which Brazza became Government Commissioner. Pacification of the complete area went on, at intervals, until the First World War, and it was not until the 1920s that the last administrative posts held by army officers were handed over to civilian officials.

One of the more curious aspects of the twentieth-century history of the Congo (Brazzaville), which had an outstanding effect on later political developments, was the growth and influence there of a series of African messianic movements which sprang up all over the sub-Saharan portion of the continent in the years following the arrival of European colonists and missionaries. The most important of these movements was that launched by André Matsoua Grenard, who had served in the French Army in the First World War, fought in the Rif campaign in Morocco and finally settled down in Paris as an accountant. The organization that Matsoua founded in 1926 would have appeared to have nothing in the least religious about it. Its title was the Friendly Society of Natives of French Equatorial Africa, it was a mutual aid body, it pledged itself to do all it could to raise the moral and intellectual level of people coming to Europe from the area for which it had made itself responsible, and it obtained recognition from the French authorities. The Friendly Society claimed to have no political background, but there seems little doubt that one of Matsoua's chief aims was to build up an African intellectual élite which would be capable of persuading the French to grant equality of rights to Blacks and Whites in the country he came from. What is more, the two delegates he sent out to the Congo in 1929, to spread news of the Friendly Society's activities and to raise money for them, spoke to great crowds about the Bakongo 'Nation', and about the future they envisaged for it. In the end, the French Governor had the two emissaries detained, while Matsoua was arrested in France and deported back home, where the three men and other Friendly Society leaders were put on trial for alleged fraud and sentenced to prison terms. And though Matsoua's shady financial deals were fully proved and his constant demands for money from his followers were notorious, his popularity as a symbol of the revolt against colonial society was not in the slightest affected. After Matsoua's disappearance behind the prison walls in 1930, the Friendly Society continued as a semi-secret organization, and when he died in captivity twelve years later, following a second arrest, his disciples refused to accept the fact. 'Matsoua will come back,' they said, 'all action without him is vain.' Matsoua's death, indeed, transformed him into a myth and a divinity, a far more powerful figure than he had ever been when he was alive. 'Jesus Matsoua' was said to be living in a palace in Paris, acting as de Gaulle's divine helper, negotiating with the General for the independence of the Congo and responsible not only for Free France's military victories, but for the colonial reforms initiated at the Brazzaville conference in 1944. As for the Friendly

Society, it turned into a religious movement, with its dogmas, its rites, its chapels and its clergy.

After the war, the Congo became entitled to representation in the French National Assembly, and for six years on from 1945, the deputy it regularly elected was Jean Félix Tchikaya, of the Congo Progressive Party, or P.P.C., who just as regularly beat the Socialist candidate, Jacques Opangault. Tchikaya may have got a majority of the voters to support him, but he never secured the backing of a majority of the electorate. When election time came round, the Bakongo voted, if they voted at all, for André Matsoua, whose name they wrote in on their ballot papers in place of the candidates put up by the regularly constituted political parties. All that changed at the January 1956 elections to the French Assembly, when thirty-nine-year-old Abbé Fulbert Youlou, a member of the Bakongo tribe of the Lari, was persuaded by a delegation of fellow-tribesmen to stand. Youlou had been forbidden by his bishop to enter politics and was deprived of the right to dispense the sacraments when he disregarded these orders. He was a complete newcomer to the political field. That did not matter. He had the incredible good fortune of being regarded by a majority of his fellow-tribesmen as 'Jesus Matsoua' come again, a belief which his professional character as a man of God must have made it easier for them to hold. True, one-third of the Bakongo votes still went to the dead leader, but in the 1957 elections to the Congo Territorial Assembly, when Youlou had launched a party of his own, a bare 535 electors had filled in Matsoua's name on their ballot papers. Youlou did not win in the January 1956 election, of course, but all the same his success was quite astonishing for one who had not the slightest record as a politician behind him. Tchikaya got in with 45,000 votes, Opangault came next with 43,000, and the Abbé secured the remarkable figure of 41,000.

Who is Fulbert Youlou? He was born in 1917 of a poor family living just outside Brazzaville. His mother named him Youlou, which in the language of his tribe means 'the heavens', and it is conceivable that this may have influenced him in his choice of a vocation. After his baptism as Fulbert, at the age of nine, he entered a school run by priests in Brazzaville and then the seminary at Yaoundé. He was ordained in 1946 and continued as a priest until at the end of 1955 the Lari delegation approached him to stand for the French Assembly.

Youlou is small and at first sight appears timid. He has a whole collection of soutanes, white, black, blue and scarlet, though he most often wears a white one with a black girdle round it. He never abandoned his ecclesiastical costume, because he was well aware that his religious aspect was just as important to his success as his political one. Indeed he also wears a huge silver ring set with a milky opal, which gives him something of an episcopal appearance. The only item of his costume that clashes with this general impression is the little round hat which he often wears, and which looks anything but clerical. Despite the fact that he had been barred from dispensing the sacraments, Youlou continued to go to Mass every day, and blessed the crowds that greeted him with the sign of the cross. He was reputed always to carry a revolver under his soutane. There is no means of knowing whether he always did. What is certain is that one day when the opposition had tabled a motion of censure on his Government in the National Assembly, he did pull a revolver out and point it at the deputies responsible. The Abbé's personality was too strong for them, and he pocketed the gun, with a broad smile, as soon as the motion had been withdrawn.

Finally, there was one interesting resemblance between his Bakongo supporters' attitude towards Youlou and that which they had adopted towards the dead Matsoua with whom they had identified him. Just as they never complained of Matsoua's dissipation of their money, they tolerated in Youlou financial practices a mere whisper of which would have discredited a Western politician over night. They went even farther. As soon as the Abbé had committed himself to politics, they happily provided him with a car, a chauffeur and a monthly living allowance so that he could pursue his chosen career without any concern for his material needs.

Youlou was soon to show that he had little to learn about playing the political game. In the January elections, a number of his young tribal supporters had been arrested for beating up electors who they had reason to believe had voted the wrong way. The Abbé secured the withdrawal of most of the prosecutions pending against them, and the few who did eventually appear in court were all acquitted. But there was another political challenge ahead. Municipal elections were due in Brazzaville and Pointe Noire in November. This was no question of a single-man fight: a new party had to be formed. Youlou duly founded it, christening it the Democratic Union for the Defence of African Interests, or U.D.D.I.A., and handed in its constitution to the authorities, as required by the law, on 17 May. November saw the U.D.D.I.A. winning twenty-three out of the thirty-seven seats on the Brazzaville council; in Pointe Noire, where Youlou had formed an opportunistic alliance with the locally powerful Socialists, the two parties between them secured all but eight of the thirty seats. Though it had been in existence for a mere matter of months, the U.D.D.I.A. found itself in possession of the only two mayoralties of the country. Youlou, who had entered politics less than a year before, became mayor of Brazzaville. He had also encouraged the formation of a European party which was to act as a 'parallel organization' to his own.

March 1957 saw the first elections to the Congo territorial assembly under a new French law which gave greater political liberty to the colonies. Its results appeared to a great extent to have followed the lines of tribal boundaries. Just over half of the country went to the Socialists and almost all the rest of it to the U.D.D.I.A. and its European team-mates, with the formerly predominant P.P.C. nowhere. With the Socialists and their allies holding twenty-three seats and Youlou and his backers twenty-two, a coalition Government was formed under Opangault. Youlou entered the Government as Minister for Agriculture. He may have known little about farming, but his choice was a shrewd one politically. It allowed him as part of his duties to make repeated trips in the countryside. He was officially received there by the local authorities, and this could hardly fail to impress the villagers. The trips could be regarded, in fact, as so many personal propaganda tours.

As early as September 1957, a Socialist deputy had gone over to the U.D.D.I.A., which had promptly demanded the head-ship of the Government, and relations between the two parties became envenomed. It was not, however, until the late autumn of 1958, after de Gaulle had granted a further stage of auto-nomy to France's colonies, that the clash came out into the open. All the colonial territories were remodelling their institutions, and the Congo Assembly met at Pointe Noire on 25 November to do the same. Unfortunately the two sides could not agree on the constitution of the Congo Republic which would obviously have to be set up, and at the height of their dispute, a Socialist deputy who had been vaccilating between them for some time suddenly announced that he was going over to the U.D.D.I.A. When the news leaked out, it was too much for the Socialists who formed the majority of the Pointe Noire population, and they invaded the Assembly hall to wreak vengeance on the defector. Police and gendarmerie had some difficulty in restoring order, but even when they had done so, the Socialist deputies flatly refused to discuss the U.D.D.I.A.'s draft constitution, and walked out. There they made a grave tactical mistake for, with the twenty-three deputies they now numbered, Youlou's supporters had exactly the required quorum to put through what measures they wished. The U.D.D.I.A. began by replacing the Opangault Cabinet by a 'provisional Government', of which Youlou was promptly designated the Premier. They then, since Pointe Noire had been so markedly unfriendly to them, decided to transfer the seat of the Assembly to Brazzaville, for which they promptly set off. The Socialist deputies met next day and declared the proceedings of the Assembly null and void, but they did nothing more about it. So in December, Youlou formed his Government, which he persuaded two Socialist deputies to enter, thus bringing the strength of his party up to twenty-five.

The Socialists' reply was to call for immediate new elections, before the U.D.D.I.A. had time to dig itself in. This plea met with less than no response, so they took a stronger line: they declared that they were ready if necessary to embark on civil war to turn out the Youlou Government, which they said represented nothing. An organized civil war did not, in fact, occur, but February saw four days of merciless mutual killing in Brazzaville between inhabitants belonging to the northern M'bochi tribes, who supported the Socialists, and those who were members of the southern Lari tribe, and backed Youlou. Dozens of innocent African women and children were hacked to death or horribly injured by knife wounds. The fact that the two sides put on their traditional tribal headgear made the massacre far easier, for it rendered them readily distinguishable one from the other, and the mere circumstance of belonging to the rival tribe was apparently sufficient provocation for its opponents to attack to kill. The trouble stopped only when the French flew in troops, who did not have to fire a shot to halt the slaughter: they simply patrolled the streets and conducted a house-to-house search for arms. Opangault was of course arrested for incitement to violence, of which he seems indeed to have been guilty, but he was never brought to trial and was released after barely five months.

The rioting was not yet over when the Assembly adopted a definitive Constitution, which among other things turned the 'provisional Government' into the Government of the Republic and gave the Premier power to dissolve Parliament. Most of the other new Governments of French Africa had laboriously worked out model constitutions patterned on carefully chosen models. Youlou's team had not time to do this. They had to act quickly in order to provide a juridical basis on which a strong administration could rely in case the troubles went on. Two months later, the Abbé used his newly conferred powers to dissolve the Assembly.

Youlou could be pretty certain of victory in the ensuing elections. The Socialists, who had been officially blamed for the February massacres in Brazzaville and had lost their leader, had been reduced to something like clandestinity in their electioneering. What is more, the Abbé could count on the benevolent neutrality of the French, who wanted stability above everything else. All the same, he was taking no chances. Electoral boundaries were redrawn on what can only be described as gerrymandering lines. And though the figures of the polling in June showed that the Socialists had got as many as 42·22 per cent. of the votes cast, against the U.D.D.I.A.'s 57·78 per cent., the Government won 51 seats in the 61-member Parliament and the opposition no more than 10. Youlou's comment on the results was an extremely conciliatory one. He said that they did not represent the victory of a party or a programme, but the beginning of national unity. As soon as the new Assembly met, two Socialist deputies were invited to join a reshuffled Ministry: the Socialists had everything to gain by an understanding with the Government party, and if

Youlou was sincere in his expressed desire to achieve national unity, such an understanding was equally necessary for the U.D.D.I.A. Just over a year later, Opangault, who had led a friendly opposition after his release from prison under the July 1959 amnesty, himself entered the Cabinet as Minister of State and Deputy Premier. This liberal attitude of the Youlou Government towards former enemies was not confined to the political field, either. A number of trade union leaders were flung into jail after the discovery in 1960 of an almost certainly apocryphal Communist plot against the régime. As soon as they were released, they were given places on the Congo Economic Council. The authorities might have introduced repressive measures, but it has not unjustly been remarked that for the Abbé's opponents, prison cells as often as not proved to be the antechambers to positions of official responsibility.

The Congo (Brazzaville) became independent in 1960, and in 1961 a new constitution was voted. Like other constitutions of former French Africa, it appeared to be to a large extent modelled on that of the Fifth French Republic. Under it, the President was directly elected for five years by the people and was head of the Government; he appointed and dismissed its ministers and they were responsible to him only. The President could also seek the people's opinion by way of a referendum, and in emergencies could exercise the same sort of powers as had been conceded to de Gaulle in France. When the time for the first presidential elections came, in March, Youlou was the only candidate. According to the official figures, those voting for him represented 88·4 per cent. of the registered electorate and 97·56 per cent. of those who had taken the trouble to go to the polls.

Now that the country had definitively adopted its political institutions, it might have been expected that the Government would have gone ahead right away with the plans for economic development and social progress that were the biggest local problems. Certain projects were indeed announced, but they advanced very slowly. The most likely reason seemed to be that Youlou had been hypnotized by the plan for a dam on the river Kouilou which, if the very large sums of capital necessary for it could be found, and certain other equally difficult conditions could be realized, might have transformed the life of the country. The dam, which had been talked about intermittently since 1956, would have cost something approaching £200 million. It would have been built on the Kouilou about fifty miles upstream from Pointe Noire and would have brought into existence an artificial lake twice the size of the Lake of Geneva. The dam would have produced seven billion kilowatt-hours per year of electric power at a bargain-basement price, and six-sevenths of this power would have been used to produce aluminium, half a million tons a year of it. All that may have sounded very well, but the difficulty was that the Congo (Brazzaville) had none of the necessary raw material itself, and would have had to obtain it from the Guinea bauxite deposits. And it was a little hard to see the Guinean President, Sekou Touré, allowing all his country's bauxite to be processed abroad. He would obviously want a similar, if smaller, Guinean dam project, that for a barrage on the river Konkouré, to be carried out first. Nevertheless, pending the materialization of support for the Kouilou river dam, Youlou made no attempt to set in motion the series of other and smaller projects which might have helped to raise the national standard of living and provide employment.

For urban unemployment was a very serious problem in the Congo. There had been demonstrations by unemployed as early as December 1960, and all that Youlou had been able to offer them had been a few days of work on hand-to-mouth relief projects, after which they were progressively dismissed; the same sort of face-saving relief work was produced on the eve of elections or of any international conference which might happen to meet in Brazzaville. The position was the more difficult since the Congo could boast of one of the highest figures of school attendance in Africa: no less than eighty-one per cent. of her school-age children were in fact at school. An unemployed man who is educated or semi-educated is liable to represent a far greater danger to the Government of his country than one who is illiterate: the latter can be got, with any luck, to regard his lot as part of the nature of things. And there were quantities of young men about in the Congo who had a certain education but could not find anyone to employ them; they were particularly numerous in Brazzaville

since, being the capital, it was regarded as the natural source
of jobs. It might have been thought that these discontented
youths would have sought a remedy for their grievances in
politics. That would have got them nowhere, for the National
Assembly, apart from the occasional timid criticism, contented
itself with setting the seal on the various decisions of the
Government. It was not necessary to buy a newspaper to be
aware of that. The Assembly's proceedings were from time to
time put on the air, and anyone who had ever listened to one
of these broadcast sessions could not fail to remember the ritual
exchanges of compliments between ministers and deputies
in which they largely consisted. The only group of men who
could advance a valid claim to speak for the people were the
leaders of the trade unions, which had not so far been taken
over by the State though they knew, as did the union movements of all the newly-independent African States, that their
independent existence was in growing danger. What is more,
the Congo unions did not confine their activities to urging their
members' wage claims. When Left-Wing President Sekou
Touré, of Guinea, visited Brazzaville in June 1963, they
mobilized their followers to demonstrate, with cries of 'Long
live the President of Africa! Down with Fulbert Youlou!' and
a number of their leaders were thrown into jail. Work for the
trade unions thus seemed to the young unemployed the only
worthwhile outlet for their energies.

One of the reasons why the Youlou Government had never
embarked on any series of smaller development projects was
that it was chronically short of money. That shortage was
partly due to extravagance in high places, and here Youlou set
no sort of example: on his first official visit to France, he is
credibly reported to have taken the equivalent of £40,000 with
him for expenses, and there was hardly a week when cocktail
party conversation in Brazzaville was not enlivened by a new
Youlou scandal story. An official report which came out after
the 1959 elections said that one minister would arrive at his
work three hours late, or spent most of his time on the watch-out
for a love affair, while another would spend his morning examining the prices of the latest type of nylon shirt in the shops.
Certain ministerial cars, the report added, were on the road
night and day, and there were ministries where waste and

nepotism reigned supreme. Nepotism was the second reason why the Youlou Government never had any money to spare. As a result of it, the civil service was swollen with often useless recruits and, in the words of one of Youlou's ministers, a high proportion of the budget was taken up in running-expenses that did no sort of good to the State. Some of these civil service recruits, the Minister said, were hardly capable of their work, yet for all that, if they disposed of influence, they could count on salaries far higher than their qualifications warranted: it was common gossip that if a man was in with the President, he could boost his pay to ten, twenty or even fifty times the normal figure for his post. That was why, the Minister concluded, the Congo could not afford to invest in development, though this sort of investment represented the only way in which the country could progress.

Corruption and nepotism were not peculiar, among the newly independent states of Africa, to the Congo (Brazzaville) alone. Scandals concerning bribery and official rake-offs had been constantly coming up in Accra, for all the civil service there was far more efficient. The trouble was that the Youlou Government had never made the least attempt to cover up its internal deficiencies by pursuing a combative foreign policy. Far from challenging colonialism and 'neo-colonialism', it had supported Tchombe and his secessionist movement in Katanga and had come out violently against the Leopoldville Government of Patrice Lumumba. Though Youlou appeared to have had some success in appeasing the inter-tribal animosities within his own country, he had consistently opposed any closer links between the countries of Central Africa, and his ostensible conversion to Pan-Africanism at the first meeting of the African Unity Organization had come so late in the day that it had seemed to many more than a little suspect. Finally he had tried to put over the idea, for which there may have been arguments, but which could hardly fail to be unpopular among Africans, that if Salazar were carefully handled, he might inaugurate a liberal policy in Portuguese Africa.

Youlou's foreign policy had largely been inspired by the team of French advisers who had been working for him since 1959 and who profited from his inexperience in these matters. One of them was Alfred Delarue, who died in 1964 and who had been involved in one of the more sensational scandals of the French Fourth Republic; sentenced to prison over this, he had come to Africa as soon as he had been released in 1956. That had not been Delarue's only experience of imprisonment, either. During the Second World War, he had been a high official at the Paris Prefecture of Police, had been arrested at liberation on a charge of working for the Germans and had been sentenced to twenty-one years' hard labour, though he managed to escape in 1947. Men with such a background are rarely if ever liberal in their politics, and Delarue's fellow-advisers professed the same kind of extreme Right-Wing views. In order to enhance the value of their services, this curious team of Frenchmen invented a danger to the Congo which almost certainly did not then exist, the Communist danger; only people with their knowledge of affairs were capable, they claimed, of coping with it. They succeeded only too well in convincing their employer of the reality of the peril. Youlou conceived a morbid fear of Communists, and his advisers imposed on him precautionary measures so strict that to some extent they cut him off from his people.

It seems likely that Youlou had been convinced for some years of the desirability of setting up a single party in his country in order to stop intertribal quarrels once for all. A year before the August 1963 riots over the issue which ended in ousting him from power, he had publicly announced his intention of fusing the existing political movements into one. What is more, he had done so not in Brazzaville, where he could count on a friendly hearing from his fellow-members of the Bakongo ethnical group who formed the majority of the population in the area, but on a tour of the northern departments, which were largely inhabited by the M'Bochi tribe. He met with no opposition at all; indeed the ministers of the two other parties immediately agreed with his proposal, though the Socialist party leader Opangault three months later resigned his Cabinet post for what he described as 'personal reasons'.

It was not till the summer of 1963, however, that Youlou took practical steps to carry into effect his plans for the installation of a single party. He convened a round-table conference to discuss the idea in Brazzaville, the participants being the leaders of the three existing parties – the moribund P.P.C., the Socialists and Youlou's own U.D.D.I.A. – the officials of the National Assembly, the heads of the three trade union organizations, Christian, Communist-linked and Socialist-linked, and representatives of the 2,000-strong Congo army. Youlou told the conference that since national unity was now an accomplished fact, with a Government of National Union at the head of the country and all the parties out after the same end, the good of the nation, there was no need of more than one political movement. And in a broadcast to the nation, the Abbé explained that the single party would be 'a brotherly party, the party of all the Congolese, whoever they may be'.

The trade unions had, however, been refractory from the start. When their leaders met Youlou towards the end of July, they had demanded what they described as a rapid reform of the State. What they wanted, in practical terms, was the installation of a new, provisional Government before the single party was set up. Youlou disagreed; he felt that any change in the Government should be decided on by a provisional national political bureau, an emanation of the single party. Moreover, he made it quite plain that he strongly disapproved of the political stand which, as the unions saw it, they had been virtually forced to take by the régime's domestication of the various political leaders. 'Trade unionism has a vital job to do going out after economic progress,' the Abbé said on 6 August, 'but I believe it would make a grave mistake if it went beyond its traditional role and mixed up in politics too. What is more, trade unionism has no mandate from anyone to do so. Only the people are qualified to choose their representatives, and this rule, which the Congo has always followed in the past, the new party will stand by too.' Fulbert Youlou's Congo, of course, had never followed any such rule.

The next day saw the Government's ban on political meetings pending the establishment of the single party followed by the unions' calling for a general strike on 13 August in protest. There is widespread agreement that when the union leaders called their men out, they had not the slightest intention of overthrowing the President. They were registering their disapproval of a particularly arbitrary attack on freedom of speech, though they would undoubtedly have been more than satisfied if their action also persuaded Youlou to get rid of some of his more notoriously corrupt ministers. The strike started off in complete calm; in Pointe Noire, the country's commercial capital, it remained quiet till the end of the day. What sparked off the trouble in Brazzaville was a seemingly small incident. Possibly because Youlou had been persuaded by his French advisers that the movement was a Communist-inspired plot, two prominent trade union leaders were arrested in their car outside the Trades and Labour Hall during the night of 12/13 August and flung into jail. As soon as the news began to spread, the comparatively small crowd that had gathered in the Place de la Gare around 7.30 in the morning was swelled to some 7,000 by the streaming in of reinforcements from the African suburbs of Poto-Poto and Bakongo. Tempers were rising. The demonstrators began rhythmically to shout such slogans as 'Let's free our leaders!', 'Down with corruption!' and even 'Youlou, resign!' Halfway through the morning, the gendarmerie opened fire, and at least two people were killed. After that the crowd went berserk. They marched on and stormed the prison, and freed all the prisoners, they broke into the radio station and beat up the director, and then they started burning the houses of ministers, deputies and people who had profited from the régime, particularly the mistresses of the men in power. In the afternoon, martial law was proclaimed and a curfew ordered, and Youlou made a broadcast denouncing what he described as a plot against State security. 'I urged understanding; I just wasn't listened to,' he said. Finally, in the evening an emergency Cabinet meeting decided immediately to set up the special criminal court for which provision had been made under a law of 1959.

The next day saw the curfew extended. Radio Brazzaville reported that more houses had been burned and official high-ups' cars too. French security forces, however, were still helping to maintain order; they had to, under the relevant agreement between the two Governments. Youlou felt strong enough to turn down a proposal by the trade unions that a completely new eight-member Government should be formed. Indeed, at midday he broadcast a statement that he had personally taken over all civil and military powers and had set up a small committee under his authority which would be responsible for the restoration of order, the resumption of work and the introduction of the necessary reforms. Calm had returned to Brazzaville. The Abbé seemed to be on top of things again.

All the same, something seemed to have cracked inside him. In the afternoon, troops started digging trenches round the presidential palace and installing obvious machine-gun posts there. What is more, a bare two hours after his first, authoritarian broadcast, Youlou went on the air again, this time with what sounded very like a climb-down. He announced that he was forming a new Government, a Government of technicians and men of good will whose main task would be national reconciliation. He added that he was postponing the establishment of the single party to a later date. Finally he ended his broadcast with the words which de Gaulle had used during the generals' *putsch* in Algiers: 'Help me!' In the mouth of the General, who was assured of the support of the sane majority of the French people, those words were a moving and irresistible appeal. On the lips of Youlou, they sounded very like a confession of weakness. What is more, though he had got rid of almost all his old ministerial team, he had retained in his new Cabinet one figure who he must have known was cordially detested by the trade unions who had been the main animators of the demonstrations, and by almost everyone else, Minister of Justice N'Zakalanda.

On 15 August, therefore – which was the third anniversary of the Congo's independence – the crowds that took advantage of the suspension of the curfew to gather in front of the presidential palace had only one slogan in their mouths: 'Resign, resign!' Youlou appeared on the balcony and invited the demonstrators to send in a delegation to discuss things with him, and the talks went on and on. Finally the little Congo Army, which by now had complete control of the capital, decided that the uncertainty had gone on long enough. Two of its senior officers burst into the President's office and summoned him to resign at once in order to avoid any further bloodshed. The Abbé had counted on his 2,000-strong Army; once that had deserted him, there was little more to be done. So putting on his most brilliant white soutane, he took his gold fountain pen and signed his resignation as President of the Republic, Head of the Government, Mayor of Brazzaville and

Deputy. For good measure, he appeared on the balcony and himself announced the news to the crowd, who applauded him for the last time. Shortly afterwards, by agreement between the Army and the trade unions, a provisional Government was installed, with Alphonse Massemba-Débat at its head. Forty-two-year-old Massemba-Débat, who had started life as a schoolteacher, was generally regarded as a moderate Socialist. He had been elected to the National Assembly in 1959 and after acting as its Speaker had been appointed to a succession of ministerial posts from which he resigned in May 1963 on account of undefined differences with Youlou. The Abbé had tried to get him out of the way by offering him the post of Ambassador in Paris, but he had refused.

In December 1963, the Congo (Brazzaville) electors went to the polls to approve a new Constitution which had been elaborated in the meantime and to elect a new and rather smaller Assembly. Though the Constitution provided for the existence of a premier as well as of a president, it was still of the presidential type: the President was described as 'defining the national policy', whereas the Premier and his Government merely carried that policy out. The big novelty of the document was, however, its establishment of a completely new governmental institution, the National Council of the Revolution. It is true that the National Council was represented as being a provisional body, in that its activities would be confined to the period during which the revolution was being consolidated. It is true that it was to be headed by the President and that members of the Government were to be *de facto* members of it. The functions allotted to it, however, were extremely sweeping. It was 'to carry out the fundamental aims of the revolution, work out the general policy of the country and inspire the action of the State in accordance with the deep aspirations of the masses', phrases very similar to those defining the position of the F.L.N. in the 1964 Algerian Constitution. What is more, the Constitution provided no sort of means for deputies to question the National Council's actions. It did, like most of the new African constitutions, commit itself to guarantees of public liberties similar to those obtaining in the West. Thus, the preamble declared the Congolese people's determination to ensure the respect of political and trade union freedom, including the right to strike, and of religious freedom and freedom of the press. Article 21 laid down that no deputy of the National Assembly could be prosecuted, arrested or tried for opinions he had expressed or divisions in which he had participated as part of his activities. All this verbiage was to reveal itself for what it was before twelve months were up.

Naturally the Constitution went through, though something like fifteen per cent. of the electorate voted against it. Equally naturally, the only fifty-five candidates standing in the elections, those of the National Revolutionary Movement, or M.N.R., as the victors of the August *coup* had christened themselves, were all returned, though more than a tenth of the voters put in spoiled papers. Just under a fortnight later, Massemba-Débat was elected unopposed as the new President, by a body consisting of deputies and local government councillors. He immediately appointed as his Premier thirty-two-year-old Pascal Lissouba, an expert in farming who had obtained French degrees in natural sciences and who had come out top of his class at the Higher School of Agriculture in Tunis. Lissouba was generally regarded as being much farther to the Left than his President; the Frenchwoman he married is described as a Communist.

All the same, the initial programme of the M.N.R. had nothing in the least revolutionary about it. Naturally the party called for a foreign policy of non-alignment and for the control of foreign trade that is common form in Africa today. Otherwise its objectives appeared to be both moderate and reasonable: the starting up of industrialization, the improvement of road and river communications, and encouragement for the formation of companies whose capital would come partly from Government and partly from private sources. It was not a mere matter of words either; practical plans that were going forward for the promotion of exports included the enlarging of an existing sugar refinery and the construction of a new one, the setting-up of a pineapple cannery with the participation of private American capital and a Franco-American plan for the exploitation of the local potash deposits. The Congo continued to accept large-scale French economic aid and remained a member of the moderate-minded organization of former French African states.

The new development measures could hardly, however, be expected to bear fruit at once. The cost of living, of which the trade unions had long complained, showed no signs of falling; indeed, Brazzaville overtook Abidjan as the most expensive town in French Africa. Pay was as low as ever and there were just as many unemployed in the streets. In the February 1964 elections to the municipal councils of Brazzaville, Pointe Noire and Dolisie, abstentions reached the astonishing figure of forty-eight per cent., and Massemba-Débat annulled the results for what he described as irregularities and 'violation of democratic and revolutionary principles'. All this played into the hands of Youlou's tribe, the Lari, and less than a week later they staged an attack on the gendarmerie where he was detained and a number of them were killed and wounded when the gendarmerie intervened. The Government reply was an appeal to 'the revolutionary youth of the Congo' to jettison sentimentality and denounce even their fathers or their brothers to the authorities should they suspect them of plotting against the régime.

There were those who discerned quite early on that the Government headed by President Massemba-Débat might be going to pursue a policy far tougher than the original programme of the M.N.R. suggested. One of them was Gilbert Pongault, leader of the Congolese Christian trade unions who had played a leading part in organizing the strike that led to Youlou's overthrow. In an interview in February 1964 with the Tunisian-owned weekly *Jeune Afrique*, which sets out to cover African affairs as a whole, Pongault said that too many new African governments were opposed to trade unionism and could only accept its existence if it was dominated by them or by the single government party. Such governments, Pongault went on, wanted power and disliked criticism. If, however, the masses could not express their criticisms after the euphoria of independence was over, they revolted. And when this happened, more or less clandestine bodies, enjoying the support of international forces, entered into the game and tried to turn the revolution to their advantage.

Six months later, Father Badila was pinpointing signs of this drift to the extreme Left in the soon-to-be-silenced *Semaine Africaine*. He pointed out that the first official visits abroad the head of the new Congo Government made were not, as might have been expected, to the country's neighbours and old friends, such as the Central African Republic and Gabon. The first foreign trips he undertook were to 'the African Marxist countries', Ghana and Algeria, and to Peking; indeed, very soon after it took power, the new Government established diplomatic relations with the Soviet Union and Communist China. Secondly, Father Badila said, the Communist Chinese Embassy, which had a staff of more than fifty, a strength quite unwarranted by routine diplomatic work in a country of less than a million inhabitants, was made to feel more at home in Brazzaville than was any other foreign mission there. Its members had free entry into the various Government departments, and were reported to be helping to select and train officers in the Army. Thirdly, individual and collective freedom was disappearing and religion was being attacked. A whole succession of Catholics were expelled from the Congo, and most of these were leaders of the Catholic youth movement, to which the majority of the young people in Brazzaville belonged: when the authorities started up a united youth movement, as they did, they did not want these priests to interfere in it. Finally, Father Badila said, the political institutions of the Congo seemed more and more to be inspired by Communist ideas.

The late autumn saw the replacement by tougher figures of the two principal moderate members of the Government, Planning and Public Works Minister Paul Kaya and Minister of Justice Pascal Okiemba. Almost immediately a series of repressive actions followed. Fulgence Biyaoula, the head of the Congolese Christian trade union movement, was arrested and tortured. The National Assembly, despite the new Constitution's formal guarantee of free speech in Parliament, decided by an overwhelming majority to raise the parliamentary immunity of a deputy who had accused the Government of violating the Constitution and failing to respect political and trade union liberties. Two deputies who were also sympathizers with the Christian trade unions promptly resigned their seats, obviously under pressure. The youth section of the single party, the J.M.N.R., broke into the Pointe Noire offices of the Christian trade unions and burned all the papers there. The offices, indeed, were not to be needed much longer, for, barely a month after the constitutive congress of what had been organized as the Congo's single trade union movement, the National Assembly passed a law which confirmed it in its monopolistic role and dissolved all other union organizations. Shortly afterwards, the Government put through a measure establishing a 'people's court' for the trial of political offences and a regulation which made it impossible for any Congolese citizen to leave the country without a police authorization stamped by the M.N.R. political bureau.

An interesting pointer to what was going forward, and how, was provided in a couple of articles by Biyaoula which the *Semaine Africaine* printed just before he was arrested. 'The authorities,' Biyaoula said, 'have reproached the Christian trade unions with being in the service of imperialists, colonialists, the Vatican and what not. Have they ever given a thought to what are the aims of the Chinese, the Russians and the Czechs, whom they made a grave mistake in not regarding as colonialists? . . . The Christian trade unions are determined to defend the nation against any totalitarian régime which would make the country the property of a few people. Yes, a few people. There aren't more than thirty of them.' The job Biyaoula held could hardly fail to give him first-hand knowledge not only of the meaning of developments in his country but, as the figure he stressed suggested, of the details of them also.

The men who made the August 1963 Congo revolution had no very clear positive idea of where they were going. They had done what they did in the first place to call a halt to the Government's authoritarian trend and to clean up corruption in high places, both of them negative objectives. There was hardly an item in the original M.N.R. programme which Youlou could not have advanced, had he had better advisers. With the arrival of the Communist Chinese Embassy, things began rapidly to change. There is no reason to believe that anything that could be called a Communist movement existed in Brazzaville when the Abbé was evicted from power. Individual Communists there were; they are to be found in every African country, mainly among young people who have pursued their university studies abroad, though such political activities as they indulge in are almost everywhere conducted *sub rosa*. All the evidence suggests that as soon as the Chinese diplomats arrived they set about contacting these young Communists and training them in the job of organizing wherever they could a disciplined network of sympathizers who could be relied on to follow their instructions. The handful of young Congolese Communists and their Chinese prompters had the clearest possible positive idea of where they were going and, in a country with no political traditions at any rate, half a dozen men who know what they want are as strong as, if not stronger than, half a million who do not.

A fact that would seem to confirm this interpretation of the post-revolution developments is the growing role played as the months passed by the J.M.N.R. The Government, indeed, got its instructions from the party, whose political bureau, itself headed by a very young man, came more and more closely to supervise the administration and the police. But the youth section of the party shared in this work of supervision, and pressure by it was universally acknowledged to be responsible for almost all of the Government's most contestable decisions, such as the legal imposition of the M.N.R. as the country's single party, the throttling of the Christian unions by the establishment of a single trade union movement and the closing of the Congo's frontiers to any citizen who could not get the permission of the political bureau to go abroad. What is more, the J.M.N.R. set up what was the equivalent of a 'people's militia', which undertook punitive expeditions against members of the opposition and at nightfall checked on all cars driving between the European town of Brazzaville and the African suburbs of Bakongo and Poto-Poto. This J.M.N.R. militia was generally credited with the kidnapping and assassination in February 1965 of the President of the Supreme Court, the Attorney-General and the Director of Information who, without being open critics of the new régime, were known to hold opinions which may well have been regarded by Communists as incompatible with the responsible posts they held. In addition, the young people made themselves responsible for moulding public opinion in a sense that could only be welcome to their Chinese Embassy backers. Their weekly *Dipanda* was constantly making violent attacks on the

Western Powers. The young people went as far as to urge that all economic co-operation with the West should be ended, though the $5,000,000 loan granted by the Chinese in May 1964 was a mere fleabite in comparison with the assistance that the Congo was receiving from France.

The Ministerial reshuffle of April 1965 further accentuated this hold of the revolutionary young people over the State apparatus. The key post of Minister of the Interior had been held by a man who plainly enjoyed the President's confidence: barely a year before Massemba-Débat had sent him as his personal representative to the Nouakchott conference of the heads of state of French-speaking Africa. That confidence did not save him. He was kicked downstairs to an insignificant job and replaced by André Hombessa, president of the J.M.N.R. – whose first act as the new Minister of the Interior was to board the next plane for Moscow. Another significant figure to enter the Government was the editor of *Dipanda*. The Speaker of the National Assembly plainly thought he knew on which side his bread was buttered. In a speech at a reception for a parliamentary delegation from Communist China, he went out of his way to encourage the young revolutionaries who had been constantly complaining of the inefficiency of the State organization, to persist in their intransigent attitude. 'Our revolution started off as a peaceful revolution,' he said. 'Today it is a revolutionary revolution, violent and armed.' Meantime President Massemba-Débat and Premier Lissouba remained virtually mute.

President and Premier alike had a great deal more to worry about than such internal divergences as there might be within the M.N.R. Since a few weeks after his deposition and arrest, the former President Youlou had been confined in a comfortable villa overlooking the Congo River. The authorities had never taken the least steps to bring him to trial, probably through fear of the reactions of his tribe, the Lari. In February 1965, Youlou escaped across the river to Léopoldville, where he was almost immediately given official asylum by Premier Tchombe. His presence, at liberty, on the other side of the Congo River represented an obvious danger for the Brazzaville régime.

For, partly despite its activities and partly because of them, that régime was hardly more popular in the Congo (Brazza-ville) that its predecessor had been. Many people who had started off by supporting the August 1963 revolution were by 1965 heartily sick of the team in power. Youlou's Lari fellow-tribesmen were as loyal to him as ever, and would certainly have welcomed and almost certainly assisted his return to office. The economic situation was as difficult as it had been under the Abbé, unemployed in Brazzaville could still be counted in thousands, indeed in tens of thousands, and the Government could count on no sympathy at all in the economic capital of Pointe Noire. Finally, the Catholics completely disapproved of much of the Government's programme, and of all its methods, and Catholicism was an important factor in the country: the work of the Catholic schools was largely responsible for the extraordinarily high percentage of literacy among its population. The new Archbishop of Brazzaville, Mgr Bemba, was a Lari like Youlou and had been ordained at the same time as him, and, with *Dipanda* waging a merciless anti-clerical campaign, many people thought of him as one of the leaders of the opposition.

This generalized discontent would not have represented such a threat to the Brazzaville authorities had Youlou remained in safe detention. It was generally agreed that no other figure in the country was capable of putting an organized force in the field against the M.N.R. Once he was free, and free in Léopoldville, the peril of such a force taking form became an immediate one. Could Tchombe consolidate his hold over the Congo (Léopoldville) the probable sequels were only too plain. Youlou would be allowed, indeed encouraged, to set up a provisional Government in exile, and all the resources of Radio Léopoldville would be put at its disposal for broad-casting its propaganda across the river. Once the moment seemed appropriate, he would be given every facility he required for crossing the Congo and re-establishing himself in power, and the facilities would quite likely include armed support. There was every reason why the Government in Brazzaville, whose heads showed no signs anyway of sharing the outlook of their young revolutionary supporters – or masters – should feel the gravest concern.

5
Gabon

A PERIOD OF thirty-six hours in February 1964 saw the
Republic of Gabon the scene of two successive and contradictory acts of political violence which have so far remained
without parallel in Africa. Three hours before dawn on
18 February, soldiers of the 400-strong Gabonese Army
occupied strategic points in the capital, Libreville, and made
President Léon Mba and most of the ministers in his Government prisoners. The quartet of junior officers who headed the
revolt had little difficulty in persuading the President to sign
his resignation and to record a statement announcing it which
was soon put out over the radio. A communiqué explaining
the *coup* which was broadcast at intervals throughout the day
said that the Army had dissolved the Government and arrested
the President and his hangers-on 'in order to prevent the outbreak of demonstrations which it would have been difficult
to halt. Public liberties have been re-established,' the communiqué went on, 'and all political prisoners freed', and it
ended by making an urgent appeal to the population to stay
completely calm and not to lay hands on anyone. There was
not the least opposition to the Army's action. Gabon had been
liberated from what was generally regarded as a dictatorial
régime without a drop of blood being shed.

The French Ambassador, Paul Cousseran, had been roused
by the noise in the streets and had checked on what had
happened, and about an hour after sunrise he rang up Jean
Hilaire Aubame, who for a decade and a half had been Mba's
chief political rival. 'There's no Government at the moment,'
the Ambassador said, 'and in view of the importance of French
interests here, there must be a civilian with whom I can discuss
matters.' Aubame replied that he knew nothing at all about
what had happened, but promised to find out and to ring back.
Midway through the morning, an Army car with one of the
four-man revolutionary committee in it called for Aubame and
drove him off to the presidency, and before the afternoon was

out, the head of the official opposition to Mba had formed a provisional Government.

That should have been the end of the story, but alas it was not. The previous year had seen a succession of plots and *coups* against the heads of French-speaking African states, and three of them had proved successful. In Togo, President Sylvanus Olympio had been assassinated; in the Congo (Brazzaville), President Fulbert Youlou had been deposed; and in Dahomey, President Hubert Maga had been evicted from office. The three men's opposite numbers in some at least of the French-speaking republics of Africa were extremely bitter at what they regarded as France's do-nothing attitude which, as they saw it, was putting them all in peril. As soon, therefore, as the news of what had happened in Gabon got out over the wires, the ambassadors of these countries in Paris got together and, under urgent instructions from home, requested General de Gaulle to take action to save Mba. Their task was made the easier since Roland Bru, a French financial magnate who had financed Mba's latest electoral campaign, and who has been described as 'the real master of Gabon', had used his influence in the same sense at the French Embassy at Libreville.

Under the circumstances, the General was bound to regard the Gabon affair as a test. It was easier for him to face up to it since the British had recently done in East Africa something which could be represented as similar to what he was being asked to do in Libreville, though the parallel was not in fact exact. He therefore decided to fly French troops to the spot at once. His aim was twofold. He wanted to put an end to what it was easy to regard from Paris as the progressive breakdown of authority in the African states, and he intended to safeguard the position of France in a country which had considerable natural resources. The first French troop-carriers landed at Libreville airport from Brazzaville before Aubame had even formed his provisional Government.

During the night, further French troop-transports landed at Libreville, coming this time from Dakar, and French paratroopers reconnoitred strategic points in the capital. Next morning the French launched an attack on the Gabonese army camp at Barake. Its defenders put up such a stiff defence that assault aircraft were called in to strafe them. In the end their ammunition gave out, and they surrendered. Their commander, Lieutenant Edou, was promptly shot. Meantime, the Provisional Government had called on the French Embassy to try to ascertain the meaning of what was going on. They got no satisfaction. The Ambassador asked Aubame to hand over Mba unhurt, and the provisional Premier promptly sent a Gabonese officer down to the countryside, where he had been deported, to find him. The Ambassador also assured the members of the Provisional Government, speaking, as he said, in the name of France, that he had not the least intention of restoring Mba to power: he was only concerned about his safety. The next few hours were to show how hollow this assurance was. Hardly had it been given when Paris announced that the French troops had taken action under the Franco-Gabonese defence agreement, which obliged France to give assistance to the legal Government of Gabon. Before the afternoon was out, those troops had occupied Libreville and surrounded all its public buildings, including the presidential palace. Shortly afterwards, Radio Libreville announced that all the rebel forces had surrendered. Twelve hours later, Mba was back again as President. His deposition had been bloodless. His restoration had cost dozens of lives. And though six months later the President had the men involved in his temporary overthrow tried and sentenced, the beginnings of 1965 saw a French garrison still stationed in Libreville. The French troops had come in to restore Mba to power. They were staying on, at his urgent request, because he could not be certain of remaining in office without their backing.

The Republic of Gabon has an area of just over 100,000 square miles, most of it consisting of tropical rain forest, and a population of less than half a million. Its capital, Libreville, has no more than 17,000 inhabitants, though it has no drains and few paved streets, and many of its residents still live on the produce of their gardens. School attendance, like that in the neighbouring Congo (Brazzaville), is extraordinarily high: eighty per cent. of the children are in primary schools, though very few of them seem to go on any further. This high school attendance is largely the work of the Church, and as many as half the people of Gabon are stated to be baptized.

Gabon has considerable natural resources, and as the 1960s opened it was one of the rare countries of tropical Africa to enjoy a favourable trade balance, with exports exceeding imports by thirty per cent. Most of this was due to its forests, for Gabon is the world's largest producer of *okoumé* wood, renowned for its excellence as plywood, as well as of mahogany. As the 1960s advanced, however, other natural assets began to come on the scene. There was iron: Gabon's known reserves of this have been put at 250 million tons, with probable reserves estimated at up to four times that figure. There was manganese and there was gold; there was petroleum which, as the 1960s opened, was bringing in more than one-third of the sums the country was getting from its wood, and above all there was uranium.

Finally, the country suffered from the ethnical divisions common to all the countries of sub-Saharan Africa. Between a quarter and a third of the population are composed of the Fang invaders, who came into the country fairly late in its history. The rest is divided between a number of Bantu tribes. No less than forty languages or dialects are current in Gabon, though French is spoken everywhere, even in the remotest villages.

As early as the sixteenth century, the Portuguese were setting up trading posts all along the coast round the Congo basin, and some of the names they gave them have survived to this day. One of these survivals is Gabon itself. The name was first given to the estuary of the Congo because its outlines suggested those of a cloak with sleeves and a hood, in Portuguese, *gabaõ*. On the eve of the French revolution, seventy French firms were doing commerce with the Gabon coast, and had acquired a lead over their European rivals in the slave trade.

The decision taken by the European Powers at the start of the nineteenth century to abolish the slave trade radically changed their relations with Central Africa. In 1830, the French decided to establish missionary, trading and naval supply posts along the Gabon coast, the object of the last-named being to see to it that the export of slaves was in fact stopped. Nine years later a local chief whose name is given as 'King Denis' ceded two small plots of land to the French for the construction of some of the fortifications involved and signed a treaty with his French opposite number, King Louis-Philippe. Treaties with other chiefs followed and in 1849 the officers of a French ship who had captured a boat carrying slaves settled these down on the right bank of the Gabon estuary, in a place which was given the appropriate name of Libreville. Libreville became the centre of French administration and influence in the area, and the Gabonese were proud of the fact that they had been French longer than had the inhabitants of Nice and Savoy. It is true they lost their privileged position at the beginning of the twentieth century, with the establishment of the federation of French Equatorial Africa, the installation of its capital in Brazzaville, the construction of the only railway in the area in Congo (Brazzaville) territory and the building of what was described as a 'federal highway' to up-country Bangui, whose starting point was not a Gabon port, but the Congolese commercial capital of Pointe Noire. The Gabonese resented their relegation into the background all the more since it was their trade surpluses which were being used to finance economic developments in the generally deficitary territories the other side of their borders.

The modern history of Gabon contains one interesting parallel to events in the neighbouring Congo (Brazzaville). This was the spread of an eclectic local religious cult – it could not with any accuracy be called Messianic – which was known as Bwiti. The existence and power of Bwiti had not a little influence on later political developments. A Gabonese writer claims that Bwiti is an age-old faith, and that its teaching is that of Hermes Trismegistus. He adds that the Bwiti faith was responsible for the greatness of the inhabitants of the engulfed continent of Atlantis, 'of whom the Negro people are the direct descendants.' There is no need to take these statements with any seriousness. The best available evidence is that the Bwiti cult first appeared among the Fang of lower Gabon in the early twentieth century, and gradually spread to the centre and north of the country. Like similar cults elsewhere in the continent, it seems to have been essentially a protest against the foreign domination which European missions no less than European administration were felt to represent. It is significant that up north, in Dahomey, Christians are called 'whites' whatever their colour. Bwiti had its secrets, which it was death to reveal, and its initiation rites. It took over from the established Christian bodies the elements which would be likely to make the greatest emotional appeal to the local population: vestments and ceremonies, hymns and church buildings. Its leaders also borrowed from Christianity such things as they thought would bring the Fang unity and strength as a group: an ecclesiastical hierarchy, the rejection of sorcery and fetishism, and an ethical code which included most of the ten commandments.

Since just after the Second World War, Jean Hilaire Aubame and Léon Mba had become rivals for the political leadership of Gabon. Their backgrounds and their characters formed a complete contrast. The only thing they had in common was their membership of the Fang tribe, though Aubame came from its northern and Mba from its southern section. Aubame, who was born in 1912, was a practising Catholic. Starting life as a schoolmaster, he had become an official in the French colonial administration and had been awarded the French Resistance medal. Between 1946 and 1958 he had represented Gabon in the French National Assembly, regularly defeating Mba at the elections; in the Assembly he had become chairman of the group of deputies who called themselves Overseas Independents. He had a curiously harsh voice, a severe appearance and what was generally agreed to be a stern character.

Mba, who was ten years older, had nothing severe about his appearance. He was, indeed, determined to get what he wanted, but he set out to win it with a smile on his face. Far from winning any medals from the French, he had for a number of years been seriously at odds with them. Because of his knowledge of Fang customary law, he had early in his career been appointed an administrative official in one of the most backward Fang areas of lower Gabon. Seeing in the Bwiti sect a means of regenerating Fang society, he joined it and was not content until he had become an extremely influential member of the cult. Bwiti temples were at this time rapidly going up all over the country, and the development alarmed both the missionaries and the administration. The former saw in it a threat to their teaching and the latter a challenge to their authority: given the circumstances of the sect's origins, it could hardly fail to have a political aspect, and in fact it was passing on to its followers instructions to disregard Government orders of which its leaders disapproved. When, therefore, Mba's position in the Bwiti Church was discovered, he was not only dismissed from his Government post, but prosecuted and exiled, and it was only after the Second World War that he returned to Gabon and set up in trade. His sufferings at the hands of the colonial power won him considerable prestige among the Fang, and were to a great extent responsible for his success when he entered politics after the war. The fact that his popular appeal was to a large degree due to his association with an indigenous religious movement gives Mba an obvious resemblance to Fulbert Youlou in the neighbouring Congo (Brazzaville).

The extent to which Mba had been successful in building himself up as a leader among his fellow-tribesmen did not, however, become apparent till the middle 1940s. In 1947, he made an outstanding contribution to the discussions in a conference on the future of the Fang organized by the French authorities in Gabon. About the same time, he founded his own political party, which was soon to be known as the Gabonese Democratic Bloc, and later was elected to the local territorial assembly. When he was elected Mayor of Libreville in 1956, political observers began to suspect that his star, as tribal spokesman for the south, was rising and that of Aubame, the northern Fang Catholic leader, was waning. In the competition between the two, Aubame suffered from the disadvantage that he was absent for much of the year in Paris. It is, indeed, true that African deputies in the French Assembly, because their votes could sometimes be mobilized to save an imperilled Government in a division concerning internal politics, could count on exercising more influence on behalf of their constituents than was available to deputies returned by the electorate in France. All the same, this card was not strong enough to trump the personality, and the persistent and patent activities on the spot, of Aubame's rival.

The real struggle between Mba and Aubame did not, however, open till 1957, just after the first elections to the Congo Territorial Assembly under the French law which gave increased political liberty to the colonies. Of the forty deputies returned, half belonged to Aubame's Democratic and Socialist Gabonese Union, or U.S.D.G., and no more than six to Mba's Gabonese Democratic Bloc, or B.D.G., while fourteen were elected as independents. The exact explanation of what followed cannot be stated for certain. The evidence suggests that the decrease since the war in the anti-European character of the Bwiti cult and the election of Mba to the mayoralty of the Gabon capital had persuaded unofficial and official Frenchmen alike that far from being a danger to French interest, the leader of the B.D.G. was a personality with whom it would be useful to come to an arrangement. Mba's financial interests in the economic development of his country were soon to come out into the open; the exploitation of its mineral resources made a special appeal to him. It was widely believed that French business circles, for whom Gabon's uranium deposits were only one attraction, and who had considerable influence locally, had brought pressure on both the uncommitted and committed members of the new Parliament to give Mba their backing. In any case, the fourteen independent deputies promptly went over to the B.D.G. side, as did two Europeans elected as representatives of the U.S.D.G. Mba was consequently elected head of the new Gabonese Government, and Aubame's party went into opposition, and conducted a vigorous campaign against the country's leadership, both in Parliament and in the country.

It did not take long for Mba to show that though his manners were kindly, his character was authoritarian. In 1960, the year which saw Gabon acceding to independence, Paul Gondjout, opposition former Speaker of the National Assembly, was arrested with a number of his friends, and Mba also cracked down on his own party, which was threatened with a split. This kind of conduct naturally aroused the indignation of politically conscious Gabonese, but it inspired confidence in French and other foreign investors, who came to regard Gabon as a 'safe' country, the more so since Europeans were treated with great friendliness there. After independence, and the election of Mba to the Presidency of the Republic, a new National Assembly voted important amendments to the Constitution which had been adopted not long before. Under these, the President alone had executive powers; he appointed and dismissed ministers, who were responsible to him only; he could dissolve the Assembly or prolong it beyond its normal term of five years; he could consult the people by referendum and could declare a state of siege or a state of alarm when he considered it necessary. It was, in fact, much the same sort of constitution as was being adopted about the same time in the Congo (Brazzaville) in favour of Fulbert Youlou.

There was, however, a liberal move not long after independence. Mba formed a coalition Government, which included four U.S.D.G. ministers, one of them being Aubame, who became Foreign Minister. The new set-up did not last indefinitely. As a result of pressure within the Government party, all but one of the U.S.D.G. ministers were dropped in 1963 and Mba appointed Aubame to the presidency of the Supreme Court. Here again there was opposition: a bill was tabled in the Assembly early in 1964 which laid down that the position of President of the Supreme Court was incompatible with that of deputy. Mba was not satisfied with the parliamentary vote on the measure, and in consequence dissolved the National Assembly. Even before he had done so, however, Aubame had made his choice. For all the material advantages that went with the new post that had been offered to him, it was his job of Chief Justice and not that of deputy which he resigned. New elections were fixed for 23 February, but the opposition decided not to take part in them. They could be pretty certain, under the circumstances, that the results would be faked against them, and in any case there was good reason to believe that Mba was about to set up a single party system which would have made any electoral campaign against him sheer waste of time. It was on the eve of the date fixed for the polls that the *coup* which for thirty-six hours evicted President Mba from office took place.

It may be argued that the fact that it was a military *putsch* and not a popular revolt which overturned Mba proved that there was no widespread public feeling against him. The contention can hardly be said to carry much weight. In armies as new as those of the nascent states of Africa, no closed military caste had had time to come into being, and the reactions of young officers could quite well have expressed those of wide sections of ordinary people. In a country which had no political traditions, and where everything was done to prevent the expression of criticisms of the régime, a military *coup* may have been the only way of giving voice to a wave of underground discontent. Indeed, events in the days and weeks that followed the abortive revolt strongly suggested that there was widespread discontent with the Mba regime. Finally, it had been a military *coup* which had resulted the previous year in the overthrow and death of President Sylvanus Olympio, of Togo, and there had been nothing in the sequel to suggest that the officers responsible had not enjoyed the fullest sympathy of the Togo population.

What is more, for the mere day that it lasted, the provisional Government which replaced Mba was taken seriously by responsible people and itself behaved in a responsible manner. Quite early on in the day of 18 February, a fairly senior official of the American Embassy in Libreville had driven to the presidential palace to see Aubame in an official car flying the Stars and Stripes. That may not, perhaps, have amounted to giving tacit approval to the revolutionary régime, but it at least conveyed that the Americans regarded its leaders as something more than a bunch of chuckle-headed roughnecks. That evening, the provisional Government became alarmed at the first landings of French troop-carriers and the lame explanations which were all the French Embassy could give. Its reaction was to summon the diplomatic corps and ask them to bring pressure on the French Ambassador to avoid useless bloodshed. It could not have taken a more level-headed step. Early the next morning, when fighting between the French expeditionary force and the tiny Gabonese Army had already begun, the Government itself called round at the Embassy. Its members did not go alone. They were accompanied by a number of local notabilities and by the Catholic bishop, and the bishop would hardly have compromised himself by going with them unless he had taken them seriously.

The Franco-Gabonese agreement under which French troops intervened to restore Mba – it had, incidentally, been signed by Aubame in his period as Foreign Minister – obliged France to give assistance to the legal Government of Gabon if requested by it to do so. Just who with the necessary authority can have made such a request still remains something of a puzzle. Mba and his ministers had been arrested while it was still night, long before the French Ambassador became aware of what had happened. The only member of the Cabinet who was certainly at liberty was Vice-President Paul-Marie Yembit. Yembit, however, was nowhere near Libreville: he was deep down in the countryside, in his native Ngounié, winding up his electoral campaign, and from Ngounié it was impossible to telephone Libreville, let alone Paris. The explanation given is that the Embassy sent down a light plane to the area where Yembit was electioneering and that the pilot got out to the the village where he was staying, informed him of what was happening and returned with a message from the Vice-President imploring France to step in to safeguard French lives and property and to restore Mba. This is not quite impossible. Because of the complete absence of road bridges in Gabon – the only way a car can cross a river is by ferry – the country has a thick network of airfields, no less than 130 of them. The big difficulty is the timetable. Ngounié is a very long way from Libreville, and it is a little hard to see how the pilot of a light plane – which would be no fast, ultramodern model in that part of the world – could have flown to the nearest airfield, driven out to see Yembit and back and returned to Libreville with the appeal for aid whose flashing to Paris could alone justify France's intervention much before the arrival of the first French troop-carriers, which landed at Libreville at two p.m. Yembit did not fly back to the capital in the light plane as might have been expected if a pilot had in fact been sent down to contact him. He returned to Libreville on the following day only, and it was not till eight in the evening that he read over the radio a statement, which bore every appearance of having been prepared for him by French officials, in which he said that it was he who had appealed to France to step in and added that Mba was about to be set free, if he had not already been liberated.

African reactions to the French operation in Gabon were varied. In the neighbouring Central African Republic, President Dacko and his ministers congratulated General de Gaulle on having honoured his obligations to the Gabonese Government. In the Congo (Léopoldville), two dailies, one governmental and the other independent, condemned France and said that what had happened would do little good to Mba, who would be regarded in future as a mere French puppet. In Nigeria, the *Lagos Daily Times* said that the French Army should also have intervened in the Togo and Dahomey *coups* the previous year, though the *West African Pilot*, founded by President Azikiwe, condemned France's action outright. In Dahomey, the *Voix du Peuple* said it was an act of cowardice on the part of any African state to appeal to the former colonial Power to intervene in an internal dispute. There was little doubt what the people of Gabon themselves felt. On 23 February, the French did their best to organize a mass demonstration to hail the President's return to power; not more than 200 people took part, and few, if any of them, appeared to be Gabonese. Immediately afterwards there was a completely spontaneous counter-demonstration, in which some thousands of Gabonese participated, and when it was officially stated that this second crowd had gathered to cheer Mba, the demonstrators started up again the next day. Under this popular pressure, Mba had it announced over loud-speakers that he was going to dissolve the Government; the people took this to mean that he was going to step down, and when they found that this was not so, they came out on the streets again, this time with shouts of: 'Mba, resign!' French troops retorted by occupying the whole town, but that did not prevent a series of further demonstrations, in one of which the French Embassy was for a while besieged. Under the circumstances, it is hardly surprising that a great deal of the ill feeling displayed by the crowds was directed against French people, scores of whom started to leave the country. It should be added that there had never previously been a trace of xenophobia among the Gabonese.

The next piece of evidence of the Gabonese people's feelings towards Mba was furnished by the results of the elections: as a result of the *coup* and the counter-*coup*, these had been postponed from their original date in February to 12 April. There could be no question, after the events of February, of Mba's critics boycotting the polls, as Aubame had originally decided that his party should do. The electorate plainly had to be given an opportunity of registering a protest against what had happened. The opposition, of course, had everything against them. Almost all of its leaders had been arrested, and even those who remained at liberty were given little chance of carrying out any propaganda. Mba had spoken in the most violent and menacing tone during the campaign: among other things, he had threatened to dissolve the new Assembly if differences should arise between its members and the Government. French troops were still occupying key points in the country, and their presence might well be expected to intimidate voters; what is more, at least some French officers had supported Mba by distributing leaflets and by other means. Serious electoral irregularities were reported. Finally, the opposition were divided among themselves: they put forward two rival lists of candidates, one of them associated with Aubame, who was of course now in prison, and one of them headed by a trade union leader. For all that, no more than thirty-one of the forty-seven seats in the new Assembly went to the Government B.D.G. Even these results, which could scarcely be called a walk-over, were far from representing the real voice of the electorate. Despite the lack of free speech and the various forms of pressure brought on the voters, well under fifty per cent. of them in fact supported Mba's party.

The trial of those arrested over the February *coup* did not take place till August, and it was staged in somewhat curious conditions. The court did not sit in Libreville as would have been expected, but in the little provincial town of Lambaréné, more than twelve hours' drive away. Quite plainly, the authorities wanted to avoid any large-scale popular demonstrations in favour of the accused; there had been strikes in protest against the Government's policy as late as May. Distant though Lambaréné was from the capital, it was still thought necessary to take additional measures against any incidents. A 'state of precautions' was decreed in the area, and under this the local prefect was empowered to maintain police surveillance over people susceptible of making trouble and to keep them under house arrest if he thought fit, to close down theatres, cinemas and bars, and if necessary to order a curfew. Special transit- or residence-permits were required for people who wanted to travel through the district, or to stay there.

The trial was, indeed, held in public, in a school building on a hill which looked down over the Ogooué river on Dr

Albert Schweitzer's leper colony. Space was, however, so limited that there was no question of admitting anything like a representative section of the public. The only people allowed to attend the proceedings were those who held a permit issued by the authorities, and even the families of the accused had a right to only one card each. There were restrictions on press coverage of the trial. The only journalists admitted to the court were the correspondents of such news agencies as had been represented in Gabon at the end of June 1964. There were restrictions on the defence facilities available to the accused. When such a trial takes place in an African country, the defendants usually try to brief counsel from Paris or London, men who will not be overawed by the local authorities. Back in May, a special decree had forbidden the appearance of any lawyers who were not members of the Gabon bar.

The prosecution had called sixty-four witnesses, but neither they nor the defendants had anything particularly new to say. Lieutenant Essone, one of the four leaders of the *coup*, said that almost all the officers and N.C.O.s of the Gabonese army had known in advance what was being prepared. Aubame repeated the story that he had known nothing about the *coup* till the French Ambassador had rung him up about it and that he had gone to the presidential palace at Couseran's request to meet the putschists because there must be a responsible civilian whom the Embassy could contact over the affair. The presiding judge later read a somewhat lame correction from the Embassy, which denied Aubame's 'interpretation' of his telephone talk with the Ambassador. Aubame said he had formed his provisional Government constitutionally, at the request of the putschists, after what he described as Mba's voluntary resignation. He also declared that the intervention of the French parachutists was an intolerable interference in Gabon's internal affairs. Jean Marc Ekoh, a former Education Minister, and Paul Gondjout, former president of the Gabon Economic and Social Council, who were also in the dock, strongly supported the view that the provisional Government's actions were legal and the French intervention illegal. The Gabonese actor, Philippe Maury, who had appeared opposite French actress Marina Vlady in the first Gabonese film, *The Cage*, flatly refused the court's request that witnesses should confine their evidence to the *coup* and the formation of the provisional Government. Maury contended that, on the contrary, France's intervention should be the centre of the proceedings. 'If we'd been able to put up a few more Gabonese soldiers against the French,' he said, 'we'd have won – and we shouldn't be here today.' The public prosecutor wound up by demanding the death penalty, or hard labour for life, for Aubame, the two officer leaders of the *putsch* who were in the dock, and the former Gabon Ambassadors to London and to Israel, who were also among the prisoners, and hard labour for life or for twenty-five years for the rest.

The court announced its findings and pronounced sentence on 9 September, and the leniency it displayed could not fail to create astonishment and inspire speculation. Not a single one of the prisoners was condemned to death. Aubame got off with ten years' hard labour, his nephew, the former Ambassador to London, with twenty, and the two officer leaders of the *putsch* in the dock with the same term. The actor Maury and one N.C.O. received six and eight years' hard labour respectively, and the remainder of the prisoners who were found guilty were sentenced to prison terms ranging from one to five years. What is more, Ekoh, Gondjout and the former Ambassador to Israel were acquitted, as were six N.C.O.s, and the court refused the Government's demand for the award of sixty-three million francs damages against the defendants. Mba's supporters maintain that he made not the slightest attempt to influence the judges' verdict and did not even see them till the hearing was over. All the same, it is a little difficult to believe that, in an African country with something very like a dictatorial régime, the court did not consult the President before passing sentence. The conviction that there was such a consultation obviously inspired a commentary on the trial in the best-informed French newspaper, the *Monde*, which many observers of the African scene will regard as a balanced pronouncement on what happened.

When a strong and representative régime spares its enemies, the *Monde* said, it is possible to talk of clemency; when the Government is weak and its authority is disputed, the leniency is generally due to political considerations. Some people had thought at the time of the February *coup* that there was nothing more behind it than a handful of embittered and ambitious officers and N.C.O.s, who were following the example of those who a little earlier had threatened the Governments of Kenya and Tanganyika. But the demonstrations of March and even more the April elections showed that this opposition had considerable support. The Lambaréné judges' verdict, the *Monde* continued, in a rather more debatable passage, reflects the anxiety to damp down angry feelings and to promote an atmosphere of reconciliation which has for some time been apparent in Libreville. Such an atmosphere would permit Mba some time in the future to form a coalition Government. The paper added that the French Government had encouraged measures of appeasement in Gabon, and here it was undoubtedly right.

It had indeed been reported as far back as April 1964 that Mba had made contact with certain opposition leaders in view of the closeness of the vote at the elections. The trouble was that, apart from the Lambaréné sentences, there was very little evidence of any desire by the authorities to promote political appeasement; on the contrary, political arrests were still going on and the prisoners taken were being mishandled in every kind of way. Thus it was alleged that a woman member of the opposition named Martine Oyane had been completely undressed after her arrest, following which the police had paraded her naked through the streets of Libreville, beating her and forcing her to shout 'Long live Léon Mba!'; and this was represented as being by no means the only case of maltreatment of women. Men suspected of opposition tendencies were stated to have been transported for many miles in the boots of Mercedes cars; a young teacher named Raymond Sontoumé was cited as one of the victims. Just before its editor was himself arrested, the *Semaine Africaine* printed a letter from a reader which talked of arrests being made on a basis no stronger than anonymous letters, of people being imprisoned without even the pretence of a trial, and of women prisoners being raped by the so-called 'gorillas', the strong-arm men among the prison warders and the police. The editor of the column in which the letter appeared went on to speak of prisoners dying after being forced to eat rice mixed with the powdered glass of broken bottle-ends, and of others perishing from the effects of pimento suppositories. Things were going no better with the men who had been sentenced at Lambaréné. Reports from two different sources said they were being regularly beaten up in order to persuade them to sign a letter saying that Aubame had dragged them into joining the February *coup* and had indeed paid them for doing so; Aubame, like his fellow-prisoners, was said to have his feet in fetters. What is more, once those involved in the *putsch* had been transferred to Libreville prison, the Catholic chaplain was no longer allowed to call in there; no very great imagination was necessary to guess the reasons. Mba was said to have been put up to these repressive measures by the French officials around him, some of whom, at any rate, seemed to have a past history as least as tarnished as certain of ex-President Youlou's French advisers. Nor was it safe to expose the authorities' conduct. The news agency correspondents in Libreville knew perfectly well that if they were to send out dispatches displeasing to the authorities, they would be expelled. Monsignor Walcker, a senior local priest, had written a letter to the press about police brutality, so a punitive expedition against his house was organized. His furniture was knocked about and, despite the fact that he was ninety-five, Mgr Walcker was mishandled by the invaders. Nor was he the only priest to be treated in this fashion.

There were, of course, arguments which could be urged in favour of Mba. He had, it is true, a financial interest in the development of his country: since January 1961, soon after he became President, he had been a director of the Company for the Mining, Industrial and Agricultural Expansion of Gabon. He had, however, built himself no luxurious palaces, nor had his wife, like the wife of one of the Ghana ministers, ever bought herself a golden bed. What is more, he had been, with President Houphouet-Boigny, of the Ivory Coast, one of the founders of the party known as the African Democratic Rally, or R.D.A., which had been the first coherent attempt in French Africa to challenge the colonial system. Over the years following the accession of Gabon to independence, he had done his best to end tribal feeling. Thus, when Aubame had been Foreign Minister, his principal private secretary and all the members of his personal staff had been Fangs, like himself; Mba's assistants had been drawn from every tribe in Gabon.

The same thing held good of the staffing of the principal ambassadorial posts: Mba laid it down that the ambassadors of his country in Paris, Washington and London must each come from a different section of the broad ethnical divisions of the country. This rule went by the board after the plot, however; since February 1964, Fang officials have been installed almost everywhere inside Gabon. They wear formal clothes, which keep them in their offices in a hot country such as Gabon is, and there are those who say that they are not so close to the ordinary people as were their French predecessors. It can, indeed, be maintained that not a few of the Gabonese peasants regret the departure of the French. Parallels to this feeling of nostalgia can be found in other countries of sub-Saharan Africa that were formerly under French rule, and, of course, in Algeria.

Mba's photograph is to be seen in hotels and shops all over the country; in Government offices it is generally hung up next to that of General de Gaulle. The omnipresence of the President's features, which is common form in single-party countries, does not mean he is liked. One sign of the lack of popular sympathy for him was the circulation, late in 1964, of a story that at a recent meeting of the Bwiti cult, his member-ship of which had aided his original accession to power, he had taken the 'fire test' – and been burned. The outstanding proof of his lack of hold on his people was that more than a year after the *coup* which had for thirty-six hours evicted him from power, French troops were still guarding his palace. What is more, they had at least once been heavily reinforced. At the time of the Lambaréné trial, an additional contingent had been flown in, and its strength may be judged from the fact that at that time the French forces had an N.C.O.s' mess no less than fifty strong. It was only as a result of Mba's insistent and repeated requests that the French garrison was being maintained in Gabon; he pleaded for it to stay on every time he flew to Paris, and on each occasion he had a little more difficulty in seeing General de Gaulle. For, as the French saw it, their parachutists had been dispatched to Libreville to restore Mba to the Presi-dency, not to keep him there. The view taken in Paris was that Mba should immediately have profited from their presence to come to some sort of accommodation with his opponents. As the months passed, and there were no signs of Mba's reaching or trying to reach such an arrangement, it began to seem increasingly likely that the General would order his men out.

It can, indeed, be urged on the Gabon President's behalf that he would need a great deal of persistence to conclude an agreement with his opponents. They did not form a united front, as did the supporters of ex-President Youlou in the Congo (Brazzaville): far from it. Even within Aubame's own party, there were those who backed him up to the hilt and those who criticized him for having entered the Mba coalition Government in which he had served as Foreign Minister. There were also deep divergencies between such figures as Paul Gondjout, who was acquitted at Lambaréné and who believed in a parliamentary system of the classic Western type, and the leaders of the General Association of Gabonese Students in France, or of the Gabonese Popular Action Movement, or M.G.A.P. The latter body, which was formed in 1958 and campaigned for a No vote at the referendum in which colonial countries were asked whether they wanted to join the new Franco-African community, later adopted a semi-clandestine existence and called itself a 'National Liberation Movement'. The M.G.A.P. spokesmen did indeed demand the release of Aubame and all the other political prisoners, but they definitely did not want to see them joining Mba in a Government of National Union; in fact, it cannot be certain that they wanted to see them in any sort of Cabinet. The young people they represented did not feel any particular confidence in politicians who had begun their public careers while Gabon still enjoyed colonial status. Not a few of them would like to see the establishment in their country of a régime like that which replaced the Youlou Government in Brazzaville. In fact the strongest argument which the champions of Mba can urge in favour of his maintenance in power is that, were he to fall, he might momentarily be replaced by Aubame, but that Aubame would within a matter of months be replaced by something very like a fellow-travelling administration.

133

6

Dahomey

THE OVERTHROW IN 1963 of President Hubert Maga of Dahomey was largely a matter of chance. Maga had not provoked by his own actions a widespread movement of popular protest, as had President Fulbert Youlou in the Congo (Brazzaville). He was not hurled from power by such a sudden military *coup* as was a few months later to remove President Mba of Gabon from office for thirty-six hours. Maga had been out of his country for some weeks on an official tour of Asia, which was to have been followed by a visit to the United States. His ministers had been unable to handle the various grievances which had arisen during his absence. When he was summoned back from Paris to cope with the situation, he could easily have put down by force the trouble he found confronting him at home. He did not want to. Under an agreement between Dahomey and France, he could just as easily have called for French military aid to maintain him in power; he did not fancy the idea. In Togo, President Sylvanus Olympio had promptly been shot by the soldiers who overthrew him. In Brazzaville, President Youlou had just as promptly been imprisoned by his successors in the government of his country. As soon as the Gabon Army putschists had got President Mba to sign his resignation, they locked him up and then deported him to the provinces. Maga, on the other hand, remained in office, as one of three Ministers of State in a provisional government, for more than a month after the Army had stepped in and taken over power. When he was eventually forced to resign and put under house arrest, it was because a commission of inquiry set up by the provisional Government had found him – and a number of his former ministers – guilty of misapplying public funds, a charge which could almost certainly be brought with equal validity against the presidents and ministers of a high proportion of newly-independent African states.

What is more, Maga's accession to power could not be ascribed to any kind of personal ambition. In Algeria, Ben

Bella had not hesitated before the risks of civil war when that seemed the only way of acceding to the leadership of his country. In Ghana, Nkrumah had plainly been out after undisputed authority from the very moment he returned home. The only reason why Maga was elected Premier of Dahomey in 1959 was that the leaders of the two rival parties in the south of the country were each determined that the other should not hold the post, and therefore agreed on him, a northerner, as a compromise candidate. Much the same reasons were responsible for the accession of Ahmadou Ahidjo to the Presidency of the Cameroon Republic. Northerner though he was, Maga displayed no sort of regional fanaticism; he had, indeed, married a woman from the south of Dahomey, and such marriages are not very common. Though he had set up in Dahomey – with the co-operation, it should be noted, of one of the southern leaders who had been responsible for his accession to office – the single-party system which is now almost universal in the newly-independent African states, he had far more reason to do so than most of his opposite numbers in Africa. The second southern leader had fomented a general strike against him, and was a few months later arrested, tried and sentenced to a prison term for plotting against Maga's life. Writing in 1962, an American specialist on Africa said of Maga that he had brought to heel, with the minimum of bloodshed, the most ungovernable of all the French-speaking West African countries, and through forging a one-party system had given it a relatively stable administration. Maga had also managed, this author went on, to reorganize local government and the judiciary, and had found time to draw up a development plan, inspired by what its authors called 'dynamic Socialism', which had been tailored to the meagreness of Dahomey's resources. 'Probably no other leader,' the American specialist concludes, 'could have resolved as satisfactorily as Maga has done, in the short time at his disposal, the many and complicated problems he has encountered in his determination to bring unity to Dahomey. ... Only he seems capable of controlling the centrifugal tendencies still so conspicuous in his country.'

Finally, though discontent among Dahomeyan students had been one of the factors that had been responsible for Maga's eviction from the Presidency, less than a year later, their

Cotonou congress was denouncing the new régime for faithfully treading in the footsteps of its predecessor. Naturally enough, the National Assembly had in March 1965 voted that the former President should be brought to trial before a specially created High Court of Justice; equally naturally, the vote had been unanimous. But it was difficult for the impartial observer to resist the conclusion that Maga had been given something of a raw deal.

The Republic of Dahomey, with an area of just over 47,000 square miles and a population of around 2,000,000, forms a narrow strip of country, rather over 400 miles long, between the states of Togo and Nigeria. Its northern neighbours are the Republics of the Upper Volta and of Niger. It has 3,200 miles of roads and 360 miles of railways. The capital, Porto Novo, has about 30,000 inhabitants, but the main commercial centre, Cotonou, is credited with more than 80,000. Dahomey is one of the poorer African countries. No mineral resources have so far been discovered there, and its principal products are palm oil, maize, millet, sorghum, copra, ground-nuts, cotton and coffee, while tobacco-planting has been started up. These export products, however, almost all come from the south; the north has to exist on a subsistence economy, For more than forty years now – with the exception of the year 1924 – Dahomey's imports have constantly exceeded its exports; in 1963, its sales overseas covered no more than thirty-eight per cent. of its purchases abroad. Nor does there seem much sign of the situation improving; indeed there are those who maintain that the country's economy is actually going downhill. Reforestation is generally agreed to be a crying need, for there has been not a little degeneration of the soil in the often over-cultivated areas of the South. Steps were indeed taken, under the Maga régime, to promote the industrialization which might obviously provide one way out. The year 1962 saw the signature of a Dahomey-Israel agreement which provided for the establishment of a company that, with Israeli expert assistance, was to build a chain of factories designed to produce a wide range of consumer goods for all the neighbouring states of French-speaking Africa.

Finally, Dahomey had a problem peculiar to itself among the other countries of French West Africa. Despite its poverty,

136

it had a very high figure of school attendance, though this did not reach the level of that found in the Congo (Brazzaville) and Gabon, and its people were naturally intelligent and enterprising. In the colonial period, the French had recruited Dahomeyans for subordinate positions in their civil service up and down Africa. A fair proportion of the educated class who did not find this sort of job emigrated on their own, because of the lack of employment at home, and found work abroad: in Dakar even today, twenty of the thirty African doctors in practice are Dahomeyans. All that changed almost overnight when Dahomey's neighbours attained independence at the turn of the 1950s and the 1960s. The 'brother African states' wanted jobs for their own young people. Sometimes the immigrants from Dahomey were forced to flee by popular demonstrations against them: in the Ivory Coast, these ranged from strong-arm attacks and murders to the burning-down of their houses. Sometimes they were simply expelled: the number forced to leave Niger in this way in 1963 was officially put at 8,000. Whatever the method adopted to turn them out, their return home aggravated yet further a problem of skilled un-employment which was already serious enough in the towns of Dahomey, and which came on top of the chronic rural under-employment which is to be found in so many African countries. The construction, under Maga's development plans, of a big deep-water harbour at Cotonou, which was designed to attract traffic from Niger and Upper Volta as well as from Dahomey itself, would undoubtedly absorb many of the town's unem-ployed labourers. It could not be expected to help Dahomey's jobless intellectuals. There were nothing like enough jobs in the civil service or in private business to fix them all up and many of them, especially those who held French university degrees, either harboured quite unrealistic political ambitions or would only accept extremely well-paid posts. Whatever government was in power in Porto Novo was bound to find in them a potential source of serious trouble.

The first European ships had called in at what is now Dahomey – it was then known as a part of the 'Slave Coast' – about the same time as they came to the Gold Coast. The French West Indies Company, founded by Louis XIII, set up two trading posts there in the seventeenth century, and a fort was built at one of these. In the middle of the nineteenth century, France established protectorate areas in three places, including Porto Novo and Cotonou. The 1880s saw the ruler of the southern kingdom of Abomey doing his best to throw the French into the sea; an expeditionary force soon put an end to that. Finally, at the end of the 'nineties, France's position in the country, whose original protectorates had by now been expanded far up-country, was recognized by Great Britain and Germany, and the frontiers of the colony of Dahomey were defined. Those frontiers, which are the same today, were not dictated by any sort of geographical or ethnical unity, but purely by the rivalry between the colonial Powers, who had each staked out their claims to this or that tract of the continent and were not going to abandon them. So though France brought together under a single administration the previously independent kingdoms which had existed in the north and the south of the country, their divergent populations never fused into a single people. The factors that divided them were, of course, to be found in a high proportion of other African countries. Six languages were spoken in Dahomey; much of the southern population was Christian, whereas the northerners were mostly Moslems, but there was nothing unusual about that in West Africa. Possibly the biggest difficulty that stood in the way of breaking the centrifugal forces was the highly individualistic character of the Dahomeyan people. Dahomey has sometimes been called the Latin Quarter of the West Coast, and the transient denizens of the real Latin Quarter are notoriously refractory to discipline, without which there could be little hope of creating a unified nation state.

The year 1945 saw France's colonial populations returning their first deputies to the French Parliament. The choice of the Africans of Dahomey fell on a thirty-two-year-old accountant, Sourou Migan Apithy. Apithy, who was a Catholic, had been educated at local mission schools and had gone on to Bordeaux and then to Paris, where he had taken degrees in political science and accountancy. Support from the Catholic missionaries in Dahomey was largely responsible for Apithy's initial success, and for twelve years on from then his political leadership in his country was almost uncontested. He had constantly been re-elected to the French National

Assembly and to presidency of the Dahomey territorial assembly.

The second big political leader of southern Dahomey was Justin Tometin Ahomadegbé. Ahomadegbé had more than one point in common with President Houphouet-Boigny of the Ivory Coast. Both men were wealthy traditional chiefs, both were graduates of the Dakar medical school and both had served for some time in the local French administration. There the resemblance between the two men ended. Ahomadegbé never sat in the French Parliament or headed a widespread political movement such as Houphouet-Boigny's African Democratic Rally, which was represented in a high proportion of the states of French Africa before they acceded to independence. His prestige was due to the fact that he was a direct descendant of the kings of Abomey who had resisted the French conquest. His influence was confined to the area over which his ancestors had ruled and he did not enter politics, and then only on a local plane, until he was elected to the Dahomey territorial assembly in 1952. As a deputy in this, he became known for his sharp criticisms of the French administration, but he might even so have remained in the background had he not hit upon the idea of allying himself with the trade union leaders of Cotonou. In the municipal elections of November 1956, Ahomadegbé was elected Mayor of Abomey, while two of his lieutenants became respectively Mayor and Deputy Mayor of Cotonou. That suggested that with the party he had founded, the Dahomey Democratic Union, or U.D.D., Ahomadegbé was on the way to becoming an important person.

The political leader of northern Dahomey, Hubert Maga, had been born of a peasant family at Parakou in 1916, completed his education at the Ponty Normal School in Dakar, and was converted to Christianity, which was not so common for a northerner. When his training was completed, he was appointed to a schoolmaster's job in Natitingou, even farther north than his home town, and he served there from 1936 to 1946. The area was extremely poor in educated leaders, and he and his southern-born wife, who was also a Christian and was a trained nurse, acquired considerable influence there. He left his job when he was elected to the Dahomey territorial assembly, where he founded a party which was first known as the Northern Ethnical Group, and in 1951 joined Apithy in the French National Assembly, when Dahomey's representation was increased by one deputy. In Paris he joined the Overseas Independents, faithfully followed the leadership of their Senegalese head, Léopold Senghor, and was rewarded by a ministerial post in the Gaillard government, the last of the Fourth Republic, which held office from November 1957 to April 1958.

It took very little effort to get a party started in the politically conscious south of Dahomey. In 1951, there were no less than six of them, though most of these were not so much organizations basing themselves on rival programmes as cliques built round rival personalities. At the 1957 elections to the territorial assembly, it became apparent that Ahomadegbé's U.D.D. had become a good deal more than a clique. It is true that of the sixty seats in the assembly it won only the seven seats allotted to the Abomey constituency, while Apithy's Republican Party of Dahomey, or P.R.D., secured a total of thirty-five. But the U.D.D., which had by now entered into a loose affiliation with Houphouet-Boigny's inter-territorial African Democratic Rally, secured as much as twenty-seven per cent. of the popular vote against the forty-three per cent. of the P.R.D., and its following included a high percentage of the working class of Cotonou, the commercial capital of the country. The next year Ahomadegbé was able to furnish practical proof of his strength, and of that of his allies among the local trade union movement which had formerly been affiliated to the Communist-dominated French C.G.T. The Cotonou members of these unions came out in sympathy with the strikers at a local oil mill, and the employers refused to give way. The Apithy Government was unable to arrange a settlement, but all the same the French Governor, after a bout of rioting and looting, had the dispute settled along the lines the unions demanded. Apithy might well resent what he regarded as the U.D.D.'s championship of organized labour to promote its party interests, but the result of the strike was a triumph for Ahomadegbé.

It was possibly this triumph which was responsible for his obduracy when in the spring of 1959 Apithy started discussions with the other party leaders in preparation for the elections fixed for April. His aim was to secure an agreement with them on the division of seats in the new assembly, and this should on the face of it have been the easiest of tasks. The three parties' strengths were evenly matched, and there seemed no reason at all why their respective shares of the total popular vote should change. It was not as if they were differentiated by rival ideologies, the infectious appeal of one of which might conceivably, at the coming polls, have swept the whole country. They were regional parties, each of which enjoyed the support of an area with much the same population as the two others. The Porto Novo region, with its high proportion of civil servants, supported Apithy; the north was almost to a man behind Maga, while the population of Abomey, with the industrial workers of Cotonou, favoured Ahomadegbé. Apithy found no difficulty at all in reaching agreement with Maga. Maga promised that members of his party, which had now been rechristened the Dahomeyan Democratic Rally, or R.D.D., should not stand outside the north; Apithy in return undertook that candidates of his P.R.D. should contest seats in the south only. The head of the Dahomey Government found Ahoma-degbé a great deal tougher to bargain with. He is reported to have insisted that his party should be allotted the same number of seats in the new assembly as the P.R.D. and the R.D.D. combined. This was pretty plainly a nonsensical proposition, so Apithy resorted to the age-old method of redrawing electoral boundaries to ensure his success and his rival's failure on election day.

He did the job almost too well. When the official figures of the results came out they showed that Apithy's P.R.D. had secured thirty-seven seats with its 144,038 votes, Maga's R.D.D. twenty-two seats for its 62,132, whereas Ahomadegbé's U.D.D., despite the 162,179 people who had pronounced for it would have no more than eleven deputies in the new assembly. There was an immediate explosion. The riots which followed the announcement of the upshot were so serious that French troops were flown in. In the circumstances, Apithy had no alternative but to climb down. At the mediation of Houphouet-Boigny he agreed to a compromise solution under which his party and Ahomadegbé's divided the eighteen seats of a contested south-western constituency between them. Once that was done, Apithy's supporters in the assembly came down to twenty-eight, Ahomadegbé's rose to twenty, while Maga's followers remained at twenty-two. After what had happened, Ahomadegbé made it plain that he was not going to stand for Apithy's remaining Premier. Apithy refused to stand down, and the result of the deadlock was that Maga was put forward as a compromise candidate for the premiership and duly voted into the post.

He could hardly have taken over power at a more difficult time; had he been moved by nothing more than personal ambition, he would never have chosen the spring of 1959 as his moment for embarking on office. Foreign investments in Dahomey were at a standstill. Unemployment was daily growing with the return home of thousands of Dahomeyans from the neighbouring countries of black Africa, under the pressure of popular demonstrations or governmental action. Under the circumstances, organized labour was naturally restless, and Maga felt it necessary to consult the trade unions before appointing a Minister of Labour. Living was so difficult that some local politicians were going as far as to urge electors to stop paying their taxes. Maga obviously had to choose his ministers very carefully, and most of the posts in his cabinet were equitably shared out among the three main parties. In view of the flare-up between the leaders of the other two parties which alone had permitted his accession to the premiership, he hardly felt that he could appoint the outgoing Premier, Apithy, to the post of Deputy Premier which he had obviously expected. Apithy was made a Minister of State without any definite assignation, while the Deputy Premiership went to his second-in-command. From an inter-party point of view, there was nothing to be said against the appointment, but Apithy could not forgive what he regarded as a personal slight, and it became pretty plain that he was ready to do anything he could to overturn the Maga Government and to return to power himself. Maga gave him very little chance. In the policy speech he made in the assembly after his accession to office, he announced a programme with which few intelligent people could quarrel. He said that he intended to do away with tribalism and regionalism and revise the status of the local tribal chiefs. He added that he would encourage investments from any kind of source, would freeze wages and prices, and would enforce austerity measures. Austerity is never a popular word, but it can at least be said that Maga had risen above the regional considerations which had up till then largely dominated Dahomey politics and had put forward a programme on a national level.

Dahomey became independent in August 1960, and for a short while it looked as if the country was about to unite solidly behind the Maga Government. For a few weeks, the country's three parties spontaneously united in what was called a 'Patriotic Action Front'. They went even farther: they agreed to a law turning Dahomey into a single electoral constituency and providing that the list of candidates which received a majority of votes in this would occupy all the seats in the legislature. The Patriotic Action Front did not last very long. Ahomadegbé broke away from it almost at once. He used the discontent among students and workers over the growing scarcity of jobs because of the mass return of Dahomeyans from abroad to inspire strikes among both. And at the end of September, he came out with a statement that only the establishment of a single-party system could save Dahomey from what he called 'its present stagnation'. Since he had just broken away from the single party which he had voluntarily joined a mere few weeks before, he was plainly out after the establishment of a monopoly party headed by himself.

Unfortunately for him, Maga, though he did not possess what could be called a magnetic personality, had a very keen sense of tactics. He started by bringing into his party newcomers like the brilliant Albert Teveodjré, a European university graduate who had published two books about Africa, had edited the organ of the Left-Wing Federation of Students from French Black Africa and had in 1959 participated in founding the pro-independence African National Liberation Movement. Teveodjré soon became Minister of Information. Maga also got Houphouet-Boigny to recognize his R.D.D. party as the authentic representative in Dahomey of Houphouet's inter-territorial African Democratic Rally. That was regarded as a blow below the belt by Ahomadegbé, who had long taken it for granted that his U.D.D. was the sole mouthpiece of the Rally in Dahomey. As September went out, he got the unions he controlled to call a general strike, while the U.D.D. deputies in the Assembly moved a vote of censure on the Government which they accused of responsibility for what they called the country's grave social unrest on two grounds: it had done nothing at all to promote a national development plan, and it had done nothing at all to ensure the welfare of the workers. The strike completely paralysed Porto Novo and Cotonou for two days, the police had to use tear gas and the trouble only finally ended when Maga brought down some of his supporters from the north of the country. One day Cotonou woke up to find itself occupied by a force of men clad in animal skins and carrying bows and arrows, men who started by taking up their stand in front of ministers' homes and patrolling the streets they later walked through as tourists. In order to defeat the parliamentary opposition, Maga could not count on his northerners; he had to make an alliance with Apithy's P.R.D. party. The two parties together mustered more than enough votes to defeat the motion of censure. As soon as it was rejected the U.D.D. Ministers were turned out of the Government and P.R.D. deputies took their places, and shortly after the P.R.D. and the R.D.D. merged to form the Dahomeyan Unity Party, or P.D.U., of which Maga was elected head. The programme it put forward included what it called rational planning and economic austerity and also, what is a commonplace in single-party African countries, a revision of the trade union movement's objectives and methods.

The next step was for the Assembly to transform itself into a constituent body and to adopt a new Constitution. The Constitution, like a high proportion of those of the newly-independent states of French Africa, seemed to draw its chief inspiration from that of the Fifth French Republic. Thus, the President could call on the National Assembly to reconsider a bill, when it must be passed by a two-thirds majority if it was to become law, and he could also submit measures to a referendum. The first elections to be held under the provisions of the document occurred on 11 December. There was nothing unexpected about the results: the P.D.U. got sixty-nine per cent. of the popular vote and the U.D.D. thirty-one per cent., while Maga was elected President and Apithy Vice-President. What must have surprised many electors was that under the

144

provisions of the electoral law which had been voted when all
the three parties had been momentarily united, every seat in
the Assembly went to the P.D.U. and not a single one to the
U.D.D. Ahomadegbé remained without a single minister in
the Government. The only effective weapons still at his
disposal were the trade unions he controlled – and their latest
strike had ended in failure – and his party's daily newspaper,
and Maga was pretty soon to deprive him of both.

With the help of his young Information Minister – Teveodjré
was no more than thirty-one when he took over the post and
the administrative secretaryship of the P.D.U. – Maga set
about tackling his opponents along a number of different lines.
Some were repressive: as 1961 came in, he got the Assembly to
pass legislation which empowered the Government to deal
summarily with the opposition press and with any people it
considered likely to foment disorders, and these powers were
soon to be used. Some were aimed at presenting the official
case more efficiently: Teveodjré announced the formation of a
corps of town criers who would keep the illiterate regularly
informed about current events from the Government point of
view, while fresh newspapers were set on foot. Some were
conciliatory: Maga took steps to win the sympathy of individual members of the U.D.D. though these did not pay off at
once. Some were organizational: such was the formation of the
General Union of Dahomeyan Workers, which the President
had helped promote as a rival to the labour movement controlled by Ahomadegbé and which almost immediately
secured recognition by the inter-state General Union of Black
African Workers as its sole authentic representative in Dahomey,
a position up till then held by Ahomadegbé's trade union
followers. Most of the U.D.D. leaders had by now come to
realize that the wind was blowing against them. Their party
newspaper, *Dahomey-Matin*, was suppressed in February under
the new security measures, and though it was promptly
replaced by the *Cotonou-Matin*, no one could be certain how
long that would be allowed to survive. At a party congress
held at the beginning of April, most of the speakers expressed
themselves in favour of merging with the Government party.
An uncompromising minority, headed by Ahomadegbé himself, held out against them, but the fact that it was only a

minority made it possible for Maga to take action. He started by suspending the surviving party newspaper. He continued by dissolving the U.D.D. Less than a week later he ordered the dissolution of the trade unions which had taken their orders from Ahomadegbé. Most of their members promptly joined his own General Union of Dahomeyan Workers. Maga ended up by declaring, with what turned out to be exaggerated optimism, that the Dahomeyan nation had at last been born.

Ahomadegbé, however, if the official version is to be believed, had not yet given up the fight. A few months before, he might have contemplated a *coup d'état* against Maga. That was a little difficult now, with organized labour no longer under his control. On 26 May, Teveodjré alleged that he had taken to conspiratorial methods. He announced that a plot had been discovered to assassinate Maga and his ministers, and that Ahomadegbé and eleven other ringleaders had been arrested. Their trial did not start till December, but it took place in public, which is by no means the case with all African political trials, while the accused were allowed to retain counsel from Paris.

The case for the prosecution may well have appeared in parts a little dubious to anyone unfamiliar with Africa. The prosecution witnesses included a number of fetishist chiefs and sorcerers, who had turned State's evidence, and who testified that they had received money from the main defendants to provide magical protection for the strong-arm men who were to carry out the necessary murders. Ahomadegbé, who denied all the charges, fastened on this point. He argued that it was highly unlikely that he, 'a man of science and a Christian', would ever have paid hard cash to those claiming the power to make men invisible and invulnerable. In fact, it was by no means as unlikely as he suggested. The highly civilized President Houphouet-Boigny, of the Ivory Coast, who is also a Christian and also a doctor by profession, is known to have his private soothsayer and to have given up air travel on his advice, and has accused the enemies involved in two plots against him of having tried to poison him by means of fetishes. Despite his defence, Ahomadegbé was found guilty and sentenced to five years' imprisonment, while the other accused received sentences ranging from one to ten years. Eleven months later they were all released, 'because of their good conduct in prison and as a gesture of conciliation', Maga stated in a broadcast. National reconciliation and national unity were, indeed, Maga's openly proclaimed objectives, but it may have been difficult for his opponents to resist the conclusion that their release was in fact a confession of his weakness.

As the summer of 1961 came in, however, Maga appeared to be in a strong position. His political rivals were either safely in jail or safely incorporated into the ranks of his P.D.U., and he was free to turn his attention towards disarming the chronically discontented sections of the population, coping with the chronic budget deficit and promoting the country's economic development. Labour had been called to heel, for the time at any rate, by the formation of the official trade union movement, and his success over that emboldened Maga to go a little farther. As part of a newly introduced austerity programme, it was decided that ten per cent. should be held back from the workers' salaries and wages till further notice. Trade unionists might grumble that since their pay had already been frozen for three years, it was unfair to impose a further burden upon them, but Maga had no real reason to feel guilty. Town workers represented a bare one per cent. of Dahomey's population, and what is more they were a privileged class, earning as they did up to twenty times as much as their fellows in the countryside. Students formed another category of the discontented. As early as 1960, he had sent home to their parents student strikers at Cotonou technical college who had downed pens in protest against the action of two of their French professors who had failed some of them in their examinations. In 1961 Maga took additional measures to secure student docility. He forced the two main youth organizations in the country, one affiliated to the World Federation of Youth and the other to the Communist-dominated World Federation of Democratic Youth, to fuse in a National Union of Dahomeyan Youth. He went even farther. He insisted that the new body should pledge itself not to seek relations with any world organization but to place itself unreservedly at the service of the P.D.U.

The development plan he soon announced was mainly designed to raise rural living-standards through regular and substantial increases in agricultural production and the local processing of its yield. It is true that the money needed to finance the plan would almost all have to come from France. Dahomey's contribution to it was to take the form of what was called 'human investment', that it to say the mobilization of the country's young people for compulsory work, largely on the land. One advantage of this human investment, as Maga's supporters saw things, was that it would check the flow of country youths to the towns, and this was a gain that nobody could sneeze at. For though the rural population of Dahomey, like that of most African states, was chronically under-employed, the country's most pressing problem consisted in the number of its skilled unemployed, and their concentration in Cotonou, whose population was estimated to have almost quadrupled between the start of the 1950s and that of the 1960s. This large body of trained but unused manpower was a political as well as an economic liability for Dahomey; it had been swelled at the turn of the 1950s and the 1960s by the expulsion from neighbouring African countries of thousands of civil servants and commercial employees, and any measure which could prevent it from expanding to an even more unmanageable size was obviously to be welcomed. With his measures to cut down Government overspending and to promote national unity behind him, and with his four-year plan drafted, Maga had a right to feel satisfied with himself when he went on a State visit to Paris in the autumn of 1961. He had come to power only because of the rivalry between the south Dahomeyan parties, he had remained in office by playing their leaders off against each other, and he had ended up by asserting his authority over both. His methods, it is true, had not always been democratic, but they had involved next to no bloodshed.

The successful execution of the four-year plan called, of course, for a great deal of hard work. The task of organizing the population to co-operate in it could fall only on the P.D.U., functioning both through its local cells and through the local government bodies which some observers felt had been in-stalled largely to facilitate this mobilization. Much about the same time, the Neo Destour, Tunisia's Government party, was setting to work to ensure the smooth working of the first

Tunisian development plan. There was, however, one big difference between the situations in the two countries. The Neo Destour, at the time the Tunisian plan was launched, had been in existence for nearly thirty years. Its ranks had been consolidated by the years-long struggle, for much of the time an underground struggle, to wrest independence from the French. That struggle had given it its heroes and its martyrs, it possessed in President Bourguiba a leader of brilliant oratorical powers and absolutely uncontested authority, and it could almost certainly be described as by far the most efficient of all the single parties of Africa. The P.D.U., on the other hand, did not begin to function as an organization till the year in which the plan was drafted. Its country-wide organization was a matter of mere months old. It had only just asserted its authority over the trade unions and the youth organizations. Its leader, Maga, had emerged as a national figure not much more than two years before, and many of those who had rallied to his standard in the south of the country had done so more from motives of expediency than because they wholeheartedly believed in his ideal of national unity. Under the circumstances, the party's hold on the country could hardly be expected to be a hundred per cent. secure. What is more, it was faced with a number of tactical problems and at least one major policy decision. What, for example, were to be the relations between the local party agents and the officials heading the newly established departmental, municipal and village councils? What role was to be attributed in the new establishment to the traditional chiefs? Finally, would it not be necessary to make a really big effort to raise the economic and educational level of the northern region to something at least approaching equality with the south? The obvious answer to the last question would appear to be Yes, but if Maga, as a northerner, were to answer it in that sense, would he not be accused of favouritism towards the inhabitants of the area he came from?

In the meantime, the expansion and tightening-up of the P.D.U. organization all over Dahomey was plainly a whole-time job. Maga, as Head of the Government, was in no position to devote all his energies to it, so the task fell to his fellow-northerner, Chabi Mama, who had become the party's Secretary-General. In the autumn of 1961, Mama made a tour of the country many hundreds of miles long, in the course of which he had talks with nearly 150 party cells. He admitted that the P.D.U. had been suffering from growing pains, but he went on: 'We know from experience that the only way for a young nation to succeed is to become organized. Just for that reason, we Dahomeyans must rally round the ideals of the P.D.U. We must put an end to overweening ambitions, to hatred, to envy, to regionalism and racism and to the person-ality cult.' It may appear paradoxical that the lieutenant of a single-party leader should have selected as targets the first and the last of the attitudes Mama named, since ambition and appetite for the personality cult are the outstanding charac-teristics of most leaders of single parties. It is probable that Mama's real mark was Ahomadegbé, and that he thought of Maga, as Maga almost certainly thought of himself, less as a dictator intent on cramming national unity down the Dahomey-ans' throats than as an authoritative chairman trying to put it over on them by persuasion backed by the minimum of coercion.

Eleven months later Maga was able to show the extent to which his authority as chairman had increased. His Vice-President, Apithy, was not an easy partner to work with. It was not only that he had his policy differences with the President. He made it pretty plain that he would never be satisfied with playing even the most honoured of second fiddles in the ranks of the Government, and the 1962 example of Senegal showed that an administration with two virtually co-equal heads was almost impossible to work, in Africa at any rate. In a Cabinet reshuffle in February 1962, Apithy added the Ministry of Planning and Development to his Vice-Presidential post; there could hardly have been a more responsible office. It did not seem to work, all the same. In August of the same year, the Vice-President, after a long tour of Eastern Europe and the Soviet Union, went to Paris as Dahomeyan Ambassador. That position also was a highly important one now that Dahomey, with the requirements of its development plan, was going to require more aid from France than ever. Many Dahomeyans, however, regarded the posting as a mild form of disgrace.

And it was Apithy who just over a year later was the first

of a number of figures who raised their voices against what they called the totalitarian nature of the Maga régime. The factor that finally unleashed the demonstrations that were to lead to Maga's downfall was no politician's utterance, however; it was an explosion of the regionalism which the President had from the beginning set out to fight. In the summer of 1963, Daniel Dessou, who had been working as an official at the Sakete sub-prefecture, had died of poison. Bohiki, the local deputy had been accused of murdering him and arrested for it. Bohiki had been released after his fellow-deputies had voted a resolution demanding that Article 37 of the Dahomey Constitution should be applied to his case; this laid down that detention or prosecution of a deputy must be suspended if the National Assembly demands it during a Parliamentary session.

The deputies may well have been acting within their rights, though it seems highly likely that if Maga had been in the country he would have dissuaded them from what the ordinary man could only regard as putting one of their number above the law. Maga was away, however, and what might have been a mild manifestation of resentment at the Assembly's vote became an explosion of popular feeling because the murdered man and his alleged murderer belonged to different ethnical groups. The victim came from a tribe living in the area of Porto Novo, the Dahomeyan capital, a tribe which was notorious for the invincible particularism of its people; the accused deputy came from another tribe in the Sakete region. Crowds turned out on the Porto Novo streets demanding that the National Assembly should rescind its vote and that Bohiki should be rearrested. The demonstrations were reasonably orderly the first day, and then the trade unions took a hand. The General Union of Dahomeyan Workers had indeed been organized by Maga, but its leaders and its members alike were still furious over the ten per cent. wage dock he had imposed on them two years before, and they saw in the exploitation of the Bohiki case a chance to advance their own interests. The second day of the demonstrations, which ended by intimidating the Assembly into voting Bohiki back into prison, was so rowdy that a curfew was imposed and the general secretary of the Government flew to Paris to explain the situation to Maga. Maga decided to cancel his American trip and return home at once. He broadcast an appeal for calm to the Dahomeyan people and he summoned a special session of the National Assembly. That did less than nothing to disarm the trade unions, or the young people whom the lack of good jobs, the lack of free speech and the Government's attempt to enforce docility on them had turned into enemies almost as bitter. Only a minority of youngsters had joined the National Union of Dahomeyan Youth, which the Government had established two years before in an attempt to ensure their safe indoctrination. When six trade unionists were arrested on the second day of the demonstrations against Bohiki, the unions called a general strike. As soon as Maga had yielded to their pressure by dismissing his Government and replacing it by a provisional one in which he invited Ahomadegbé to sit alongside Apithy, they summoned their followers out on the streets to boo the new team. It was not all booing, either: two people were killed in Cotonou in clashes between the demonstrators there and armed north Dahomeyans who had descended on the economic capital to support Maga. Finally, Colonel Christopher Soglo, Chief of Staff of the Army, announced that the armed forces were taking over power in order to avert civil war. He told a crowd of 10,000 in Cotonou that the Government had been dismissed, the National Assembly had been dissolved and the 1960 Constitution had been suspended. His next move was to form a new provisional Government himself, in which Maga, Apithy and Ahomadegbé all became Ministers of State. Finally, he banned all meetings and demonstrations.

The new Government was never likely to have been a harmonious one, as one of its first actions made pretty plain: this was the setting-up of a committee which was charged with investigating the conduct in office of the members of the late Maga Cabinet, and such an inquiry could have only one object, to pave the way for their arraignment. The committee carried out check-ups in a number of ministries and in former ministers' homes, and armed gendarmes wearing steel helmets were posted in front of the latter. By the second half of November, the committee was ordering the arrest of the former Minister of National Economy on charges of dipping into public funds, the prosecution of the ex-Finance Minister and the blocking of the bank accounts and the temporary sequestration of the other property of all the one-time Maga ministers. Meantime, the provisional Government dissolved the single party which Maga had established three years before and announced the formation of a new national political movement, the Dahomeyan Democratic Party, or P.D.D., under the joint leadership of Maga and his two rivals. It also announced that a referendum would be held on 15 December on the new Constitution which was in process of being elaborated.

It was not till the turn of November and December, however, that the break between the new régime and the old became complete. Colonel Soglo made known the discovery of what he described as a plot to murder him and a number of his ministers, with the aim of restoring the former set-up, and he called on the people of Dahomey to regard themselves as mobilized against any counter-revolutionary movement. A day or two later, Maga was forced to resign and put under house-arrest in the provinces, as were four more of his former cabinet colleagues. All of them were accused, on the evidence of the committee of inquiry, of having misused public funds, and it was also alleged that Maga's supporters, if not he himself, had been the instigators of the plot against Soglo. It is difficult to resist the conclusion that the second charge, if not the whole story of the conspiracy, was a put-up job designed by Maga's enemies to ensure his final eviction from office, for when the National Assembly more than a year later voted for the former President's arraignment before a specially-created court, not a word was said about this accusation.

The trade unions had been the principal artisans of what had now become the complete overthrow of Maga. His disappearance from politics represented an outstanding victory for them, and they immediately set up 'vigilance committees' both to emphasize what they regarded as their position of authority and to defend their achievement against any possible reaction. It may be asked what lay behind their bitter feelings for the late President. The parlous position of the Dahomey budget provided a not unreasonable excuse for the ten per cent. hold-back on pay he had ordered. As for the workers' complaint that the minimum wage had not been increased since

1958, the rate payable to the most highly-skilled category of Dahomeyan labour was exceeded only in Senegal and the Ivory Coast, both of them much richer countries, in which the cost of living had risen far more rapidly than it had in Dahomey. The best justification for the unions' discontent lay in the prestige expenditure on which it had seen the Maga Government embarking at the same time as it had called for sacrifices from the wage-earners: the building of a costly presidential palace, for example, and long, expensive and not manifestly necessary trips abroad by the high-ups of the régime. What is more, the Maga ministers had given the impression of living on a luxurious scale. It is true that there were few if any African countries where similar grievances could not be raised, but the Dahomeyans were notorious for their difficult characters. If there is not enough money in the state coffers, the labour leaders had argued, the sacrifices necessary to cope with the situation should not be imposed on the workers alone, but should be shared by everyone, the Government included.

Victorious though they might have been in the deposition of Maga, the trade unions were by no means to have it all their own way in the sequel. Their first rebuff came from the sixty-man commission which had been preparing a new constitution, the referendum on which had been postponed till January 1964 as the result of the December crisis. The commission did indeed reject a federal-type draft put up by Chabi Mama, former Secretary-General of the now defunct P.D.U. and at the time minister in Soglo's provisional Government, which provided for a certain decentralization in favour of the northern population to which he belonged. It also, however, flatly turned down a classical parliamentary Constitution which had the whole-hearted backing of the unions and the young people. And the draft the commission finally did adopt was far too much of a presidential kind to please the labour leaders, who had insisted that their country's premier should be voted into office by the Assembly, which should also have the power to supervise his policy as a whole. The new Constitution, which secured an overwhelming majority at the January referendum, was, indeed, a rather unusual one for West Africa. Under it, the President and the Vice-President were both elected by universal suffrage, but while the President was Head of State and took the chair at Cabinet meetings, it was the Vice-President, who was also Premier, who decided on and carried out the national policy, chose the ministers, appointed officials, issued decrees and was responsible for the Army and the police. What is more, though the Assembly could criticize the Government's policy, it had no power at all to vote a Government down, while its legislative powers were confined, as were those of the Assembly in the 1958 French Constitution, to an enumerated list of subjects, everything outside which would be dealt with by decrees. The only points over which the unions did get satisfaction were a provision which implied the tolerance of more than one political party – the union leaders were resolutely opposed to the single-party system – and another which guaranteed freedom of speech, of the press and of trade union activities. The latter provision, however, is common form in African constitutions, and is almost nowhere observed.

Before the month was up, Apithy had been elected President of Dahomey and Ahomadegbé Vice-President, and the latter had chosen his ministers: these were almost all technicians and included a jurist, an agronomist, a public works engineer, a teacher and two doctors. For his Minister of Labour, Ahomadegbé had little choice. He had to pick someone who could say No to wage claims with some chance of a hearing, and the only man in that position was the Secretary-General of the General Union of Dahomeyan Workers. In his inaugural speech to the new Assembly, the number of whose deputies had been reduced, for economy reasons to forty-two, the new Premier put forward an ambitious programme, most of which, was still awaiting implementation a year later. The Government, he said, would put new life into agriculture, increase industrial crops and associate farming with cattle-breeding, and he promised such other novelties as the establishment of low-price 'pilot shops', the founding of co-operative villages for unemployed young people, a full-scale battle against illiteracy and the opening of a University of Dahomey, and added that an effort would be made to improve the ordinary man's living-conditions and to share out the national income more equitably. All this, of course, implied the same sort of austerity policy as had won Maga so much unpopularity, and by the end of January, Government spending was already going down. Even so, February went out with the new Finance Minister flying to Paris to ask France for a loan to cover the continuing budget deficit.

The Dahomeyan labour movement had certainly not expected a continuance of cheeseparing from the Government it had been largely responsible for installing in office. Its members were, indeed, still pressing both for the cessation of the ten per cent. deduction from their pay-packets and for an all-round wage-increase, over which they were not to get satisfaction for a long while yet. What is more, in February, bank employees came out on a forty-eight-hour strike in order to obtain the 'thirteenth month', a bonus of an extra month's pay a year, a privilege that even in developed countries is enjoyed by a minority of workers only. There was no wonder that a delegation of officials and university graduates which called on the Premier about the same time protested against the way in which certain trade unionists were keeping up 'an ill-considered social agitation'. As for Ahomadegbé, he made no bones about calling for an end to this sort of claim. The workers should know, he said, that every year Dahomey had to appeal to France to help balance her budget, sixty-four per cent. of which was spent on officials' pay. They might say Dahomey was independent, but independence on this sort of basis was no more than a word. Under the circumstances, the union leaders felt themselves to be in something of the position of the French settlers who had organized the 13 May 1958 insurrection in Algiers, only to find General de Gaulle going far farther in his concessions to the F.L.N. than the Government they had overturned would ever have dared to go. 'We made the October revolution in Porto Novo,' a union spokesman summed the situation up, 'and now the Government wants to stamp on us.'

March came in with the Government facing something a good deal more serious than a strike. Violence broke out in Parakou, the largest town in Northern Dahomey and the birthplace of Maga. A number of houses belonging to southern residents there were sacked or destroyed, while telephone lines were cut and rails removed from the railway to prevent troops from being sent in. Chabi Mama, Maga's right-hand man in the deceased single party, and later a minister in the Soglo provisional Government, was responsible for the outbreak. Ahomadegbé suggested in a broadcast that his motive was resentment that he had failed to be returned to the Assembly when he had stood at Parakou in the January elections. 'If he won only 20 votes against the 160 and the 120 of his two rivals, that was no fault of the Government party, though,' the Premier added, with a marked lack of ingenuity. When the Army did eventually reach Parakou, it opened fire on the rebels and a number were killed, but the fighting did not go on for long. Mama and nearly 200 of his supporters were arrested and flown down south, and it was announced once more that Maga and all his former ministers were to be put on trial, this time for malversation only. It is true that a young examining magistrate put a spoke in the wheel of these proceedings by finding that there was no case against Maga, but he was promptly relieved of his post.

When the first anniversary of Dahomey's October revolution came round, it was a little difficult to see just what the revolutionaries had gained. They had, it is true, granted the local press a freedom that is rare in Africa, though one paper which was accused of abusing the Government found itself suppressed. There had been no improvement in the chronic economic stagnation, however; things had got even worse. More Dahomeyans expelled from neighbouring African countries had streamed home to swell the mass of workless, and the French troops who had been stationed in the north of the country, and who had provided a considerable amount of employment and of income, had been evacuated under a plan for regrouping France's armed forces. Ahomadegbé had visited Paris, where he had seen everyone from de Gaulle down, and had pleaded that the discontent that had led to the revolution was now over, that there was no more ill feeling between the north and south of the country and that he and his Cabinet had taken a series of austerity measures which should assuredly pave the way to an economic revival: they had cut the number of ministers from seventeen to nine; they had automatically pensioned off all civil servants with more than thirty years of service or more than fifty-five years old; National Assembly deputies' pay had been cut by half, and the number of Dahomeyan Embassies abroad had been reduced to six. All the same, he obviously felt no sort of certainty that he would get the increased French aid he asked for: he left Paris not to return home, but on a hat-in-hand tour of other European capitals. And though responsible foreign observers agreed that Dahomey was on the verge of bankruptcy, with more than 10,000 unemployed in Cotonou, Ahomadegbé ended up by agreeing to a twelve per cent. increase in the minimum wage.

Naturally that did not satisfy labour. A few days after he had made his wage concession, the Premier was deporting two union leaders to the north of the country on a charge of 'subversive activities'. The young people were no more satisfied. Their August congress vigorously condemned Ahomadegbé and made it pretty plain that what they wanted out of him was a faithful imitation of the extreme Left-Wing policy which the successors of Fulbert Youlou in the Congo (Brazzaville) were by this time following. The congress did not only call on the Government to fight for the achievement of what they called a real African unity. They summoned it to enter into diplomatic relations with Cuba, Communist China and East Germany, and to back what they described as 'the Vietnamese people's struggle for freedom'. Though the radio and the official news agency criticized these demands as being violent and excessive, the students had their way over one thing. The end of December 1964 saw a Communist Chinese chargé d'affaires arriving in Dahomey to open up an embassy there.

Things were made no easier by the fact that Apithy as President and Ahomadegbé as Vice-President and Premier appeared to be at constant loggerheads. This was no matter of mere gossip: a figure as responsible as the General-Secretary of the Government party admitted the gravity of the differences between the two at a party conference, and indeed said that they could well lead to a split in the party ranks. The veterans of the Dahomeyan nationalist movement, fifty-odd strong, all the same tried to bring about a reconciliation between the two leaders, and between 'the intransigent young people who formed Ahomadegbé's friends, and who wanted wider and wider responsibilities, and the old stagers of politics, whose chief was President Apithy'. The means they picked on for their mediation was a 'council of wise men' consisting of eighteen of their number and presided over by Paul Hazoumé, a former member of the Council of the French Union. Hazoumé, speaking at the first congress of the Association of Veterans, put his finger on the two principal problems that were worrying them. First, he said, after a ritual denunciation of the abuses of the Maga régime, the 1963 revolution had not yielded all the fruits that had been expected of it. Second, he regretted the way in which young people were turning down the jobs for which they had been trained in the hope of getting more highly paid political or administrative posts – a complaint that could be made in many if not most of the newly-independent African countries.

The feelings between the two leaders were not made any warmer by the fact that Ahomadegbé must have increasingly come to realize that he had accepted rather a raw deal over the allocation of responsibilities under the new Constitution. Apithy, as President, was not responsible for the day-to-day conduct of affairs; as Premier, Ahomadegbé was. He had made a highly optimistic programme speech on his accession to office, but neither he nor his friends had apparently given much thought to the finance they would require to carry it out. In the months that had followed his impressive promises, he had been able to translate few of them into facts. By June 1965, he was being forced to call on the National Assembly for further measures of austerity, including tax-increases and cuts in the pay of officials, and to present the deputies with what can only be called a catastrophic balance-sheet. 'We are facing bankruptcy at any moment,' Ahomadegbé said. 'In plain language, we may at any moment find it impossible to settle officials' pay-cheques.' It is true that Apithy also had issued similar warnings: 'We've far more civil servants than we can afford,' he had said. Apithy, however, could not be blamed for carrying out the policy which his statements appeared to warrant; Ahomadegbé could be and was.

The differences between the two men would not have mattered so much if the Government party, the P.D.D., had been able to consolidate itself and become a firmly-based political organization on the Western pattern. Many British Conservatives strongly disapproved of the then Lord Home's succession to Mr Macmillan as party leader and Prime Minister, but that did not split the party in two. African parties which enjoy the stability of British Conservatism are, however, difficult to find. Within an organization of a less stable character, the divergencies between the President and the Premier of Dahomey could easily result in one of them seeking to eliminate the other, with a new *coup* a quite possible outcome.

As 1965 opened, there was a new complication in the Dahomeyan political scene: the foundation of an opposition party, the Rally of National Interests, or R.I.N. The new party had been established in the constituency of Valentin Djirode Aplogan, President of the Dahomey Supreme Court and former Speaker of the National Assembly, and when the executive of the Government party next met, it examined a charge against Aplogan of having given moral and material support to the founders of the R.I.N. and forbade him to engage in any political activity till further notice. Since, however, the new Dahomeyan Constitution does not specifically forbid the formation of opposition parties, Aplogan remained temporarily President of the Supreme Court. He was arrested and removed from his position only when he was suspected of complicity with the self-styled 'Committee of 104', an underground opposition to the new régime, and charged with plotting against the State. All in all, the political situation in Dahomey, eighteen months after the disappearance of Maga, seemed far less settled than it had been before his eviction from power.

7

Malawi

AT MIDNIGHT ON the night of 5/6 July 1964, the State of Malawi, formerly the British protectorate of Nyasaland, formally achieved independence. With the Duke of Edinburgh standing beside him, the new head of State, sixty-two-year-old Dr Hastings Kamuzu Banda, looked on while the Union Jack was lowered for the last time and the Malawi flag hoisted for the first. After the new flag had been raised, there was a display of fireworks which illuminated a huge portrait of Banda and the ceremony concluded with a song of praise, 'Everything belongs to Kamuzu Banda,' led by Dr Kanyama Chiume, the Minister in charge of the celebrations. At a civic lunch on 7 July, after the instruments of Government had been handed over, the Duke said he hoped tolerance, stability and good government would bring Malawi the investments it needed, though this was insignificant when compared with the achievement of independence. 'Poverty is preferable to tyranny,' the royal visitor said. Incidentally, Portuguese wines were served to the guests at the lunch and a Portuguese pavilion was a feature of the impressive independence trade fair: the Malawi festivities were the first African freedom celebrations the Portuguese had ever been invited to attend.

Exactly two months later, at the beginning of the second week in September, three ministers of the first Cabinet of independent Malawi were dismissed and another three resigned. Back in August the thirty-two-year-old Scot who had been the only European member of the nine-man Government had also handed in his resignation. A spokesman for the dismissed and resigning ministers said that the trouble had followed some weeks of disagreement in the Cabinet between Dr Banda and themselves. He added that the points of friction between the two sides had included the salaries of African civil servants, which the Premier had decided to peg, the signing of a trade agreement with Portugal, and the appointment of an honorary Malawi consul in Portuguese-owned

L   161

Mozambique. Portugal's treatment of her colonies on the continent is an understandable theme of indignation among the leaders of African states, but Banda had a not unreasonable excuse for his action: the Portuguese control Malawi's sole outlet to the sea. The spokesman for the ministers finally agreed that Banda's decision to introduce a preventive detention law had something to do with the crisis. It was known to have lain behind the resignation of the European member of the Cabinet.

The day after the split in the Government had come out into the open, Banda appeared before Parliament and presented his own version of what had happened. Even by the standards of Africa's not always mature Parliaments, it was a somewhat curious story. 'The Ministers wanted to get rid of me,' he said. 'If they could have murdered me and got away with it, they would have murdered me in cold blood. If they could have forced me to resign and got away with it, they would have done that – but they knew the people wanted me.' It says something for the hold Banda had got over his people, and for the vanity of his accusations against his former collaborators, that when it came to the final vote, the motion of confidence went through unanimously. The ministers who had been dismissed or had resigned did not merely abstain in the division: they urged other members to vote for the Government.

The strangest thing about the whole story is that two at least of the outgoing members of the Cabinet had back in the 'fifties been responsible for Banda's return to his home country, from which he had been absent for more than forty years. They had done so because the then leadership of the local nationalist party was, in their opinion, unsatisfactory: it had no outstanding personality, and they felt themselves too young to fill the vacuum. Banda, who was then practising as a doctor in London, had made himself known among the intellectuals in the nationalist movement of what was then Nyasaland by his opposition to the proposal to set up a federation of his country with Northern and Southern Rhodesia which became a fact in 1953. The federation had been unanimously condemned by all politically conscious Africans in the three territories concerned. The men who had summoned Banda back had warned him that it would be necessary by propaganda to build him up as an outstanding personality, and this they had conscientiously done after his return home in July 1958. In the Nyasaland Legislative Council in December 1958, Masauko Chipembere, who had played a leading part in securing Banda's return, had referred to him as 'our Mahatma', 'our Messiah' and 'our Saviour'. Chipembere was one of the ministers who had resigned in August 1964 and, less than two months later, he was put under house arrest in his home village. When he disappeared from there, Banda called for his recovery 'alive if possible, but if not, in any other way'. Banda had in fact treated the men who had invited him back to assume their leadership in exactly the same way as Nkrumah had treated Dr Danquah, who had called him back to Ghana for much the same reason. The process had gone through a little faster in Malawi; that was the main difference. It was not till more than a year after Ghana became independent that the first Preventive Detention Act became law; another three years were to pass before Nkrumah got rid of the ministers who had been his principal lieutenants in the fight for national freedom. In Malawi, something that could not unfairly be called a police state had been established within less than six months after independence.

Malawi has an area of just over 46,000 square miles, about the size of Scotland, though nearer a quarter than a fifth of its territory consists of the waters of Lake Nyasa. Its population is more than 3,000,000. The resources of the country, which has no access to the sea, are almost entirely agricultural and are not capable, as they are worked at the moment, of providing its population either with sufficient work or with any reasonable standard of living. Only 10,000 square miles of its territory, mainly in the south, are regarded as suitable for production on a commercial scale. The great majority of the people are therefore engaged in subsistence farming, and the main Government drive, in 1964, was to convert this into cash farming along co-operative lines. Of the export crops, tea, tobacco, cotton and ground-nuts, which have been bringing in about £11,000,000 a year between them, are the most important, while rice, tungoil, coffee and maize production are being expanded. The most important manufacturing industries in the past have been the handling of tea and tobacco, though in 1964, new light industries were springing up, and a £4,000,000 sugar scheme was under way.

Because of the lack of opportunities at home, a high proportion of Malawi's able-bodied men have been emigrating in search of work. Not more than 130,000 of them are in wage-earning employment within the country, as against around 160,000 employed outside, mostly in Southern Rhodesia, but some in Northern Rhodesia and South Africa. This circumstance explains the Banda Government's desire to maintain friendly relations with Southern Rhodesia. If by any chance the thousands of men working there were to be forced back, it would greatly aggravate the internal employment problem, as happened in Dahomey as a result of such a mass repatriation, and also deprive Malawi of the £2,000,000 a year they send home in family remittances.

Well over eighty per cent. of Malawi's people are still illiterate, but among those who have been able to attend school, the educational level is high. Natives of Malawi are to be found teaching in schools all over Central Africa, while Kenneth Kaunda, President of Northern Rhodesia, comes from there, as do two of the ministers of President Julius Nyerere, in neighbouring Tanzania. Malawi is one of the very few countries in sub-Saharan Africa which are not plagued by recurrent inter-tribal disputes. It is also unique among the states of the British Commonwealth in that the British Government is helping it to meet not only its development planning costs but also its regular budgetary expenditure after independence: eight shillings in every pound spent by the Malawi authorities come direct from Britain.

Malawi, which means 'flames' in the chief vernacular language of the country, was the name of a fourteenth-century empire which covered Nyasaland and parts of Northern and Southern Rhodesia, and stretched as far north as Mombasa in Kenya. By the end of the eighteenth century, the Malawi empire had split up into four fragments, and the process of disintegration had gone even further when Livingstone visited what was later to become Nyasaland as an explorer in 1859. He found no kingdom, but a medley of small tribes which were constantly fighting and preying upon each other. Their hostilities were not the result of any inborn antagonism; they were the fruit of the slave trade. The Arabs who ran this trade had started by supplying Asian rulers and only later turned their attention to the American market, and they bought their wares with cloth, beads and guns. The guns stimulated the trading and also made for inter-tribal warfare. Tribes without guns became victims of the slave-traders, and chiefs would therefore sell their subjects to obtain guns and then use the weapons to capture human merchandise from their neighbours. The trade was on a pretty large scale: Livingstone quotes the British Political Agent and Consul in Zanzibar as telling him that 19,000 slaves from the Nyasa country alone passed annually through the customs house of the island.

British missionaries had arrived in the country by the middle of the nineteenth century, and clashes between them and the Arab slave-traders – which for a while forced them to withdraw to Zanzibar – brought the first British consuls there in 1883. It was not, however, till six years later that the British Government sent Mr, later Sir, Harry Johnston out to Nyasaland to negotiate treaties with the local chiefs. Finally, after agreements had been signed with the Germans and the Portuguese, Nyasaland was proclaimed a British protectorate in 1891. Johnston was put in charge, as Commissioner and Consul-General responsible to the Foreign Office. With the aid of gunboats and Indian troops he suppressed slave-trading and put an end to such tribal conflicts as had survived the days of the trade, and before the end of the century the process of pacification had been completed.

European settlers came in, and though they never approached the numbers of those in the two Rhodesias, they made a vital contribution to the economy of the country in its early days. By 1907 they were sitting on the newly-created Legislative Council, to which the first Africans were not appointed till more than forty years later. By 1923, they were producing four-fifths of the exported tobacco, all the tea and more than half the cotton, on a value basis: the Africans' backwardness in production has been ascribed, among other things, to the debilitating effects of tropical diseases, to ignorance and to poverty, which prevented them from spotting and seizing economic opportunities. Even before that date, Nyasaland had experienced its first outbreak of nationalism, which took the form of an anti-white insurrection. This originated with one of the African Messianic movements which sprang up over a great part of the continent in the early part of the twentieth century, as a spontaneous form of resistance to alien authority, both temporal and spiritual. The leader of the rising was John Chilembwe, who had been educated in the United States and who on his return had founded an anti-European sect, the Providence Industrial Mission, in which he had preached independence for Africans. Other separatist Churches saw the light, and the agitation came to a head in 1915, when Chilembwe led an open revolt in which three Europeans were killed. One of them was a descendant of Dr Livingstone, and Chilembwe delivered a sermon with this Livingstone's head stuck on a pole near the pulpit.

It was not until the 1940s, however, that nationalism began to assume real importance in Nyasaland, and the stimulus responsible was the resuscitation of the proposal for a federation of Nyasaland with Northern and Southern Rhodesia. Nyasaland might easily have come under Cecil Rhodes's British South African Company, like the two Rhodesias, fifty years before, and some sort of administrative union between the three countries seemed plain common sense. It would have permitted considerable economies in Governmental expenditure and made for greater efficiency. None of the three countries had an individual population much exceeding 3,000,000, and Nkrumah has expressed his opinion – it is one of his arguments for continental unity – that an African country must have many more inhabitants than this if it is to be viable. Together, the three territories would have a population of around 9,000,000. What is more, Nyasaland stood to gain far more than the two other partners from a federation. As a separate state, she did indeed pay her way, in the sense that her budget could just about be balanced; but her economy was a rudimentary one and could not support more than an austere administration. With federation, all that would change. Expenditure on such services as health and education could be pushed up far beyond the possibilities of Nyasaland herself, for the finance for the balance would be provided by the Federal Government from resources in the other two countries.

There was much talk of a federation of the three territories in the 1920s and 1930s, and a number of commissions were appointed to go into the question. It was not till the turn of the 1940s and 1950s, however, that it began to appear a serious issue, and the effect inside Nyasaland was immediate. The Nyasaland National Congress, which had been established in 1944, set up a Supreme Council to direct its anti-federation campaign, and the membership of Congress grew by many thousands. Chiefs, villagers and the emerging middle class were united in their opposition to the plan. Some of the reasons that inspired them came out at a conference called at Victoria Falls, at which the Nyasaland African delegates firmly opposed any closer association with the other two territories, particularly with Southern Rhodesia: Nyasalanders had emigrated there, they admitted, because the wages were high and there were not enough jobs at home, but apart from these considerations, it was not the sort of place that any African could conceivably choose to live in. Some of the reasons were explained in a pamphlet which was brought out jointly by two Africans, one a Nyasalander and the other a Northern Rhodesian. Federation, the authors argued, would not be in the interests of the Africans of Northern Rhodesia and Nyasaland for four reasons. First, it would deprive them of direct political and cultural ties with Britain. Second, it would replace British tutelage by Southern Rhodesian domination, for since Southern Rhodesia had by far the largest European population of the three countries, the proposed Federation's native policy would largely be determined by the settlers there. Third, it would extend to Nyasaland and Northern Rhodesia the policy of segregation and discrimination – the pass laws were an obvious example – from which the Africans of Southern Rhodesia were already suffering. Finally, it would enable the settlers of Southern Rhodesia to claim Dominion status for the Federation, and this would give them the same sort of authority over the Africans of Central Africa as the whites of South Africa had over the African population there.

The Nyasaland co-author of the pamphlet was Dr Banda. Banda is a teetotal, non-smoking bachelor of extremely simple tastes, and he owes his success entirely to his own capabilities and efforts. Born in 1902 of a poor family, he started as a pupil at a Nyasaland mission school, hiked to South Africa in 1915 – the year of the Chilembwe rebellion – to obtain further education and then earned enough money by working as a clerk in a gold-mining company to pay his fare to the United States, where he continued his studies. Banda obtained a degree in history and political science at the University of Chicago, and then took up medicine, was awarded a medical degree and went on to complete his medical training at Edinburgh, where he became an elder of the Church of Scotland (it should be said that Scottish missionaries are very influential in Nyasaland). At the end of 1937, he went to Liverpool and started to practise there, later transferring first to Tynemouth and then to London, where he worked as a doctor from 1945 to 1953. He never lost interest in Nyasaland affairs, however, and his few countrymen in London looked up to him as a leader in their political discussions.

In August 1953, the year when Federation came into effect, Banda left London for Ghana, where he continued his medical practice. He said he wanted to give the new set-up a chance: if he had stayed on in London he would have been in honour bound to continue his open opposition to it. A far more likely reason for his departure was that he was involved as co-respondent in what turned out to be a successful divorce case. By 1956, he was satisfied that Federation had won no substantial support from African opinion in Nyasaland, and he began to pay more attention to the letters which had begun to reach him from there urging him to return home and take a lead in the struggle against it. Far the most insistent of these letters came from Masauko Chipembere who, though only in his early thirties, was already one of the Nyasaland National Congress leaders. What Nyasaland needed if it was to win its freedom, he wrote, was a kind of saviour. It might, indeed, be wrong to be led by a single man placed in a powerful position, yet human nature was such that it needed a hero to be hero-worshipped if a political struggle was to succeed. Under African conditions, that hero could not be a young man, either. What was needed was a figure about fifty or sixty years old, an intellectual with a character combining nationalism with honesty, self-denial and a spirit of co-operativeness. Chipembere did not attempt to conceal the fact that Banda's reputation would have to be built up if he was successfully to fill the role allotted to him. At the moment he was little more than a name to most of his compatriots, a highly educated doctor of Nyasaland birth who had practised in London. Educated people might have heard something about his political feelings and abilities, but little was known about him among the masses. Banda must not therefore be frightened, Chipembere wrote, if, in the event of his return, he was built up as a political Messiah. Publicity of this sort would cause great excitement and should precipitate a revolution in political thought in Nyasaland. Nkrumah had been invited back to Ghana to organize the nationalist party, not to head it. Chipembere and his party colleagues Kanyama Chiume and Orton Chirwa were deliberately asking Banda to return home to assume not the position with which Nkrumah had started off in Accra, but that which he had won for himself by nearly four years of mob oratory and political manoeuvring at the service of his limitless ambition. The time was coming when they were to realize that they had created a political Frankenstein's monster.

Banda arrived home on 6 July 1958. A British journalist who was with him on the plane records him as saying: 'I have no illusions about the difficulties ahead. I may not see the end of it in my lifetime.' His first words after he had stepped out on the airfield were: 'I'm not anti-white or anti-European. I come to bridge the gulf between the races.' It is true that when he asked members of the British administration to lunch, they did not even reply to his invitation, though he does not appear to have held it against them. In the eyes of his fellow-Africans, however, he had quite a number of strong points. He was old enough by 1958 to merit the special respect which is shown in tribal societies to those of mature age, yet he was still exceedingly active. The title of doctor which he bore could be trusted to win him special respect in Nyasaland – far more than would those of Lord or General – on account of the revered figures, such as Livingstone, who had borne it in the past. Like Chilembwe, chief among the dead heroes of local nationalism, he had completed his education in the United States. Finally, the fact that he had been forty years out of his country was more of an asset than a liability to him. He had been prominent in the opposition to federation in England, but he had not been involved in any local political rivalries and he had never, as an adult, been subject to the authority of colonial government. There were other examples to show that the way to the top in Nyasaland was quick for those who had lived abroad. Within six months of his return from Uganda, Chiume had become a member of the Nyasaland Legislative Council. Within one month of his return from England, Banda was President of the Nyasaland African Congress.

Congress held its annual general meeting on 1 August, and Banda was elected President on his own terms. These were the adoption of a new party constitution which gave him sole power to appoint the other officers of Congress and the members of its executive committee. Other African leaders may in fact possess this authority, but few if any have got it set down on paper. The choices Banda made could be viewed as a victory for the Left Wing in the party, which had been responsible for bringing him back. Two of the principal offices went to Chipembere and Chiume, while Y. K. Chisiza, one of two brilliant brothers, was summoned back from England, where he had been at a university, to become Secretary-General. Banda did not dispute the criticism that in selecting his colleagues he had ignored the older, more experienced and more moderate leaders and had taken on the younger, more volatile and extreme people. He explained that while he might find it necessary from time to time to curb the excesses of youth, he was in general sympathy with the feelings of the young, and preferred them as colleagues to the older people, whom he regarded as failures. It is, of course, also possible that he had asked himself whether the older generation would be prepared to truckle to him, as the young for some years did.

Banda had thus become, within four weeks, the undisputed leader of Congress. He had naturally started touring the country, and he was already regarded as the greatest of Nyasaland's sons, whose gifts made him the equal of any European. His colleagues had fulfilled their promise and started creating around him a legendary atmosphere which raised him, in the eyes of Africans, above any ordinary leader. Indeed, he had come to be looked on as the one man who could deliver Nyasaland from alien domination. Huge crowds flocked to all his meetings and displayed enormous enthusiasm, and this was the more surprising since, alone among African nationalist leaders, he could speak hardly a word of the main language of his country (Ben Bella was not too fluent in Arabic when he returned to Algeria, but at least he could make himself understood). Banda spoke nothing but English, and every word he said had to be interpreted, but that did not seem to diminish the impact of his oratory. He had considerable histrionic talents, and these went over; in Tunisia, President Bourguiba's gifts as an orator are such that foreign journalists who do not understand a word of Arabic can listen to him speaking in that language for an hour and a half on end and never feel bored. As Banda wrote to a friend, he found himself gifted with an unexpected gift for mob oratory, and he obviously enjoyed the sensation of power over a crowd. It was not only rhetoric that he contributed to the nationalist cause, either. He gave the Nyasaland African Congress a united leadership after a period of squabbles, and he brought with him some new ideas which enlarged the appeal of the movement, such as the formation of a women's league and a youth league.

For all that, after his first three or four months of speech-making were over, Banda started to take it easy. At the beginning of November, he settled down to establish a medical practice, and his surgery kept him pretty busy; after November, he found time for speech-making at weekends only. The detailed work of party organization he seemed content to leave to his lieutenants, and he rarely if ever presided at party meetings, even those of the so-called 'Congress cabinet', possibly because he could speak nothing but English. No doubt he thought his subordinates would refer to him everything that mattered, says a contemporary English commentary, and to all appearances they did so. But in fact his three principal assistants were men with minds and ambitions of their own. They probably saw no necessity to tell Banda everything that was going on and consulted him only when they had some reason to invoke his authority, while before they did so, they are likely to have made sure that the decision would be the one they wanted, not such a difficult operation since Banda was amenable to flattery. This sort of formula could work while Banda was treating his political work as a part-time activity; once he had decided to devote his whole time to politics, the authoritarian character he had rapidly developed made it impossible.

When he first landed back in Nyasaland, Banda had emphasized that he was in no sense anti-European. He had changed his tune a lot when he returned from a meeting in Accra six months later. Civil disobedience and passive resistance were going to be Congress policy from then on, he said. 'We mean to be masters in Nyasaland, and if that is treasonable, make the most of it,' he declared. The report of a British commission of inquiry a few months later suggested that the adulation with which Banda had been surrounded since his original homecoming had turned his head. In fairness to him, it should be recorded that he had received less than no encouragement from British officials to pursue the policy of bridging the gulf between the two races. Even in 1959, the claims he advanced for his country could hardly be called extreme. He was not asking for immediate independence for Nyasaland: his minimum demands were an African majority on the Legislative Council and parity of Africans with Europeans on the Executive Council, and Ghana had been granted a great deal more than that five years before. The trouble was that the British were not prepared to grant even the limited sort of constitutional concessions Banda wanted, because these would have enabled him to disrupt the Federation, the maintenance of which was still the policy of the Government in London. So, as 1959 opened, disorders began to break out in Nyasaland. Illegal meetings were held, a prison was broken into and European homes were threatened and attacked. Banda said in a speech that moderate leaders were no good now. Chisiza, the new Congress Secretary-General, said that they were out to make trouble about their programme. Negotiations would not do, and they intended to create disturbances up and down Nyasaland, even if this meant that every man and woman in the country died. Faced with this sort of agitation, the authorities felt they had no choice. Congress was outlawed at midnight on 2 March, and the hours that followed saw the mounting of 'Operation Sunrise', in which security forces were given the task of arresting all the influential nationalist leaders in the country, to the number of 208. African reaction surprised the Government by its violence: angry crowds set on the security forces and more than fifty people were killed. Almost immediately a commission of inquiry came out from England and, among other things, reported most unfavourably on the methods the authorities had employed.

It was not long before the Government began to release the detainees, and when Orton Chirwa came out in August 1959, he got permission to form a new political organization, which was christened the Malawi Congress Party. The party's immediate objective was to get all the prisoners freed, and it was made plain that as soon as Banda was released, he could be invited to take over the leadership. Banda was liberated in April 1960, during the visit of Colonial Secretary Iain Macleod, and he made an immediate radio appeal for calm and duly replaced Chirwa as leader of the new party. Four months later, complete agreement on a new Constitution for Nyasaland was reached at a conference in London. The provisions of the document gave Banda almost everything he had asked for. Under it the Legislative Council was to consist of twenty-eight unofficial members, twenty elected on a lower, or African roll, and eight on a higher roll, and five official members; the advisory Executive Council was to be composed of eight members, five official and five unofficial, at least three of whom would be Africans and all of whom would enjoy ministerial status. It was originally stated that the new Constitution would not come into effect till after the conference which had been called in London the following December to review the future of the Federation of which Nyasaland was such a reluctant member, but when this was adjourned after the African nationalist leaders had walked out, the condition was dropped. This Constitution became effective on 4 July 1961, three years almost to a day after Banda's homecoming. The first elections under it took place on 15 August, and they resulted in a complete victory for the Malawi Congress Party. Its candidates won all the seats on the lower roll and two on the upper roll, while one independent candidate was returned with M.C.P. support. One circumstance about the election campaign could have been regarded as a pointer to the authoritarian line Banda was soon to be taking. A number of candidates were put up by the Catholic-inspired Christian Liberation Party. The M.C.P. organ accused the Church of

'Vatican imperialism' in tolerating its foundation, and the house of its leader was burned down.

After the elections, the Governor chose four M.C.P. leaders and the independent elected with M.C.P. support to fill the five unofficial places on the Executive Council. Banda chose the portfolio of Land and Natural Resources, much the same choice as Fulbert Youlou had made in the Congo (Brazzaville) four years earlier. Banda's first major reform was to sweep away the existing Land Husbandry Ordinance. Before a year had passed, peasant crops had increased by one-third, without any significant increase in capital investment.

Banda's chief aim, however, was to free Nyasaland from what he regarded as the yoke of the Federation with the two Rhodesias, and in little more than a year he had achieved it. Following a second Nyasaland Constitutional conference in London at the end of 1962, the British Government made two decisions: it granted Nyasaland the right of cabinet government under a prime minister, with the Legislative Council becoming the Legislative Assembly and the Governor's right to nominate to it being withdrawn; and the Government announced that it had agreed in principle to Nyasaland's leaving the Federation. As the summer of 1963 went out, it was officially stated that the country would accede to independence on 6 July 1964, the sixth anniversary of Banda's return to his homeland.

There were, indeed, already a number of small signs which suggested that independence in Nyasaland might not be synonymous with freedom and security. Some of this evidence might be discounted on account of the partiality of its source: thus in the summer of 1963, the Minister of Law of the now doomed Federation alleged that Europeans and Asians had been beaten up by supporters of the Malawi Congress Party, and in particular by the private party police, and expressed his fear that this pointed to the erosion of the rule of law as a result of Banda's attitude. A one-party system on the Ghana model was already being set up, the Minister said. Some of the pointers to the way things were going were matters of simple fact. Not long after the Federal Minister had spoken, the Malawi Legislative Assembly passed a law debarring accused persons from being legally represented in local courts without the permission of the Minister of Justice. Banda explained that if law were allowed to be administered in these courts according to European ideas, 'justice would not seem to be done' in the eyes of his people. A little later the Assembly adopted a measure requiring motorists and cyclists to pull in to the side of the road and stop when Banda's police-escorted convoy approached, under pain of fines and possible imprisonment. Members were told that this was necessary to show respect for the Prime Minister and to safeguard his life, and the Scot who was then Transport Minister explained that two leading M.C.P. members had recently been killed in car crashes. What is more, Banda never from the beginning attempted to conceal his desire for an authoritarian form of rule. 'My only means of building the nation successfully is by imposing and insisting on strict discipline, and if that is dictatorship, I am quite prepared to accept the title of Dictator of Malawi,' he said on one occasion, and he complacently accepted the title of *Ngwazi*, or Chief of Chiefs, which the population had begun to use of him. 'I decide everything without consulting anyone, and that's how things are going to be in Malawi,' he told a mass meeting six weeks before independence. Banda tended to fly into a rage when things irritated him: he would brook no contradiction or criticism, and he once described the press as 'a pack of liars'. All this made things a little difficult, to say the least of it, for members of his Cabinet. He had been known to hit Foreign Minister Chiume over the head with a fly-whisk at a public meeting to shut him up, and at the moment of independence, he said of his new Finance Minister – the first non-European ever to occupy the post – 'He is learning very well, and so too are all of my boys in this House.' Banda was in fact treating his collaborators as if he were a schoolmaster and they pupils in his sixth form. Nevertheless, on the eve of independence, Banda's three main ministerial lieutenants, who had been understood to have had their occasional differences with him, said publicly that they had 'laid down their stones': they used the phrase because lapidation was locally the most popular way of showing violent dissent.

Thus at midsummer 1964 there was no outward sign to indicate that Malawi was on the eve of a major political crisis. No opposition voice had been heard from a public platform since the 1961 electoral campaign, and even then, the fact that the Malawi Congress Party secured ninety-five per cent. of the votes at the polls suggested that such critics as there were had not got a very wide hearing. At the May 1964 elections, nobody at all came forward to challenge the official candidates, every one of whom had been personally selected by Banda, and though not far short of two million electors had a little earlier registered their names in less than three weeks, a triumph for single-party organization, the M.C.P. team was declared to be returned unopposed without the formality of a vote. The trade unions and the youth league were firmly under control, a position which is not achieved in most African countries till some time after their independence, and the press was notably discreet. The only person who even hinted in public that trouble might lie ahead was the Duke of Edinburgh in his speech at the Independence Day lunch.

The composition of independent Malawi's first Government was announced on 7 July, when it was seen that Banda had added three more to the number of portfolios he already held. Then, a month later, came the first sign that anything was wrong. Colin Cameron, the Scot who had recently acceded to the Ministry of Works, resigned; he said he had no option but to leave the Cabinet when a proposal came up there of which he could not approve, but he refused at the moment to give any other explanation. Now Cameron's departure was very significant. He was not only a man of intelligence, he was a man with a conscience: he and his wife had cheerfully put up with two years of ostracism from the European community on account of their support of the nationalist cause. Moreover, though he had previously been elected to the Legislative Council on the special roll, he refused to accept nomination in this way in the elections which preceded independence, and in order to have him in his Cabinet, Banda had been forced to insist on the right to appoint not more than three ministers from outside what had now become the Assembly. Less than a fortnight later, the reason for Cameron's resignation became evident. It was stated that when the first working session of the Assembly opened in September, three amendments to the Malawi Constitution would be presented to it, and that one of these would provide for the issue of detention orders 'in the interests of defence, public safety or public order'. Cameron commented later: 'I was against preventive detention under the colonial régime, and I'm against it now.'

On 7 September the crisis came out into the open. An announcement that three members of the nine-man Cabinet had been dismissed was followed a quarter of an hour later by the resignation of three others. The Government House statement added that the only woman in the Malawi Parliament, Mrs Rose Chibambo, had also been removed from her post as Parliamentary Secretary to the Ministry of Natural Resources. Mrs Chibambo was a member of the Malawi Congress Party national executive and National Chairman of the League of Malawi Women. The ministers who were on the way out could none of them be described as second-line figures. The three who had been dismissed included Minister of Justice Chirwa, who had founded the Malawi Congress Party and presided over it till Banda was released from detention, and who was now its legal adviser, and Foreign Minister Chiume, another member of the party executive, who had been one of those responsible for inviting Banda to return to Nyasaland. Those who had offered their resignations included Yatuta Chisiza, whom Banda had ordered back from his studies in England six years before to take over the running of the party. One of the less important of the resigning ministers did, it is true, withdraw his resignation within a matter of hours, but that made less than no difference. In the short interval before the matter came before the Assembly, Education Minister Chipembere had returned from a visit to Canada and by taking a seat on a back bench when he entered the House, amid applause from the public galleries, signified that he too had left the Government.

Some of the issues over which Banda and his colleagues were in conflict were comparatively simple. The six departing ministers objected to his plan to transfer the capital up-country from Zomba to Lilongwe. It was true that Zomba's mountainous site was something of a disadvantage to it, but the move would cost several millions of, as they thought, unnecessary pounds. They viewed with disfavour his friendly attitude to the Portuguese: a trade treaty with them had already been signed and stories were circulating of negotiations with Portugal for the cession or lease to Malawi of a strip of land running through Mozambique territory to the sea, with a port at the end of it. They did not much like the trade agreement he had concluded with Southern Rhodesia. But the action of Banda's which aroused perhaps the strongest resentment, among both the ministers and the informed and interested public, was the Prime Minister's decision to put into effect part of the recommendations of the Skinner Committee, which a year earlier had suggested means of making Nyasaland viable after its secession from the Central African Federation. The committee had recommended, among other things, the imposition of a threepenny health charge in hospitals, a pay standstill for all but the lower ranks of the civil service, and the introduction of compulsory savings through the establishment of a contributory pensions and development fund. These recommendations had all been adopted, and the first the civil servants had heard of the implementation of the last item was a brief official circular, in independence week, of all times, notifying them that 7·5 per cent. of their pay was to be docked from then on for the purpose. The Skinner Committee had also, however, urged that its report should be published immediately, and that the Government should launch an intensive propaganda campaign to explain to the ordinary man what was being done, and why, while they had also said that it was essential promptly to offer Malawians the chance of serving in senior official posts and to appoint them as supernumeraries to understudy British civil servants. Banda had done nothing whatever to carry out these last proposals.

It was not, however, Banda who had turned tough on the morrow of independence; it was his ministers who had done so. The Prime Minister made a number of at the least questionable assertions when he appeared before the Assembly to ask for a vote of confidence, but one thing he said was incontestable: all the proposals over which his ministers were now seeking issue with him had been brought up by him at Cabinet meetings and in speeches before independence, and they had raised no objections. Two reasons for their sudden *volte-face* have been suggested. First, they may well have thought that if they had turned on Banda before independence, the British Government, with its residual powers, might have taken his side. Second, they quite possibly imagined that after all the years of adulation Banda had received, he would never have the courage to reveal to the public the gap that had opened between him and his closest collaborators.

The second point was implicit in the speech with which the Prime Minister opened the debate before the National Assembly on 8 September. He said that the dismissed ministers had attacked him 'viciously and violently' in a Cabinet meeting on 26 August, but that when he had offered his resignation, they had refused to accept it. The real reason for their opposition, he alleged, was that 'they wanted to introduce bribery and corruption into ministerial posts, as had happened in other African countries'. This almost neurotic concern, which was constantly coming up in Banda's statements, seemed to show that he had learned negative as well as positive lessons from his experience in Ghana. The Prime Minister went on to say that the ministers had been influenced by the Chinese Ambassador in Dar-es-Salaam, whom they had visited together the previous month, and who through them had offered Malawi an £18,000,000 development loan if she would recognize the Peking régime. When they came back from this trip, they had told him that he must stop running the country as if it were his own private estate. 'I will surrender my power only at the wish of the people of this country, the people of the villages,' Banda concluded his attack on the men whom he had denounced as conspirators. 'I won't surrender it to Kanyama Chiume. We don't want this place to be a second Congo.' After the speech, the whole House except the rebels rose and cheered and sang 'Kamuzu is the Lion of Malawi', in which they were joined by the public galleries, which were packed with party members and Young Pioneers who had been brought into Zomba by the lorryload for the sitting.

The debate could never have been an exciting or indeed a significant one. All the Malawi Congress Party members were Banda's personal nominees, and could lay no sort of claim to represent feeling in the country. The ministers naturally defended themselves. Chisiza said that some of those now claiming he had been a traitor had not been on the spot, as he had, in the darkest days of the nationalist struggle. Mrs Chibambo, who also denied the charge of conspiracy, said the

179

complaints she had expressed had been grievances voiced by the women in her constituency: surely the main reason she was in the House was to pass such grievances on and to secure their redress. Chiume made two main points: he had merely told Banda the truth when he had warned him that some of his policies were not too popular with the people, and the fact that he had passed on the Chinese Ambassador's offer of an £18,000,000 loan to Malawi could not with any sort of reason be construed as meaning he was a Communist. He would have failed in his duty as Foreign Minister if he had not reported the proposal to the Premier. At one point in the debate, which went on for two days, Banda danced in front of the Government benches, waving a fly-whisk and shouting: 'Decision!' On the second day, applause for the Prime Minister was much less enthusiastic, and the loud-speakers which had relayed the first day's proceedings to the crowds outside had been taken down. Chirwa and Chipembere both made conciliatory speeches and told the House that they were still willing to serve under Banda in any capacity. The complaint Chipembere did make was that the Premier had changed his old habit of listening to both sides of the question when allegations were made. 'Ministers like myself,' he said, 'have again and again been approached by M.P.s and members of the party executive to put complaints before the Prime Minister' – a form of words which testifies sufficiently well to Banda's difficult character – 'and we have summoned up the courage to do so. But if we leave our Prime Minister to do everything alone, we are perfectly convinced we shall lead this country into chaos.' Dismissed Housing Minister Bwanami urged members to support the motion of confidence, said that the fact that he and his colleagues had refused Banda's offer to resign furnished ample proof that they had not been 'power-hungry' and contended that he had done no more than his duty by informing the Prime Minister of certain popular complaints. The dissident ministers followed his advice, the motion of confidence was voted unanimously and Banda was cheered to the echo when he emerged from the Parliament building, though a separate section of the crowd, composed partly of civil servants who resented the docking of their pay, gave a welcome every bit as enthusiastic to Chipembere. The relaxed atmosphere in which the proceedings in the Assembly had concluded persuaded many people that only a face-saving formula was necessary to permit the rebel Ministers to return to the Cabinet. Indeed, at a press conference a few days later, Banda declared that the crisis was only a family squabble, and that he was not at the moment filling the posts of the ministers who had resigned because he was convinced that some of them would want to come back. 'I have given strict instructions,' he added, 'that there shall be no trouble for anyone, even for the ministers who have been disloyal.'

The reconciliation did not come off. The most likely reason is that the 'rebels' insisted that they would not come back unless all of them were reinstated in office, and Banda had set his mind against the return of Foreign Minister Chiume, whom he had denounced in his speech in the Assembly. So public polemics started up. Speaking in his Fort Johnston constituency, Chipembere accused the Government of cheating the people. 'When we were elected,' he said, 'we promised them that all jobs being done by Europeans would be given to Africans. But Europeans who shot our people, jailed them, burned their houses and ill-treated them are still holding the high posts in Zomba.' The Government party retorted by an attempt to silence the six ex-ministers. It suspended them all from membership till a full inquiry into their activities had been held, which meant that in the interval party members were prohibited from attending their meetings. The ban had no effect at all. On 20 September, four of the 'rebels', including Chipembere, were cheered at a midnight meeting in Blantyre, and sufficient money was collected from the audience to pay for 100 telegrams to Banda demanding that all the former ministers, who were described as 'these loyal and courageous men,' should be taken back into the Cabinet. Far the biggest ovation was given to Chipembere, who said he had not the faintest intention of complying with the ban on his holding meetings, and had told Banda so. 'I was a politician here, and holding meetings, before Dr Banda ever came,' he declared with comprehensible bitterness. The ex-ministers all said they had no plans to oust the Premier or to form an opposition, but they declared that they would not go back to Zomba till he had showed a change of heart over such matters as the Africanization of senior posts in the civil service, the annulment of the standstill on officials' pay and a review of the country's policy towards Southern Rhodesia and Mozambique. Their curiously ambiguous attitude provided Banda with an admirable opportunity for holding them up to ridicule, but he simply did not take it. Instead, he made himself ridiculous, in the eyes of the Western world, at any rate, by accusing the six of trying to kill him by witchcraft. 'They sent people to witch-doctors to ask for medicine,' he said, 'so that when they shook hands with me, Kamuzu would die.'

In the last week of September, disorders started to break out. They began with crowds defying an official prohibition of all meetings in the southern half of Malawi. Then the Zomba headquarters of the Malawi Congress Party was burned down and one of the ministers whom Banda had just appointed to fill the gaps in his Government was beaten up and taken to hospital, while Malawi flags were burned in a number of places. Next, civil servants in Zomba struck, complaining of attacks by Young Pioneers, the youth branch of the Government party. People in the streets were carrying knobkerries or pangas for self-defence, and a high proportion of those in and around Zomba, which was the most vocal centre of discontent, were wearing a strip of cloth round their left arms to show their sympathy with the rebel ministers. An African intellectual commented that people were no longer speaking of *Kwacha*, an independence slogan meaning 'dawn', but of *Kwada* – 'dusk'.

It was then that the dissidents made what seems their biggest mistake. One by one, with the exception of Chipembere, they started leaving the country, first for Northern Rhodesia and then for Tanzania. Their position had, of course, its weaknesses. They could probably count on pretty solid support from the intelligentsia of Malawi, the civil servants and the African middle class in their differences with Banda, but informed opinion held that the mass of the population was still behind the Prime Minister, as the liberator of Malawi. Again, the ex-ministers had never come out with any plan of action: they complained of Banda's dictatorial attitude, but in all their speeches, they had not even suggested the launching of an open opposition movement. Again, conditions inside the country held out little hope of any success for an attempt to reconcile the two sides: former Minister of Justice Chirwa, who had responded to a suggestion that he should see Banda in Zomba and talk things over, was beaten up outside the Premier's palace gates when the discussions broke down. All the same, the critics were losing any chance of taking a political initiative and forfeiting the confidence of their supporters when they fled from Malawi for no obvious reason, and Banda promptly cashed in on their confession of failure. He issued an order, under a four-year-old pre-home rule ordinance, restricting Chipembere, who had not fled the country, to an area within four miles of his Fort Johnston home. He gazetted new regulations which enabled him to put people under house-arrest in the interests of public security. He imposed a muzzle on the press by regulations authorizing a £500 fine or imprisonment up to five years for anyone publishing news or comment likely to prejudice public security or to undermine confidence in the Government. Meantime a purge was started in the civil service and the Government party, a detention camp was being opened up for political prisoners, and organized intimidation by lorry-loads of the Malawi Youth League was forcing ex-minister Colin Cameron and two other British citizens, all of them consistent liberals and supporters of Banda till he broke with his colleagues, to leave the country.

The Malawi Congress Party conference did what was expected of it by giving Banda an uproarious welcome, and by calling for a number of repressive measures, the mildest of which was the enforcement of regulations to prevent civil servants from engaging in active politics. Banda repaid it by representing the country as being in danger and accusing ex-Foreign Minister Chiume of plotting against him from Dar-es-Salaam. 'We must be ready for everything,' the Premier declared. 'Every man and woman, every boy and girl will have to know how to use a gun – even a machine-gun.' When he was informed that Chipembere had escaped from house-arrest, Banda said he must be recovered alive or dead. But official claims that the one rebel minister who had not left the country enjoyed no popular support were belied a week or two later, when police and troops were sent to the Fort Johnston area on the grounds that the local population, some 250,000 of them, were not co-operating with the Government. They were reported, in fact, to be refusing to pay taxes, and six chiefs were deposed on the grounds of 'disloyalty'. Measures of repression were also the principal items on the agenda when Parliament met for its autumn session. Banda asked for the voting of amendments to Malawi's three-month-old independence Constitution. One would permit him to detain anyone without trial in the interests of defence, public safety and public order, another provided for the exclusion from Parliament of any M.P.s who had ceased to represent the party for which they had been elected; naturally the amendments went through. The Prime Minister also announced another step to which the rebel ministers had objected, the moving of the capital up-country to Lilongwe, which he said was central, near Lake Nyasa, and possessed an airport which it would be easier to enlarge. Zomba could be compensated for its loss of status by the establishment of a university, and the project, which it would take three years to execute, would cost some millions of pounds. Naturally the M.P.s did not imitate the absent former ministers in their opposition to the plan.

Naturally too Banda continued to drum in the story that his country was in danger. When he went on tour near the Tanzania border in November, he sent ahead of him units of his Women's League, who were as militant as the Malawi Youth League and the Young Pioneers, and whom he had christened his 'Amazon Army', to guard against the danger of an invasion there. As the year went out, the official *Malawi News* printed a story that the Tanzania authorities had organized a camp where discontented Malawians crossing the frontier were trained in subversive activities. The Tanzania press showed rather more of a sense of humour in its counter-accusations. The Government newspaper, *The Nationalist*, claimed that Banda was so swayed by superstition that he walked with a limp, because of a human molar he had been advised to keep under his toe to counter witchcraft. There was continuing trouble at home, too. As 1965 opened, the Fort Johnston area, where Chipembere had escaped from his detention, saw something that might have been taken as the first act in a civil war. Raiders entered the town, captured dozens of rifles from the police and retreated into the forest-clad mountains, and whatever official statements might say the Government forces were not strong enough to hunt them down. Discontent among officials persisted, and if the civil servants' association wrote to Banda pledging their loyalty, hoping in return for a promise, which they did not get, that the purge in their ranks would be halted, that was because he had unleashed what might politely be called 'direct action' against them, had in fact given the Malawi Youth League and the Young Pioneers a free hand to beat them up and burn their homes.

Banda did indeed have his successes. He got an excellent reception in the United Nations when he acknowledged the speeches welcoming his country's membership and explained that Malawi was landlocked and therefore had to have dealings with Mozambique and Portugal, though, he added, 'no one resents this more bitterly than I do'. He got a sympathetic hearing at the State Department and the World Bank when he appealed for support for the £45,000,000 Malawi five-year development plan, and explained that he wanted the money for agriculture and not for prestige projects. In London, the Minister for Overseas Development promised him £6,250,000 towards the recurrent budget deficit Malawi was facing following her breach with the Federation – which was running in 1964 at the rate of £4,500,000 annually, though it was hoped to absorb it within six or seven years – and £3,000,000 towards the 1965 development programme. The Minister added that the British Government was considering the possibility of granting aid towards the proposed University of Malawi.

All this was progress, but it was progress on a basis that no one could call really stable. It was true that the European population were solidly behind Banda, though most of them felt he had handled his differences with his collaborators clumsily: by the end of 1964, whites who had expressed their terror of the single-party system when the possibility of it had begun to emerge two years before were showing even greater concern at the distant danger of a two-party régime. On the other hand, the number of whites in the country was steadily dwindling. It was true that Malawi's five-year plan was regarded by outside experts as a serious job of work. On the other hand, one British and one Southern Rhodesian firm had put their projects under it into cold storage when the crisis broke out. It was true that Banda's ex-minister critics had nothing to set against the achievements he could claim: the breaking-up of the hated Federation and the achievement of independence within six years of his coming home. On the other hand, their departure had robbed his Front Bench of most of its talent, and he had lost almost all his graduate collaborators. It was true that only one of those critics had shown the courage to stay in the country and continue his struggle, even though it had to be an underground one. On the other hand, Chipembere was someone to be reckoned with: when he had emerged from detention after the 1959 troubles, he had got a far bigger reception than Banda had. Chipembere was a liberal too, for what that is worth in the Africa of today: he was known to feel not the least enthusiasm about Nkrumah's policies. Banda, on the other hand, had been deeply marked by his stay on the West Coast. He was on record as having said that Malawi was going to be the Ghana of Central Africa. Possibly that may be ascribed in part to the fact that, after his forty years in the United States and England, he had seen it from the outside. After all, the extremely shrewd President Nyerere of Tanzania had once said of him: 'The trouble about Banda is that he's not an African.'

A brief diagnosis of what was later to go wrong with Banda was furnished in general terms, in a pamphlet brought out in 1962 by the brilliant young Dunduku Chisiza, brother of the resigning Minister for Home Affairs, who died in a car crash the same year. Dunduku Chisiza, who tried, among other things, to explain the intolerance of the new Government parties in Africa, gave three reasons why so many African heads of state tended to turn into dictators. They did so, he suggested, either because they had been accorded too much trust, or because too little trust had been reposed in them, or because they were afflicted with neurotic ambition. Pretty plainly, Banda was suffering from too much trust and from neurosis. An excellent after-the-event account of the background to and the consequences of Malawi's post independence crisis was given on his return to England by Colin Cameron, the young Scot who had resigned from Banda's Cabinet because he would not agree to the introduction of a preventive detention law. Cameron started by saying – and he was incapable of insincerity – that he retained his liking and respect for Banda, but he added that he deeply regretted the way in which the Prime Minister's policies were driving not only African ministers and civil servants, but businessmen and teachers into leaving the country. If things went on the same way, he stated, there would soon be no architects or civil engineers in Malawi, and very few building firms.

Cameron put the trouble down to Banda's obviously neurotic distrust of his African ministers and civil servants, whom he seemed constantly to suspect of being open to corruption. One result was that all the senior posts in the civil service, the Army and the police were filled with whites, and the Premier flatly refused to have Africans trained to take their posts. Another was that Banda insisted on taking all decisions himself, which meant that his ministers were hamstrung in doing their jobs and that he himself was so immersed in petty detail that he had no time left to reflect at leisure on the country's long-term needs. This attitude gravely compromised the influx of foreign capital, which Banda was as anxious to attract to his country as was any other African head of state. According to Cameron, the Premier made a point of seeing the potential investors himself, and 'virtually chased firms out of his office', so terrified was he of his collaborators taking bribes.

Cameron thought, and most competent observers were agreed with him, that Banda's distrust of his colleagues was completely without foundation. He described the ministers who had gone, and whom he had known from day-to-day personal and official contacts, as an exceptionally able group of young men, who would have been perfectly willing to work under Banda if they had been allowed to run their departments to the best of their abilities, and if he had tolerated free discussion in Cabinet meetings. They made no sort of demand that their own solutions to problems should be automatically adopted; all they asked was that they should be allowed to put their ideas forward, and that the final decision should be the fruit of a consensus of opinion.

There is a general similarity in the attitudes and characters of the heads of the newly-independent African states, but

Banda stood out from them for often quite contradictory reasons. He was by no means alone among them in his dictatorial attitude towards his ministers – but he went much further than most of them in this authoritarian approach. He used the same instruments as they did to underline his importance, the impressive titles by which he had himself greeted and the imposing palace, well-guarded and surrounded by high walls, in which he lived – but when he went to London, he was content with a modest hotel, and often enough did not go out at night, but sat in his room reading. The thing that differentiated him completely from his opposite numbers was his resolute refusal progressively to fill the high posts in the administration with his fellow-Africans. Elsewhere on the continent, the extent and the speed of this Africanization was regarded as a test of the degree to which nominal independence had become a reality. Banda was not interested in such tests. 'I'm not going to allow ignorant Africans to take over senior posts,' he said. 'While I'm here, promotion is going to go by merit, and by merit only.' His position on the issue was unique in Africa, and it might have been thought that it could hardly fail to lead in the end to dangerous discontent.

That discontent was in 1965, however, confined to the intellectuals, who formed a far smaller minority in Malawi than they did in Ghana or in Dahomey. Responsible opinion was unanimous that 'one-man Banda', as he was sometimes known, was in no danger at all of eviction from office. It was generally agreed that he was treating the new ministers appointed after the crisis of September 1964 in a far more human fashion than he had their predecessors. All the same, it was a little difficult to envisage Banda deliberately grooming anyone else to step into his shoes, and succession to the headship of the state can easily raise difficult problems in a country with no political traditions. There were some who thought that the Premier's choice might conceivably fall on twenty-five-year-old Aleke Banda, who was no relation at all, and whom his chief had chosen to accompany him to the Commonwealth Prime Ministers' conference three days after independence. Aleke, who had been running the party newspaper, the radio and the Youth League, was an extremely capable organizer; on the other hand, he was very young, many people were jealous of him, and he was widely disliked, because he was regarded as a tale-bearer. There were those who felt that, were Banda to die, the most likely successor to him among the members of his Cabinet would be Minister of Natural Resources Nyasulu, former Speaker of Parliament. Among the opposition leaders, the only man who was generally regarded as having the timbre of a new head of state was Chipembere. As 1965 opened, he was obviously still popular, and there had never been any doubt about his intelligence, character or patriotism. He had one physical weakness: he was a diabetic. If he could hold out, he might well assume the succession of the man he had summoned back from abroad and had deliberately groomed to become, as it turned out, the tyrant who had sent out troops to hunt him down.

8

Conclusions

WE HAVE JUST examined the case-histories of six newly-independent African countries. We shall now have to ask ourselves, among other things, whether the personal ambitions of the men who became their heads of state were responsible for the events in them, or whether these men were constrained to their attitudes by what appeared to be the imperatives of the positions in which they found themselves.

Of the six heads of state concerned, only one, the man who was in 1965 President Nkrumah of Ghana, would appear, even before he acceded to office or indeed returned to his homeland, to have shown signs of the dictatorial attitude all of them displayed when they found themselves in authority. It will be remembered that members of the revolutionary African students group which he founded in London pledged themselves to 'irrevocably obey and act upon the orders of the Grand Council of The Circle', of which Nkrumah was chairman. It will also be recalled that in the preface to his *Autobiography*, written before Ghana became independent under his premiership, Nkrumah said that the democratic system of a newly free underdeveloped country might need backing up, during the period following independence, by emergency measures of a totalitarian kind.

It is true that Dr Banda, in Malawi, treated the men who had summoned him back to head the local nationalist movement in much the same way as Nkrumah had behaved to the Ghanaians who had recalled him for a not dissimilar purpose. The invitations to the two men were not, however, couched in identical terms. Banda had been invited not to help organize a party, as Nkrumah had, but to become its chief. There is nothing to suggest that without that invitation he would ever have returned to what was then Nyasaland or taken up politics. Finally, it was not he who built himself up as a Messiah. His followers did it for him, for what they considered excellent political reasons, as they warned him in advance they would, and he would have been less than human if he had not first accepted and then developed the character they had invented for him. As for his distrust of his assistants when he finally got into the saddle, that could be accounted for, even without the undoubted neurotic element in his character, by the fact that he had lived in newly-independent Ghana and had seen something of the corruption there, while his half-century of absence from Africa made it easier for him to take the same view of Africans' characters as did Europeans of his own age.

Ben Bella is the third and last figure among our six who when he returned to his country was a virtual stranger to its internal politics; that was probably one reason why, as soon as he was released from captivity, the commanders of the A.L.N. on the Tunisian and Moroccan frontiers, who shared his lack of contact with developments back home and his radical outlook, teamed up with him. Ben Bella, however, would never have achieved the presidency of Algeria alone: he had none of Nkrumah's hypnotic eloquence. In the weeks that passed between his sudden departure from Tunis for Libya and his triumphant return to Algiers, he was surrounded and supported by a little group of highly intelligent Algerians of every political tendency, without whose aid he would have been a very isolated figure, though he progressively dropped them over the months and years which followed his accession to power. It is true that Ben Bella had not hesitated before the risks of civil war when that seemed the only way of defeating his rival Ben Khedda. But an excellent testimony to his apparent lack of dictatorial ambitions before he returned to his country comes from Hervé Bourges, the Frenchman who was appointed to an important position on his private secretariat three months after Algeria achieved independence. At the moment he accepted the post, Bourges had been editor of the French Catholic weekly *Témoignage Chrétien*, which had always taken a liberal attitude towards the Algerian war, but that was by no means all the story. Before he acceded to his editorial post, he had been principal private secretary to Edmond Michelet, who was for a while Minister of Justice under General de Gaulle. In that capacity, Bourges had regularly gone down and visited in their captivity Ben Bella and the four other Algerian nationalist leaders who were imprisoned with him, and he had been so much impressed that he had leapt at the opportunity to work for the first Algerian premier and had soon after applied for and been granted Algerian nationality. When the author remarked in the autumn of 1962 that some people were accusing Ben Bella of dictatorial ambitions, Bourges said he thought it was absolutely false. If he had had the least reason to believe in the accusation, he added, he would never have accepted his then job.

President Fulbert Youlou of the Congo (Brazzaville) was far closer in his way of living to the common idea of a dictator than most of his fellow African heads of state. In debauchery, he is represented as having been the equal of an Ataturk, and his corruption was just as notorious. On the other hand, there is nothing to suggest that he had accepted his vocation as a priest with the least idea of cashing in on it politically, or indeed that he had harboured any ambitions to national leadership before he actually entered politics, though the invitation to stand for the French Assembly that was the start of his political life could, of course, have been arranged. Once he had embarked on that life, it is true, he revealed himself an extremely talented political tactician. But it should be remembered that he would never have had the chance of acceding to the supreme office in his country if it had not been for the tribal conflicts which rent it, that his successful start in appeasing these won him the respect of the French, and that within a year of sweeping the board in his first elections as Premier, he had initiated a series of liberal measures towards his former opponents which testified to an attitude very different from that of Nkrumah and Ben Bella. Finally, it should be recalled that his original proposals for settling inter-tribal quarrels for good by setting up a single party were deliberately put forward not in his own tribal area, where he would have been certain of an enthusiastic hearing, but outside it, where he was far more likely to meet with the criticism which only the more intelligent even of democratic politicians welcome.

There was even less sign of personal ambition about President Hubert Maga of Dahomey. He again would never have won the leadership of his country if it had not been for inter-regional rivalries, and students from across the Atlantic have paid tribute to the talent he showed in bringing some sort of stability to a land that was extremely difficult to rule. And it should be remembered that before he had fused his own party with one of its rivals to form a single party, and taken the repressive measures which generally accompany this step, he had got all the country's big three parties spontaneously to unite, and that this voluntary coalition had broken up only when one of the partners had left it in order, as he plainly stated, to form a monopoly party of his own.

Léon Mba, in Gabon, was alone among the leaders in our six case-histories in that he not only enjoyed the support of the former colonial power once he was in office; his original accession to responsibility seems to have been largely due to the influence of the ex-colonists, who regarded him as a trusty. This circumstance is by no means rare in the newly-independent African countries. What makes Mba stand out from other similar selections of the former régime is that, more than twenty years before he had scored his first political success, he had been dismissed from his minor administrative post, prosecuted and exiled because of his adherence to the nationalist Bwiti Church. It seems extremely unlikely that as a young man back in the 1930s he can have foreseen the political profit this was going to reap for him two decades later, and if that interpretation of his actions is dismissed, we can only regard him as having been an idealist. It is true that, in the post-war period, the anti-European spirit of the Bwiti cult had tended to fade out, and that this was one of the reasons why the French in Gabon felt that Mba, as one of its leaders, would be a useful person to deal with. There is nothing to suggest, however, that Mba had dictated the new moderation in the nationalistic angle of Bwiti in order to promote his political career: the change was a natural response to the greater opportunities offered to Africans to run their own affairs after 1945. Once he had attained power, Mba did indeed display one of the characteristics commonly associated with dictators. His private life did not provide material for cocktail party gossip as did that of Fulbert Youlou, but his personal financial interest in the development of his country was notorious. Nevertheless, Mba too had his period of

193

political liberalism, when members of what had become the opposition party were for a while admitted into a coalition Government.

Our six case-histories would seem to suggest that, taking African single-party régimes as a whole, it is less the party leader who sets out to establish himself as a dictator than the system whose summit he reaches that makes him one. Whatever may be the arguments in favour of the single-party system as an instrument for coping with certain particular problems – and we shall soon be examining some of those urged on behalf of its peculiar utility in African conditions – it is never liked anywhere. It is difficult to conceive of a human society in which all the decisions of the authorities are at all times accepted by all the citizens without a murmur of criticism. The disposition to criticize, when occasion arises, is part of human nature, but criticism, like opposition, is a thing the single-party state cannot tolerate. So almost as soon as it is established, almost everywhere, a system of repressive measures has to be introduced, which begins with a press censorship and ends with preventive detention laws.

A single party can come into existence in more than one way, by imposition from above, as in Ghana, Algeria and Malawi, or by the voluntary merger of existing bodies, as in Dahomey and Kenya. But a permanent government party will earn just as much unpopularity if its monopoly of power is a *de facto* one as it would if its dominant position were institutionalized, as is happening in more and more African countries. There is nothing on paper to give the True Whig Party a permanent lien on political authority in Liberia. In fact it has ruled the country continuously since 1869, or exactly twice the period of Communist party domination in Russia. And that uninterrupted monopoly of power would seem as good a reason as any for the three plots against President Tubman which were reported between 1955 and 1963. It is true that at his last re-election to the presidency, Tubman got in by 555,044 votes out of the 570,000 cast, but the figures were a little too one-sided to be convincing, though they were something of an improvement on those of 1959, when the President was represented as having been returned by 260,000 votes to 16.

This is the sort of voting figure, the ninety-plus per cent. majority, to which the student of African single-party politics must become accustomed. It may be asked why the authorities should take the trouble to invent these figures: they cannot impress the outside world, and the internal public is only too well aware of the omission of No votes and abstentions that were necessary to produce the official results. Perhaps one reason is that African leaders are still to an extent dominated by the prestige of the Western ideas which form the theoretical basis of their political systems. In England and France, figures have to be published before anyone begins to take election results seriously, and a big majority for a party's candidates is rightly regarded as indicating big popular support for them. There are, of course, African states that have got beyond this susceptibility to Western opinion. There was only one list of candidates in Malawi's 1964 pre-independence elections, and the electorate was therefore not called on to go to the polls. The future M.P.s were declared returned unopposed, and the same formula was followed in May 1965 in Ghana's first post-independence parliamentary elections.

One justification for this flight from figures of conflicting opinions, and indeed for the single-party system as a whole, was put forward by Julius Nyerere, now President of Tanzania, in an article first published in 1961. To Western minds, Nyerere wrote, the idea of an *organized* opposition group has become so familiar that its absence promptly raises a cry of 'dictatorship'. Yet when a group of a hundred (African) equals have sat and talked together until they have agreed to dig a well (and 'until they have agreed' implies that they have produced many conflicting opinions before agreeing) they have, surely, practised democracy. Westerners will ask whether the opposition was organized, and therefore automatic, or spontaneous, and therefore free; only if it is automatic will they admit the existence of democracy. Basically, democracy is government by discussion as opposed to government by force, and under the tribal system, whether there was a chief or not, African society was a society of equals and conducted its business by discussion.

This may be thought to present an idealized picture of what went on in African societies in the pre-colonial period, but

Nyerere went on: This 'pure' democracy is too clumsy a way of conducting the affairs of a large modern state. The need to organize a 'government by discussion' does not necessarily imply the need to organize an opposition party as part of the system. In Anglo-Saxon countries, the existence of distinct classes in society and the struggle between them resulted in the growth of the two-party system. But with rare exceptions, the idea of class is foreign to Africa – a somewhat questionable assertion which will be taken up later – and the fight has been against *foreign* domination, not against a dominant class at home.

These remarks, of course, refer to a quite limited period of African history. In any case, Nyerere continued: The huge problems before them confront the new African countries with a position of national emergency. Under the circumstances, any opposition must be responsible. In fact, the opposition in the new African countries comes only too often from irresponsible individuals with no alternative policy who exploit the democratic freedoms for their own self-aggrandisement. In such circumstances, the Government must deal firmly and promptly with the troublemakers.

And Nyerere wound up by saying that this did not mean that a genuine and responsible opposition could not arise in time, or that such an opposition would be less welcome in Africa than it was in Europe or America. Indeed, in the Tanzanian elections of September 1965, he took what might be regarded as a first step towards facilitating the emergence of such an opposition in his own country: he authorized the local single party, the T.A.N.U., to put up two candidates in all but a handful of constituencies. The result might have been foreseen. More than half the sitting M.P.s, including six ministers, were defeated: they simply had not taken the trouble to keep in touch with their constituents' demands. How distant is the tomorrow which will see the generalization of even such limited opportunities for the appearance of an opposition is another matter. At least some responsible Africans doubt whether it will ever come. Chief Obafemi Awolowo, founder of the Nigerian party known as the Action Group, and former Premier of the Western Region of Nigeria, had something to say about the point in the autobiography he published in 1961: subsequently he disappeared behind prison walls, having been convicted, naturally, of treasonable activities. 'Under a one-party system,' Awolowo wrote, 'the party in power arrogates to itself the right to be the only ruling party for all time. All other parties, therefore, which differ from it or are in opposition to it are either suppressed or absorbed. At subsequent elections, if there are any, the consent of the people cannot be said to be genuinely and freely given, because there is only one choice open to the electorate.' In any case Nyerere's 1961 statement and Awolowo's accusation open the way for us to examine the arguments for and against the single-party system which they sketched out; there are about half a dozen of these on either side.

The first argument in favour of the single-party system as it is now practised in Africa is that the single party alone permits the assertion – or creation – of a sense of nationhood in the newly-independent countries, and a fairly plausible justification can be produced for those who do not see the utility of bringing such a sense into existence. There is a growing aspiration towards African unity today among African intellectuals, and it is not confined to the supporters of Nkrumah and Nasser, whose motive for wanting a united Africa is that it would enable them to become the dictators of a continent instead of a country. The potential economic advantages of African economic unity go without saying. Now internationalism cannot exist without nationalism as a base. It should not prove too difficult a task to unite the thirty-odd nation-states into which Africa is now divided once they are conscious of their identity, whereas welding into any sort of unity the hundreds of tribes which people the continent would be a very different kettle of fish.

Why should it be necessary to create a sense of nationhood? In most European countries, the existence of the nation which is the basis of the state is taken for granted. In Africa, the arbitrary frontiers imposed by the former colonial powers have, it is true, divided one state from another and given rise to local parliamentary institutions and, to some extent, led to common ways of thinking, but they are far from having laid really solid bases for nationhood. What is more, south of the Sahara, there is almost always a multiplicity of often quite

197

small ethnical groups within a state's frontiers. In such conditions, it is argued, the units in a multi-party system will inevitably base themselves on tribes and other elements which are described as retrograde, and will be bound to split the population in a way that can never happen in a country where citizens have long taken their common nationhood for granted, while the ideological platforms of the parties, if in fact they have these, will speedily fade out before individual and tribal quarrels. Not a few African leaders have hoisted themselves into power, or done a lot to keep themselves there, even after the establishment of the single-party system in their countries, by mobilizing the members of their own ethnical group to support them. And it is argued that the establishment of a single party, which extends over the whole national territory and includes in its ranks members of every tribe and every class, brings it home to people that they belong to the same national entity.

This argument, of course, has no validity outside sub-Saharan Africa. In the Maghreb, to the north of the desert, the one ethnical difference which exists has had next to no effect on local political developments. There are, indeed, Berber-speaking minorities in Algeria and Morocco – the Berbers formed the mass of the population at the moment of the Arab invasions – but though the Kabyles, the Berbers of Algeria, supported Ait Ahmed's rising, there is no reason to believe they would have done so if there had not been grievances against the Ben Bella Government quite unconnected with their local complaints. The position to the south of the Sahara is very different. In little Dahomey, with an area less than that of England, to take one not untypical example, there are no less than six different languages spoken; the half-million population of Gabon speak forty separate dialects.

There is, however, one just as important defence of the single-party system which has equal force north and south of the Sahara: this is that its existence is a key factor in bringing about the economic development which African countries need more than anything else. If such development is to take place, hard work is necessary, austerity is necessary, and it is also necessary that the population shall be mobilized for the effort required and shall have the objectives of the national plan explained to them, even if they do not take a hand in framing these. The single party, it is urged, is the ideal instrument for achieving this sort of purpose. How, it is asked, can a people be persuaded to work for years with no immediately apparent result in view if anyone who is discontented can set up a new party when he likes and overthrow the Government? The ruling-out of opposition sabotage of development is a negative argument in favour of the single-party system; a positive argument just as strong emerges from a simple factual comparison which makes plain the extraordinary value of the single party as an instrument for getting the ordinary man to work on the development jobs that have got to be done if the backward countries are to make any progress. Single-party Tunisia has not the slightest difficulty in roping people in to construct schools, build roads and dig wells, though it should be added that the single party there is the oldest-established and probably the most efficient of any in Africa. In neighbouring no-party Libya, villagers have had to be offered money to repair irrigation works which American experts had installed for them gratis.

Another justification of the single-party system is that it is the only efficient means of preventing the dispersion of an underdeveloped country's cadres. Everywhere in Africa, the number of university graduates and technicians is still desperately low: when the Congo (Léopoldville) became independent, there was not a single Congolese doctor. The middle class, which played such an important part in the development of the European countries, is almost non-existent in a good part of sub-Saharan Africa. Therefore, the argument goes, it would appear merely childish to champion the existence of a number of parties in a country where it is already hard enough to find cadres for one. If these cadres are divided among themselves, they will waste their time in personal quarrels with no gain at all for democracy. What is more, supporters of this position say, it is an open question whether the fact that he can choose his parliamentary representative freely and criticize the Government in the press represents the ideal of democracy for a citizen who has not got enough to eat, is often – if he is a town-dweller – hunting jobs from one year's end to another, and who lives in a slum. To which it might be retorted that the

African is just as likely to be jobless and hungry under a single-party system.

Again, it can be pleaded that the single party forms the best obstacle to what might be called the demagogic opposition so easily aroused in under-developed countries by the sometimes unpopular measures dictated by the process of development. The destruction of certain sterilizing customs and traditions, the requirements of increased productivity and the big sacrifices called for if the necessary investments are to be rounded up are, it is urged, so many factors which a demagogic opposition can exploit against the best-intentioned government in order to alienate from it the sympathy of ill-informed populations. It matters little whether the opposition comes from intellectuals out to safeguard or increase their personal privileges, or from justifiably evicted feudal landowners, or from simple peasants who do not understand just what is being asked of them; it matters just as little whether the opposition takes the form of calumnies on the authorities or, as happened in the Cameroons under the multi-party system, the offer of red wine by the barrel to electors to persuade them to vote the right way. The result is the same, and the single-party system is represented as the best way of putting paid to this sterile form of opposition. For, it is argued, if Western political thinkers speak of the constructive role played by opposition parties in their countries, this is because the members of these have reached sufficient intellectual maturity to be able to pronounce objectively on Government policy, which can hardly be expected in African lands.

A further argument in favour of the single party will be stated merely in order to be dismissed. It is that rival political parties represent conflicting class interests, and that since there are no such conflicting classes in Africa, there is no need for a multi-party system to speak for them. Of course, there are social classes in Africa as there are in any other continent, though colonialism may have appeared for a while to have ironed them out in a brotherhood of subjection. Once independence was won, there was no reason to expect that this class solidarity would continue indefinitely. To quote an African comment, it is merely asking for trouble to hope to unite under the same party flag a feudal proprietor, a greedy bourgeois, an unemployed workman and a landless peasant – and the two last categories are no rarity in Africa.

Finally it is argued that the single party forms a solid and irreplaceable link between the Government and the people. In a country where the techniques of news dissemination are undeveloped and where there is not the discussion there is among Western peoples, this argument runs, the single party forms an ideal transmission belt between the Government and the people. Government is not only deciding, it is also informing and being informed. The single party, it is claimed, can explain to the people the decisions of the Government and can also make the Government aware of the wishes and reactions of the people.

Alas, it does not always succeed. In 1963, three years after President Maga had set up his single-party system in Dahomey, his government signed an agreement with the Nationalist Chinese under which they were to teach Dahomeyans rice-growing, and a dozen Chinese experts arrived and started work twenty-five miles from the capital. That should have been sufficiently close for the transmission belt to work. For three months the peasants of the area turned up daily in their hundreds and worked under their Chinese instructors. Then, one day, they downed tools; they felt they ought to be paid for the work they were putting in at their lessons. The single party had not been able to put over the value of this experiment for a very poor country; the Minister of Agriculture had no more success when he came down and explained that once the peasants had learned the job of rice-growing, they would be made partners in a great co-operative farm, producing thousands of tons of rice a year, from which they would all profit handsomely. The local inhabitants refused to start work again; indeed they beat up the Chinese instructors and burned down the experimental farm buildings, containing the first year's crop of rice. The transmission belt had simply failed.

All the champions of the single-party system embody one proviso in their defence of it: the single party may have no outside critics, but there must be free speech within its ranks. Its leaders must, among other things, take into account the people's demands, even if these may sometimes appear to be unreasonable. A single party run in this way will, it is argued, in the course of the years prepare its own succession. When a new generation adapted to the demands of modern life grows up, the lessons their fathers have learned within its ranks will permit the flowering of new parties corresponding to different points of view.

At least one reason for believing that this inner democracy is not so often found in the African single party has been advanced earlier: the association in a number of the plots of the last two or three years of leading figures in the régimes concerned who would never have needed to conspire if they could have got a free hearing for their views, as leaders, at any rate, in a Western political organization are always able to do. At a lower level, there is evidence that young people who have gone into some monopoly parties on the understanding that they would be able to speak freely within them have found themselves in a trap. What is more, though democracy within the single party may be practised for a while, before or just after it has conquered independence, recent history seems to indicate that when this period is over, the cadres in positions of responsibility cease to think of anything but staying where they are and imposing their points of view. Yet it can plausibly be argued that the multi-party system is in the best interests not only of the people of a country at large and of politicians who are not holding office but also of a government which has been in power over a continuous period of years. A period in opposition gives such a party the chance, which the detailed day-to-day cares of office rule out, of sitting back and examining its ideology with a critical eye and bringing it up to date in the light of the constantly changing demands of the modern world. Few British Conservatives would dispute that their defeat in the 1945 elections was a blessing in disguise. It enabled them to revise their programme in such a way that it was a completely new party that won the suffrages of the electorate in 1951. And there is little reason to doubt that the new period of opposition on which the Conservatives embarked in 1964 will be equally profitable to the interests of their party.

Now for the arguments against the single-party system. The first is that, whatever may be said about its potentialities for the future – the American Professor Immanuel Wallerstein seriously maintained in a work published in 1961 that the one-party system in the African context is often a significant step towards the liberal state, not a first step away from it – in fact, in almost every country where the single party has taken power, this has led to the suppression of democratic freedoms and the installation of a police state. The Constitution of the Republic of the Ivory Coast guarantees freedom of speech and of the press, as do almost all the African constitutions, but a not untypical law passed there in August 1959 provides from one to three years' imprisonment, and heavy fines, for anyone circulating false news, even if he does so in good faith, where such news has lowered the morale of the population or led to disobedience of the law or reflected discredit on political leaders and officials. The danger of the personalization of the governing party will obviously be greater in countries where a high percentage of the population is illiterate, since it is easier for simple people to identify themselves with a man than with an ideology or an abstract entity such as a party.

There are, of course, defenders of the monopoly party who maintain that African single-party leaders are not dictators. Such was the position taken by Madeira Keita, at the time Mali Minister of the Interior, in a speech delivered in Paris in 1960. Far from being dictators, he said, Modibo Keita in Mali and Leopold Senghor in Senegal were obliged to follow the opinions of their respective parties' political bureaux. The author has heard it maintained that there was comparatively recently free speech within the Guinea and Dahomey single parties, but as far as Senegal was concerned, facts were to belie Madeira Keita's somewhat rash assertion less than two years later. It was President Senghor's refusal to comply with the views of the political bureau of his party – which did not enjoy monopoly status on paper, but which in fact held all but one of the seats in the local Assembly – which led to the so-called Senegal plot of December 1962. The story is worth recounting briefly, because it was one of the infrequent cases among the plots reported from Africa in recent years about which many competent foreign observers were agreed that there had never been any conspiracy at all. There had, indeed, been growing friction for some time between the supporters of President Senghor and of Premier Mamadou Dia, and this came out into the open in the middle of December 1962, when forty of the eighty deputies had tabled a motion of censure on the latter. Dia claimed that this motion was out of order because, among other reasons, the party leadership, which had nominated him to his position and had also nominated the deputies, had not been consulted, and when the political bureau met, it backed him up. It decided that discussion of the parliamentary motion of censure should be delayed pending a meeting of the National Council – a small-scale delegate conference – of the party. It was generally agreed that the Premier would have been able to swing the National Council to his point of view. That is probably why anti-Dia deputies took the first step towards what was later represented as a Dia plot: they set about stirring up the Dakar crowds and trying to organize a meeting of the Assembly despite the decision of the party leadership. Dia's reply, which hardly seems conspiratorial in view of the political bureau's pronouncement, was to order four of the trouble-making deputies to be confined to their homes and to surround the Assembly building with armed guards. And this led to a day of orders and counter-orders between Senghor and Dia, which was interrupted by a meeting in a private house of the forty deputies, who unanimously voted the motion of censure, and which ended up with Dia's arrest on a charge of plotting against the security of the State. Nobody was killed or wounded, indeed, not a shot was fired, and Dia never left his office during the whole of the day. All the same, he was found guilty and sentenced to life imprisonment by a court made up of deputies who were his political enemies, despite the fact that the public prosecutor had left a way out for his acquittal. Probably the best explanation of what happened was given by Senghor in a speech announcing the formation of his new cabinet which completely contradicted Madeira Keita's statement that he was only *primus inter pares* in his party's leadership, and in which he said that the crisis proved that 'in Africa, for the moment, an executive with two men at the helm is impossible'. So steps were swiftly taken to rule out any possibility of a future challenge to the man who was in fact the party's single leader. At a plebiscite in March, the Sengalese electorate ratified by an overwhelming majority – whose figures were widely agreed to have been faked – a new

Constitution, under which the President became simultaneously Premier and Commander-in-Chief of the armed forces, and any possibility of proposing a vote of censure on him, let alone overthrowing him, vanished.

A second argument against the single party is that its authoritarian powers are only too likely to be misused. These authoritarian powers are, of course, represented as being necessary in order to promote the quickest possible solution of the whole series of problems with which an underdeveloped country is simultaneously confronted when it attains independence. It is also argued that the sacrifice of certain freedoms, which is depicted as being temporary only, is a small price to pay for raising the standard of living. Critics of the single-party system urge that, whatever the excuses put forward for the wide prerogatives with which the governing party is endowed, the facts show that it runs a grave risk of becoming an instrument of domination at the disposal of a handful of privileged people. That is what is happening, these critics claim, in certain African countries where the so-called élite which controls public affairs is using the absence of any opposition and the enormous powers with which it has got itself endowed to preserve and increase its personal advantages without a thought for the people about whom it is always talking. Madeira Keita, in the speech already quoted, acknowledged the danger of corruption in a single-party régime, and indeed it is present at every level. In one French-speaking West African country, the President has been forced to jail officials in the highest grade of the civil service on charges of corruption. In another such country, the Minister for Trade regularly received foreign businessmen who seemed interested in investing locally, sent them up-country to see things for themselves and, when they returned, told them bluntly that he would be delighted to see them invest, but if they wanted to obtain the profit transfer and other guarantees normally offered, it would cost them ten million francs. The author can speak of the behaviour of an Algerian police chief, undoubtedly a former member of the Resistance and an influential local member of the F.L.N., saluted by common or garden cops all along the country roads over which he drove, who exacted a ten thousand-franc bribe from a visiting foreign journalist, telling him bluntly that he would not be allowed to cross the frontier for which he was bound unless the money was paid over. He must have known that the journalist would be aware, as an ordinary traveller might not be, that foreigners who are arrested in the Algeria of today tend to remain rather a long time in prison before they are brought up for trial. Nkrumah's 1961 ruling that no member of his single party should own more than two houses of a combined value of £20,000 or more than two motor-cars was not issued without reason. Up and down the continent, even in the states which profess an advanced Socialism, there are ministers who use the advantages of their position to have houses built for them and then let them out to foreign embassies, the rent, of course, being paid into a bank in Europe.

One of the stronger arguments for the single-party system in sub-Saharan Africa is that it puts an end to tribalism and regionalism. There are of course those, like Nkrumah's exiled opponent, Dr Busia, who defend associations of tribes which have sought special constitutional arrangements in recognition of their group solidarity. Identifying as such tribes the Ashanti of Ghana, the Yoruba and Ibo of Nigeria and the Baganda of Uganda, Busia says that far from being reactionary groups, they are among the most progressive in Africa. This, Busia maintains, compels scrutiny of the assumptions that tribalism is reactionary and is necessarily incompatible with nationhood. Most students of the African scene would probably agree, however, that tribalism is the gangrene of sub-Saharan Africa, and the contention that the single-party system is the most efficient weapon against it is open to serious doubt. Critics assert that the head of the single-party state is far from being a man who acts as an arbitrator and who treats everyone fairly, no matter what his ethnic origin. On the contrary, he only too often deliberately selects as his assistants members of his tribe, his clan or his family. It is they who get the big jobs and who use the single party as an instrument of repression or propaganda for their own purposes.

There is just as vigorous criticism of another major argument for the usefulness of the single-party system, that it promotes efficiency in planning economic development. That efficiency, it is claimed, simply does not exist. Production is stationary in a number of African countries and falling in some. The only states in French-speaking sub-Saharan Africa which had a favourable balance of trade in 1964 were the Ivory Coast and Gabon; Dahomey's 1964 trade deficit was equal to its entire civil service expenditure. What is more, the imports include food products which the African countries could readily turn out themselves. Foreign residents in Gabon who cannot get their vegetables and poultry from a farm run by an ageing French couple just outside the capital, which is the only farm of its kind in the country, are forced to queue up every week when a plane arrives from the Cameroons with the products of a similar French farm there.

All this would seem to suggest that, despite the single party's guiding influence, such development plans as exist are not being vigorously enough exploited, or that they are remaining a dead letter, or that they are being angled on the wrong objectives. Not a few African countries' planners have become hypnotized by instruments of development which have been successful in the West but which often do not fit into African conditions; the tractor is one of these. The cost of a tractor's transport up-country is considerable, in many tropical areas it can work no more than a few weeks in a year, it needs skilled maintenance, which in many places will mean the employment of highly-paid European technicians, and it tends to increase rural unemployment. These considerations might be discounted if the tractor could be relied on to significantly to increase production in Africa, but it cannot. In his *L'Afrique Noire est mal partie*, René Dumont, the French agricultural expert, names eight African countries where the use of the tractor has been found uneconomic.

Moreover, under the single-party set-up, private citizens who agree to put up capital for new industries tend to be cosseted in a way which could never be possible if there was an opposition which could examine every bit of expenditure with a critical eye. In one single-party country, a European textile expert had a talk with a local capitalist who had been persuaded to invest money in a mill which produced blue overalls and women's dress material, and who admitted he sold only sixty per cent. of the products he turned out: the rest went into stock.

'How do you place your stuff?' the European expert asked him.

'Through travellers.'

'Excellent; how do you pay them?'

'On commission.'

'Very good: how many travellers have you got?'

'None.'

The local capitalist said that when his stock got too large to be tolerable, he would go and see the President about it, presumably to have it taken off his hands.

The complete failure of Russian agriculture to score any progress in the first four and a half decades of the Soviet régime is only one of the factors that should inspire Africans to ask how economic planning can possibly be efficient unless there is a constructive local opposition capable of criticizing the plan, or the application of the plan, or the absence of a plan, and of putting forward an alternative programme. It is easy enough to find African examples of the sort of thing that may happen if such an opposition is not there. A European expert then in an African country was called on to be present when a plan was put up to the local President for moving the central railway station of the capital some way out of town. The plan had already been agreed to by everyone and only needed the final, formal approval of the Head of State to go through, but it had one disadvantage: it would cost tens of thousands of not particularly necessary pounds. The European expert told the other members of the committee frankly that he was against the proposal, and the chairman warned him in serious tones: 'It's a very grave thing to go against the wishes of the President.' When the President appeared, the members of the committee stated their views, all, of course, favourable to the project, and the European ended up by excusing himself for differing from the others and explaining his reasons. Railway passenger traffic, he said, was falling all over the world in favour of long-distance bus traffic, and it was ridiculous at such a time to invest a huge sum in a completely new railway station. He therefore recommended that the existing station should be enlarged and the area round it cleared. The members of the committee waited for the expected explosion: it never came. 'But our European friend is quite right,' the President said. A piece of extravagant and unnecessary expenditure had been rejected only because of the presence at the meeting which was to have decided on it of a man who was not afraid to speak his mind. The fact that he had been there was, however, a pure chance. And critics of the single-party system urge that the only way in which such extravagances and other planning errors can be ruled out with any certainty is the granting of legal status to an opposition, with a right to its own seats in Parliament, if it can win them, with its own newspapers and with complete freedom to express itself in public.

A final argument against the single-party state was put forward in November 1963 in the Paris-printed, Tunisian-owned weekly *Jeune Afrique* in an article which opened a long discussion on the subject. The author was Albert Teveodjré, who entered Dahomey politics as Maga's Information Minister and who in 1964 joined the International Affairs Centre at Harvard University. Back in the 1950s, Teveodjré wrote, Africans used to say that when a people was prevented from expressing its opinion by means of a ballot paper, it tended to express itself by means of a revolver: that was the justification of the revolts against the colonial régime. A decade later, the single-party African state was leaning in exactly the same direction.

Who had forgotten, Teveodjré continued, that bombs appeared in Ghana almost at the moment when the Parliament there was offering Nkrumah the life presidency? That was more than a mere coincidence. Whatever the benefits of the single-party system, it was better for a head of state to give play to freedom than to run the risk of being assassinated by subjects who had been reduced to silence. It was better, when this was possible, to discuss things with an opposition party able to express itself freely than to maintain monolithic organs whose only function was to approve and applaud.

'A legal strike is better than a plot or a revolt,' Teveodjré summed up.

For it is not as if the single-party system puts an end to political differences. It merely forces them to assume a new form. Instead of a struggle between opposing parties, we find a struggle for the control of the single party. That was undoubtedly the significance of the two so-called plots in the

Ivory Coast in 1963. But since partisan politics are officially banned, the struggle is driven underground and becomes far more dangerous: the cadres who are excluded from taking the vital decisions can seize control of the party by force only. An opposition that can express itself publicly loses half its danger for the régime.

What is more, the force that has more than once played a leading part in displacing or threatening African governments in the last three years has been a force which, as Western opinion sees it, should be at almost any price excluded from politics: the Army. The new African régimes have done everything they can to make the lives of their usually miniature armies agreeable, with training abroad for the officers and reasonable pay and other advantages for all ranks. That has not stopped the trouble, whose danger is all the greater since more and more of the officers are members of a younger generation which seems to have less and less sympathy with its political bosses. There were junior officers involved in the 1962 plot against President Bourguiba of Tunisia, the plot that resulted in the death of President Sylvanus Olympio of Togo was an Army affair, the Ivory Coast Army was implicated in the second of the two 1963 plots there, and the *coup* that overthrew President Ben Bella of Algeria in June 1965 was carried out entirely by the Algerian Army, whose head, Colonel Boumedienne, believed himself to be threatened with dismissal. The Army played a very big part in the Congo (Brazzaville) *coup*, young Gabonese just out of the French military college of St Cyr were leaders in the movement that for thirty-six hours removed President Mba from power, and of course there were the Army disturbances in Uganda, Kenya and Tanzania.

An excellent summing-up of the arguments for and against the single-party system was given by Bechir ben Yahmed, the Tunisian owner and editor of *Jeune Afrique*, in an article which concluded a series of contributions on the subject which the paper printed in 1963 and 1964. Ben Yahmed is anything but a run-of-the-mill journalist. He was independent Tunisia's first Minister of Information, and left that post to become editor of a Government party paper, *L'Action*, which can be called the grandparent of the present *Jeune Afrique*. *L'Action* had been forced to suspend publication in 1958 after printing a series of criticisms of the Bourguiba Government's policy which reached its climax in a denunciation of what the paper described as the totally unnecessary prosecution of a former Tunisian Premier. Two years later, the weekly reappeared under the new title of *Afrique-Action*, which was later changed to that of *Jeune Afrique*, and in October 1961 it came out with what appeared to be a scarcely veiled attack on President Bourguiba in an editorial which discussed the issue of personal power. The article was generally agreed to have been inspired by the circumstances of Bourguiba's offer to France of peace negotiations over the Bizerta crisis, an offer which he had made at a press conference without any previous consultation with his Cabinet. The editorial, which talked of 'omnipresent police' and 'imprisonment without trial' under personal power systems, culminated with the assertion that personal power could be effective only over a short period, after which it must decline into dictatorship or mount the difficult slope to democracy. It added that because the holder of personal power developed conceit and contempt for others and his entourage developed servility, it was a menace to the moral health of a nation. Not very long afterwards, the weekly moved its editorial offices across the Mediterranean from Tunis.

Ben Yahmed began his 1964 summing up of the arguments over the single party by saying that the single-party system in Africa was due to the social and economic situation which had obtained at the moment of independence. Colonialism had constantly tried to break up the unity of the nationalist movements, and when the new countries became independent, they wanted unity more than anything else. Moreover, they looked on independence as no more than a means which would permit them to build a modern state and set about working for national development, and this called for a strong and stable government disposing of exceptional powers. Africans agreed all the more readily to sacrifice the liberties they had just won since they were entrusting their fate to the men who had freed them from colonialism.

Ben Yahmed went on to distinguish very briefly between two kinds of single party. There was the single party which was an instrument of progress, in its early years at any rate. There was also the single party which was a screen, from the beginning, for immobilism and a sterile dictatorship, which was an instrument of the domination of a social class over the nation as a whole.

For what was the single party, Ben Yahmed asked. He answered himself by defining it as an exceptional concentration of powers in the hands of a man assisted and influenced by a group. Since the man and the group around him disposed of coercion, they had no need to persuade people: what they thought to be good for the country they did with no more ado. They started off as rulers; they ended by becoming a group of interests.

Thus, even in the best of events, Ben Yahmed argued, the single party and personal power could serve a country only during a transitional period, the period which saw the building up of the state, the consolidation of national unity and the establishment of new economic structures. After this phase, the single party became an intolerable institution, which led to sclerosis of thinking, social stagnation and, of course, political troubles too.

Moreover, once the single party was installed in power, it was the last to see any need for it to disappear or change. It was for all practical purposes incapable of democratizing itself or democratizing the country. Accustomed as it was to silencing any opposition, it completely failed to understand the necessity of concessions to opinion. In these circumstances, what had been a motive force and an incomparable instrument of progress became a brake. Hardly had the State been set in place than it became corrupt. Trust between former comrades in the nationalist struggle for liberty faded away. The prisons started to fill up, and young people drifted out of politics or revolted.

Ben Yahmed can hardly be said to have put forward any very convincing way out of the single-party system, whose evils he denounced so eloquently. In fact, it amounts to little more than the 'Jam tomorrow? Quite possibly' of so many defenders of the set-up. The transition from the single-party system to democracy, he argued, was going to be as difficult as the transition from underdevelopment to development. A country could not be industrialized without aches and pains;

no more could it be democratized without struggles and adjustments. The question was just how was this process of democratization to be brought about.

Ben Yahmed answered that democracy was the child of education, and fortunately education was spreading like wildfire in Africa today. Education, he maintained, developed a civic spirit and a national outlook. Rather than plotting to overthrow a man and a group only in order to replace them – inevitably – by another man and another group, the younger people of Africa must struggle for a better and more widely-disseminated education for their juniors. Just as the older generation had fought and suffered for independence, the Africans of today must fight, and suffer if need be, for democracy.

Finally Ben Yahmed answered in advance – as he had to, coming from a country which had once been under the domination of France – the argument that the absurdity of democracy had been demonstrated once for all by the multi-party form it had assumed under the Third and the Fourth French Republics. What he and his friends stood for, Ben Yahmed said, was the only form of democracy that had ever succeeded: a single majority party in the Government and an opposition, also united within one single party, which watched over the Government's actions and was ready to take its place.

Ben Yahmed's prescription for getting rid of the single-party system would seem at once too pessimistic and too optimistic. It is quite true that none of the *coups* which have so far occurred in Africa, including those we have examined, has resulted in replacing the overturned government by anything better or more liberal. It is also true that a high proportion of the plots which failed would probably have achieved nothing more impressive had they succeeded: whatever their grievances, the men who plotted against President Bourguiba of Tunisia did not seem to have a single positive political idea in their head, and the most prominent figure among them was an illiterate. On the other hand, the leaders of Morocco's National Union of Popular Forces, who were falsely accused of plotting against King Hassan's Government in 1963, had quite a number of ideas to their credit. Is it beyond the reach of possibility that one of these days an African *coup*, planned by a group of men with ideals and ideas, may overthrow the group in power and replace them not by the same sort of crew, but by a government that not only cares for the interests of its people, but is determined to give it every sort of opportunity to express its desires freely?

The hope that more education may open a door out of single-party tyranny would seem a little optimistic. More than three-quarters of the children of the Congo (Brazzaville) and of Gabon are today attending schools, but that has not saved their countries from dictatorship. The vast majority of Soviet children were attending school throughout the Stalin epoch, but that did not spell the end of the Great Leader and Teacher. For education can be and is angled. Dictators with the right sort of staff at their command ensure that it is: think of the Ghana children who begin their school-day with a litany of praise for Nkrumah. In countries where educators take this sort of line, more children at school will tend merely to mean that more children are being indoctrinated to believe in the infallibility of their ruler and the clique around him.

There are Africans who see a way out towards freedom in trade unionism. Alas, there is hardly an African country today where the unions are free from the control of the single party, though there are some defenders of the single-party system who express this association in what would appear to be a somewhat simple-minded way. 'It is not impossible,' says Madeira Keita, in the speech already quoted, 'that if the party is really the expression of the popular will, trade unions and other organizations will want to work in with it.' To hope for the springing-up of a free press is just as vain. There are countries, like Nigeria, where press freedom still exists, but by and large it is on the way out in Africa, and it would need a whole series of revolutions to restore it. In Tunisia, which is less oppressive in its atmosphere than any other single-party state, the last papers which could be called free, in the sense that they printed news and comment that did not fall in with the official line were, paradoxically enough, organs of the minuscular Communist party. They were suppressed following the 1962 plot against Bourguiba, though the Communists had nothing at all to do with it, probably because the authorities welcomed the opportunity to suppress sheets which were printing information on such unwelcome topics as the luxurious palaces being built for the President. In Algiers, the unreadability of the F.L.N. French-language daily, *Le Peuple* was such that the authorities took two successive steps to eliminate competition to it. First, they suppressed the French-owned *Dépêche d'Algérie* which, though it faithfully followed the official line, presented the same news so much more attractively that it sold ten or twelve times as many copies. Then they started by emasculating and finally amalgamated with the *Peuple* the fellow-travelling *Alger Républicain*, which must have been one of the few Communist-inspired papers in the world which its readers bought from choice, and which for a long time printed a correspondence column where there appeared grass-root criticisms of the failures of the régime such as could be found nowhere else.

What may be a pointer to a way out from the single-party system in Africa occurs in a criticism of it by Sheikh Anta Diop which appeared in 1963 in *The Ideologies of the Developing Nations*. Diop wrote: 'The single parties we are going to create may be parties of the Latin American type; i.e., we may be creating petty ephemeral dictatorships that will be dominated by foreign capital in a very insidious fashion. Then Africans will live in a state of division and permanent weakness, exactly as Latin America does.'

It may be worth while, therefore, to glance briefly at the history of Latin America since it threw off the European yoke a century-and-a-half ago, and to see whether there are any common reasons for the chronic political instability which has afflicted it since then and the instability from which the African countries have been suffering in the short space of time since they attained independence.

9

The Latin American Parallel

Since the beginning of the twentieth century, governments of the states of Latin America have been overthrown by force about eighty times. This is more than the equivalent of a revolution a year, and there are some countries where the pattern of successive *coups* is still continuing. Bolivia, for example, had violent changes of Government in 1920, 1930, 1934, 1936, 1937, 1946, 1951, 1952 and 1964.

Most of these revolutions have, however, been completely lacking in social content. They have been, like the majority of those we have recorded in Africa, no more than palace revolutions, in the course of which one clique in the ruling class, usually with the support of the Army, replaces another. The split among the rulers which is responsible for the *coup*, as often as not a completely bloodless affair, may be touched off by personal rivalry between two politically prominent figures: it has been remarked that almost every 'ism' in Latin America is a somebody-ism. Again, the trouble may be due to regionalism. Latin Americans have developed historical loyalties to their regions, and these loyalties on occasion take precedence over national sentiments. Both of these factors in the origins of violent changes of government are present in Africa, as we have seen. And the phrase one author has used of the typical Latin American revolution could be used equally well of the typical overthrow of a government in Africa: 'It is not a revolution at all. In a sense it is a proclamation that true revolution has not yet come.' The difference between the two continents is that in Latin America political revolutions with a social and economic content are not a thing of the future: they have already begun. They started in Mexico in 1911, continued in Bolivia in 1952 and then struck successively in Guatemala, in Cuba and in the Dominican Republic, though it is true that they have had to face up to counter-revolutionary movements and have indeed more than once gone down before these.

What is there in common between the historical and social backgrounds of the states of Africa and of Latin America? The revolutions that brought independence to the Latin American states were not the work of and did not for many decades profit the original inhabitants of the continent, the American Indians, nor of course the Negroes who had been imported as slaves. They were naturally the work of an under-privileged class, but that class was separated by no ethnical difference from the men against whom it rose. It consisted of the so-called Creoles, the Spaniards born in the new world, and the fact that they had for three centuries been allowed so little hand in the running of their countries, which were ruled direct from Madrid and Lisbon, was largely responsible for the movement for independence. The only visible effect of the revolutions was that power was transferred from the hands of officials appointed from Europe to those of a locally-born oligarchy. That, of course, is true of many of the newly-independent African states.

The constitutions of the Latin American states, like those of the African countries, were almost without exception highly liberal documents, copied from those of the United States or France. They provided guarantees of the rights of man and they established the separation of powers and all the normal safeguards of democracy. In fact these constitutions, with few exceptions, were dead letters. It may be asked why the oligarchies who had the task of operating them could not settle their quarrels by parliamentary means, as happened in eighteenth-century England. One answer is that there was no parliamentary tradition in Latin America, any more than there was in Spain or is in Africa. In any case, dictatorships sprang up almost everywhere, and from the start the local armies played a leading part in establishing them and replacing them. The wars that had brought independence had been long-drawn-out and devastating, and by the time they were over, military men were used to interfering in political affairs and were often the sole force, except for the Church, capable of saving their countries from internal chaos. Only one African country, Algeria, has known a revolutionary struggle anything like as protracted as those in Latin America, and it will be remembered that there the Army of National Liberation played the main part in installing Ben Bella in office in 1962 and deposed him single-handed three years later.

It is not merely in one country of Latin America, however, but right over the continent that armies have, almost to the present day, been continuing to intervene in internal politics, in season and out of season. The reason smilingly advanced in one capital for these extra-curricular activities was that: 'The soldiers have got to have *something* to do. Since no one's threatening us from outside, the Army has become one more political party.' The same reasons would justify armies becoming political parties in most African lands.

Another reason why Latin American politicians have resorted to violence rather than to discussion to settle their rivalries for power is that the position of president of a Latin American country is worth so much. There is no one in the world, says the French author of a book published in 1960, who has more powers than a Latin American president. The predominant role played by the president in the whole business of governing and the subordinate position of the legislature are the most outstanding characteristics of Latin American democracy. The president, who is elected by universal suffrage, has no sort of counter-balance. The constitutions of most countries allow him to assume extraordinary powers and in certain circumstances to suspend the constitutional guarantees. What has just been said of Latin American presidents is just as true of most African presidents, and helps to explain why in both continents the contest for the supreme office has so often taken violent forms. The one difference has been that dictators in Latin America have not till recent years resorted to the single-party system to mobilize their supporters, undoubtedly because the value of the single party formula for dictatorial government was not fully realized till it had spread from the Soviet Union to the Eastern European satellite states after the war.

The reasons advanced by writers on Latin America for the failure of real democracy to flower in its countries and for the chronic political instability there are much the same as those that are agreed to be responsible for the same phenomena in Africa. One, of course, is illiteracy, which is less widespread than in Africa, but is still high. A Mexican review stated in

1962 that 50,000,000 people over the age of fifteen in Latin America could not read or write, and since the total population of the continent is around 200,000,000 and the birth-rate is very high, that represents a considerable percentage. Primary-school attendance in sixteen Latin American States in the year 1956–7 was represented as ranging from seventy-two per cent. in Paraguay and sixty-nine per cent. in Argentina to forty-four per cent. in Brazil, thirty-eight per cent. in Bolivia, twenty-eight per cent. in Guatemala and twenty-four per cent. in Haiti. The highest figures are rather lower than those reported from Gabon or the Congo (Brazzaville), though the population of Argentina is something like fifteen times those of the two countries put together; the middle figures are higher than most of those reported from Africa and even the lowest are higher than those found in the African states with the lowest school-attendance records. The overall position is, however, much the same: there is not a large enough educated electorate in most countries to make a real democracy work. Moreover, Latin American illiterates tend to be unaware of their membership of the nation to which they belong – the lack of a sense of nationality is another feature common to the ordinary populations of the Latin American and the new African states – and, being unfamiliar with political affairs and accustomed to give their loyalty to individual employers or landlords, they transfer this custom to public life and thus strengthen the personalist tradition in politics; the Indian tends to be loyal to his tribe or linguistic group.

Another factor making against democracy which is common to both continents is economic under-development. A 1962 United Nations publication represents the annual income per head in the various Latin American countries as ranging downwards from $540 in Venezuela, $460 in Argentina and $440 in Uruguay to $120 in Peru, $75 in Bolivia and $64 in Haiti, just over half the states falling within a middle reach, in which the income per head ranged from $150 to $250. Now it is true that these averages are about double those reported from the newly-independent African states. But some at least of those acquainted with Latin American affairs contend that they mean little, since real income is divided between a very rich minority and a mass of extremely poor people on a scale which is not yet to be found in Africa.

The other reasons given for the tardy flowering of democracy and the long persistance of unstable dictatorships in Latin America are much the same as those that can be advanced for the same phenomena in Africa. One is the lack of democratic training and civic maturity, alike among the privileged and the underprivileged. The gap here is probably wider in Latin America, whose inhabitants lack the experience of tribal democracy which is still a good deal more than a memory in Africa. Another reason is the tradition of rule from above: the Africans, it is true, can look back to a few years only of dictatorship by their own fellows, but all the new states have behind them at least half a century of government from Europe, whose decisions it was very difficult to question till the last decade or two before independence. In the Latin American countries there has been a relative lack of political organization among the masses, though the growing influence of trade unions, which are still free, has tended to change this position of recent years; in very few African countries did any meaningful political organizations exist till the eve of independence. In Latin America, political life has been centred far more on individual leaders and on feelings for or against them than on principles and on ideas; that has been equally true of the brief political life of the newly-independent states of Africa. Finally, it has been said of Latin America that a weakness among its people that to some extent unfits them for the intelligent choice between programmes that is the only real form of democracy is their sensitivity to slogans and sentimental appeals. That is equally true of the people of Africa, and its nationalist leaders played on it during the campaign for independence. Tom Mboya, later Kenya's Minister of Economic Planning, wrote of this period: 'There had to be a simplification of the struggle into one distinct idea which everyone could grasp without arguing about the details of policy or of the Government's programme after independence.' It was inevitable that African leaders who had found this way of handling crowds so effective in the period before independence should continue to resort to it when the crowds became the electorate. President Bourguiba of Tunisia is as much of a dictator as any African leader, but he is almost alone among his fellows in that his speeches, eloquent though they are, take the form not of appeals to emotion, but of painstaking, logical explanations of what he represents as the necessity of a given policy.

Just as in Africa, too, a high proportion of the governing classes in Latin America appear to be lacking alike in civic spirit and in confidence in the future of their governments and their countries. They transfer enormous sums abroad, investing them in the United States, Canada or Switzerland. An estimate published in the spring of 1962 put the sum of these transfers in the ten preceding years at $10,000 million.

There are thus a whole series of parallels between political life and its background in Latin America and in Africa. That may embolden us to hope that another and comparatively recent political development in Latin American politics will before long have its parallel in those of Africa. Within the last decade or two, Latin American palace revolutions have been diminishing in number, and in more and more countries it looks as if something like a stable democratic system, ensuring the orderly replacement of regularly elected Governments, has begun to take root. What lies behind the change? The end of the nineteenth century and the opening of the twentieth saw the United States and the Western European states seeking not only for new sources of raw materials and new markets for their goods, but new places in which to invest their rapidly accumulating capital. Some of the resultant investments were placed in Latin America, and this led to the development there of railways and public utility services to start with and then, beginning with the First World War, of local manufacturing industries. This in turn led to the growth of a middle class and of an urban working-class, and as a result there was an increasing and, in the end, irresistible pressure for democracy. It was the identical factors which led to the establishment of democratic institutions in Western Europe in the nineteenth century or to the increasingly wider base accorded to those that already existed. The same social process has already started in Africa, and there seems no reason to believe that the same political results will not eventually ensue.

There will of course be certain brakes on the rapidity of

the process. In Latin America many civilians still have a feeling that when they have lost an election, the proper thing to do is to turn to their friends in the officer caste for aid in seizing the power they think should rightfully be theirs. There are just as many who find it hard to conceive that their rivals may have won an election fairly, and who interpret any opposition to the government in power, or even criticism of it, as subversion. In Africa, there is the difficulty that the transfer of power there will have to be conceded not by a class, but by a clique, and a clique parts with its privileges far less readily than a class does. What is more, the clique has at its disposal an instrument for maintaining itself in power, the single-party system, of whose efficacity Latin American dictators only recently became conscious.

Whatever the strength of that instrument, however, history would seem to show that institutions almost always end by yielding to social and economic pressures, to such pressures as have been developing in Latin America over recent decades and which are developing in Africa today. What is more, the course of events in the mid-twentieth century is advancing more rapidly than it has ever done before. The freedom which it took a century and a half to win for those countries of Latin America that have achieved it may, with any luck, require not much more than a tenth of that time to secure in Africa.

A final word may perhaps be necessary. This book has endeavoured to be objective about the not always pleasing facts of contemporary political life in Africa, but the statement of these facts should not be taken as implying any sort of prejudice against its people or their rulers. They almost all of them have a hard row to hoe. The artificial boundaries with which most of them came into existence, boundaries inherited from the former colonial powers, as often as not took no account of ethnical considerations and split peoples into two; that put a ready-made instrument of subversion into the hands of ill-intentioned neighbours and made it all the harder for the leaders of truncated lands to build up in the sense of national identity without which it is difficult to run a democratic state. This problem is not peculiar to Africa, however. There are European countries where the sense of nationhood does not date back further than a hundred years, in no country of Europe has such a sense existed for as long as a millenium, and Belgium, with its 130-year-old national status, is faced today with the same sort of linguistic if not ethnical conflict as made the first years of independence so hazardous for its former colony of the Congo. The universal suffrage which is the only basis for genuine democracy is not yet a hundred years old in any European country, neither is the universal education without which democracy cannot in any real sense function. Something has been said about the administrative corruption that plagues almost every African state and that has made the head of one of them, Dr Banda, of Malawi, extremely reluctant to transfer administrative responsibility from the remaining European officials to his fellow-countrymen. That is nothing peculiar to Africa: even in England, the tradition of civil service incorruptibility has barely a century of acceptance behind it.

Africa is, in a sense, a young continent. Writing is comparatively new to it. So are urban-centred civilizations. So is the sense of nationality. But if the local novelty of these assets by comparison with their old establishment in Europe is set within the framework of the ages over which the human race has come to flowering, it will be seen that our Western seniority means little. And with the increasingly rapid pace at which humanity is advancing, there is some reason to hope that within a decade or two the African States will have achieved the degree of political freedom about which we pride ourselves in the West.